Diverse Identities

Diverse Identities
Classic Multicultural Essays

James D. Lester
Austin Peay State University

NTC Publishing Group
Lincolnwood, Illinois USA

Executive Editor: John T. Nolan
Sponsoring Editor: Marisa L. L'Heureux
Cover and interior design: Ophelia M. Chambliss
Cover art: Celia Johnson/Gerald & Cullen Rapp, Inc.
Production Manager: Rosemary Dolinski

Acknowledgments for literary selections begin on page 251, which is to be considered an extension of the copyright page.

ISBN 0-8442-5884-9 (student text)
ISBN 0-8442-5885-7 (instructor's edition)

Published by NTC Publishing Group
© 1996 NTC Publishing Group, 4255 West Touhy Avenue
Lincolnwood (Chicago), Illinois 60646-1975 U.S.A.

Library of Congress Cataloging-in-Publication Data

Lester, James D., 1935–
    Diverse identities: classic multicultural essays / James D. Lester.
        p.   cm.
    "NTC's library of classic essays."
    Includes index.
    ISBN 0-8442-5884-9 (pbk.)
    1. Minorities—United States.   2. Pluralism (Social sciences)—
United States.   3. United States—Ethnic relations.   4. United
States—Race relations.   I. Title.
E184.A1L46   1995
305.8'00973—dc20   95-11019
                                                                    CIP

5 6 7 8 9 VP 0 9 8 7 6 5 4 3 2 1

Contents

Classic Multicultural Essays about A Sense of Place   115

Classic Multicultural Essays about The Importance of Language   143

Classic Multicultural Essays about Combating Prejudice   207

Preface

❧

NTC's Library of Classic Essays

This is a four-volume collection of some of the finest essays ever written, providing a broad yet in-depth overview of the development and scope of the genre. In essence, an essay is a short prose composition, usually exploring one subject and often presenting the personal view of the author. An essay may take a variety of forms (from narration to description to autobiography) and may reflect any number of moods (from critical to reflective to whimsical).

Although we recognize a few early works by Plato, Aristotle, and others as essays, it was really Michel de Montaigne, a French philosopher and writer, who substantially defined the form when he published two volumes of his own essays under the title *Essais* in 1580. Montaigne considered himself to be representative of humankind in general; thus, his essays, though they are to be read as general treatises on the human condition, are largely reflective of Montaigne's own attitudes and experiences.

The essay proved to be a most adaptable form. In the eighteenth century, both journalists and philosophers in England and pamphleteers and patriots in the American colonies quickly discovered the power of a well-crafted and provocative essay. By the middle of the nineteenth century, the essay was the form of choice for such brilliant writers as the American Ralph Waldo Emerson and the British George Eliot. In the twentieth century, the essay has become the most widely read genre—from personal essays in periodicals to scholarly essays in scientific journals to argumentative essays on the editorial pages of newspapers worldwide.

Diverse Identities:
Classic Multicultural Essays

This volume contains twenty-nine classic essays that illustrate the richness of the multicultural experience in the United States and elsewhere. Organized by theme, these essays explore an amazing diversity of topics. If, however, one of your favorites is not included here, it may well be in one of the other volumes: *Plato's Heirs: Classic Essays; Daughters of the Revolution: Classic Essays by Women;* or *Of Bunsen Burners, Bones, and Belles Lettres: Classic Essays across the Curriculum.*

This volume brings you essays that explore how writers think and write about their life experiences and how those experiences have been shaped and influenced by the writers' racial or cultural heritage. It is our hope that this collection will allow you to examine who you are and better enable you to explore your place—and the place of others—in the universe.

CLASSIC MULTICULTURAL ESSAYS ABOUT

Childhood and Families

Wandering

ZORA NEALE HURSTON

Zora Neale Hurston (1903–1960) was born in Eatonville, Florida. She attended Howard University from 1923 to 1924 but ultimately earned a B.A. degree from Barnard College in 1928. Though she lived principally in Fort Pierce, Florida, she traveled extensively and held a variety of jobs—librarian at the Library of Congress, instructor of drama at Bethune-Cookman College and North Carolina College for Negroes (now known as North Carolina Central University), staff writer at Paramount Studios, and as assistant to the writer Fannie Hurst.

While at Barnard College, Hurston studied anthropology under Franz Boas, who encouraged her to study black mythology. She plunged into the task with zeal. Her folklore study, *Mules and Men* (1935), featured an introduction by Boas. Her novels also provide insight into black myth and legend, especially *Their Eyes Were Watching God* (1937) and *Moses, Man of the Mountain* (1939).

Hurston wrote "Wandering" as part of her 1942 autobiography, *Dust Tracks on a Road*. For the first thirteen years of her life, Hurston lived in Eatonville, Florida, the first all-black incorporated town in the United States. At age thirteen, she was sent to Jacksonville to care for the young children of her brothers. There, in an integrated community, she discovered her color, but she argues in "How It Feels to Be Colored Me," "I do not belong to the sobbing school of Negrohood who hold that nature somehow has given them a lowdown dirty deal and whose feelings are all hurt about it." She argues that most of the time she has no sense of race—"I am *me*."

1   I knew that Mama was sick. She kept getting thinner and thinner and her chest cold never got any better. Finally, she took to bed.

2   She had come home from Alabama that way. She had gone back to her old home to be with her sister during her sister's last illness. Aunt Dinky had lasted on for two months after Mama got there, and so Mama had stayed on till the last.

3   It seems that there had been other things there that worried her. Down underneath, it appeared that Grandma had never quite forgiven her for the move she had made twenty-one years before in marrying Papa. So that when Mama suggested that the old Potts place be sold so that she could bring her share back with her to Florida, her mother, urged on by Uncle Bud, Mama's oldest brother, refused. Not until Grandma's head was cold, was an acre of the place to be sold. She had long since quit living on it, and it was pretty well run down, but she wouldn't, that was all. Mama could just go on back to that yaller rascal she had married like she came. I do not think that the money part worried Mama as much as the injustice and spitefulness of the thing.

4   Then Cousin Jimmie's death seemed to come back on Mama during her visit. How he came to his death is an unsolved mystery. He went to a party and started home. The next morning his headless body was found beside the railroad track. There was no blood, so the train couldn't have killed him. This had happened before I was born. He was said to have been a very handsome young man, and very popular with the girls. He was my mother's favorite nephew and she took it hard. She had probably numbed over her misery, but going back there seemed to freshen up her grief. Some said that he had been waylaid by three other young fellows and killed in a jealous rage. But nothing could be proved. It was whispered that he had been shot in the head by a white man unintentionally, and then beheaded to hide the wound. He had been shot from ambush, because his assailant mistook him for a certain white man. It was night. The attacker expected the white man to pass that way, but not Jimmie. When he found out his mistake, he had forced a certain Negro to help him move the body to the railroad track without the head, so that it would look as if he had been run over by the train. Anyway, that is what the Negro wrote back after he had moved to Texas years later. There was never any move to prove the charge, for obvious reasons. Mama took the whole thing very hard.

It was not long after Mama came home that she began to be less active. Then she took to bed. I knew she was ailing, but she was always frail, so I did not take it too much to heart. I was nine years old, and even though she had talked to me very earnestly one night, I could not conceive of Mama actually dying. She had talked of it many times.

6   That day, September 18th, she had called me and given me certain instructions. I was not to let them take the pillow from under her head until she was dead. The clock was not to be covered, nor the looking-glass. She trusted me to see to it that these things were not done. I promised her as solemnly as nine years could do, that I would see to it.

7   What years of agony that promise gave me! In the first place, I had no idea that it would be soon. But that same day near sundown I was called upon to set my will against my father, the village dames and village custom. I know now that I could not have succeeded.

8   I had left Mama and was playing outside for a little while when I noted a number of women going inside Mama's room and staying. It looked strange. So I went on in. Papa was standing at the foot of the bed looking down on my mother, who was breathing hard. As I crowded in, they lifted up the bed and turned it around so that Mama's eyes would face the east. I thought that she looked to me as the head of the bed was reversed. Her mouth was slightly open, but her breathing took up so much of her strength that she could not talk. But she looked at me, or so I felt, to speak for her. She depended on me for a voice.

9   The Master-Maker in His making had made Old Death. Made him with big, soft feet and square toes. Made him with a face that reflects the face of all things, but neither changes itself, nor is mirrored anywhere. Made the body of Death out of infinite hunger. Made a weapon for his hand to satisfy his needs. This was the morning of the day of the beginning of things.

10   But Death had no home and he knew it at once.

11   "And where shall I dwell in my dwelling?" Old Death asked, for he was already old when he was made.

12   "You shall build you a place close to the living, yet far out of the sight of eyes. Wherever there is a building, there you have your platform that comprehends the four roads of the winds. For your hunger, I give you the first and last taste of all things."

13   We had been born, so Death had had his first taste of us. We had built things, so he had his platform in our yard.

14   And now, Death stirred from his platform in his secret place in our yard, and came inside the house.

15   Somebody reached for the clock, while Mrs. Mattie Clarke put her hand to the pillow to take it away.

16   "Don't!" I cried out. "Don't take the pillow from under Mama's head! She said she didn't want it moved!"

17   I made to stop Mrs. Mattie, but Papa pulled me away. Others were trying to silence me. I could see the huge drop of sweat collected in the hollow at Mama's elbow and it hurt me so. They were covering the clock and the mirror.

18   "Don't cover up that clock! Leave that looking-glass like it is! Lemme put Mama's pillow back where it was!"

19   But Papa held me tight and the others frowned me down. Mama was still rasping out the last morsel of her life. I think she was trying to say something, and I think she was trying to speak to me. What was she trying to tell me? What wouldn't I give to know! Perhaps she was telling me that it was better for the pillow to be moved so that she could die easy, as they said. Perhaps she was accusing me of weakness and failure in carrying out her last wish. I do not know. I shall never know.

20   Just then, Death finished his prowling through the house on his padded feet and entered the room. He bowed to Mama in his way, and she made her manners and left us to act out our ceremonies over unimportant things.

21   I was to agonize over that moment for years to come. In the midst of play, in wakeful moments after midnight, on the way home from parties, and even in the classroom during lectures. My thoughts would escape occasionally from their confines and stare me down.

22   Now, I know that I could not have had my way against the world. The world we lived in required those acts. Anything else would have been sacrilege, and no nine-year-old voice was going to thwart them. My father was with the mores. He had restrained me physically from outraging the ceremonies established for the dying. If there is any consciousness after death, I hope that Mama knows that I did my best. She must know how I have suffered for my failure.

23   But life picked me up from the foot of Mama's bed, grief, self-despisement and all, and set my feet in strange ways. That moment was the end of a phase in my life. I was old before my time with grief of loss, of failure, and of remorse. No matter what the others did, my mother had put her trust in me. She had felt that I could

and would carry out her wishes, and I had not. And then in that sunset time, I failed her. It seemed as she died that the sun went down on purpose to flee away from me.

24   That hour began my wanderings. Not so much in geography, but in time. Then not so much in time as in spirit.

25   Mama died at sundown and changed a world. That is, the world which had been built out of her body and her heart. Even the physical aspects fell apart with a suddenness that was startling.

26   My oldest brother was up in Jacksonville in school, and he arrived home after Mama had passed. By then, she had been washed and dressed and laid out on the ironing-board in the parlor.

27   Practically all of the village was in the front yard and on the porch, talking in low tones and waiting. They were not especially waiting for my brother Bob. They were doing that kind of waiting that people do around death. It is a kind of sipping up the drama of the thing. However, if they were asked, they would say it was the sadness of the occasion which drew them. In reality it is a kind of feast of the Passover.

28   Bob's grief was awful when he realized that he was too late. He could not conceive at first that nothing could be done to straighten things out. There was no ear for his excuse nor explanation—no way to ease what was in him. Finally it must have come to him that what he had inside, he must take with him wherever he went. Mama was there on the cooling board with the sheet draped over her blowing gently in the wind. Nothing there seemed to hear him at all.

29   There was my sister Sarah in the kitchen crying and trying to quiet Everett, who was just past two years old. She was crying and trying to make him hush at the same time. He was crying because he sensed the grief around him. And then, Sarah, who was fifteen, had been his nurse and he would respond to her mood, whatever it was. We were all grubby bales of misery, huddled about lamps.

30   I have often wished I had been old enough at the time to look into Papa's heart that night. If I could know what that moment meant to him, I could have set my compass towards him and been sure. I know that I did love him in a way, and that I admired many things about him. He had a poetry about him that I loved. That had made him a successful preacher. He could hit ninety-seven out of a hundred with a gun. He could swim Lake Maitland from Maitland to Winter Park, and no man in the village could put my father's shoulders to the ground. We were so certain of Papa's invincibility

in combat that when a village woman scolded Everett for some misdemeanor, and told him that God would punish him, Everett, just two years old, reared back and told her, "He better not bother me. Papa will shoot Him down." He found out better later on, but that goes to show you how big our Papa looked to us. We had seen him bring down bears and panthers with his gun, and chin the bar more times than any man in competing distance. He had to our knowledge licked two men who Mama told him had to be licked. All that part was just fine with me. But I was Mama's child. I knew that she had not always been happy, and I wanted to know just how sad he was that night.

31   I have repeatedly called up that picture and questioned it. Papa cried some too, as he moved in his awkward way about the place. From the kitchen to the front porch and back again. He kept saying, "Poor thing! She suffered so much." I do not know what he meant by that. It could have been love and pity for her suffering ending at last. It could have been remorse mixed with relief. The hard-driving force was no longer opposed to his easy-going pace. He could put his potentialities to sleep and be happy in the laugh of the day. He could do next year or never, what Mama would have insisted must be done today. Rome, the eternal city, meant two different things to my parents. To Mama, it meant, you must build it today so it could last through eternity. To Papa, it meant that you could plan to lay some bricks today and you have the rest of eternity to finish it. With all time, why hurry? God had made more time than anything else, anyway. Why act so stingy about it?

32   Then too, I used to notice how Mama used to snatch Papa. That is, he would start to put up an argument that would have been terrific on the store porch, but Mama would pitch in with a single word or a sentence and mess it all up. You could tell he was mad as fire with no words to blow it out with. He would sit over in the corner and cut his eyes at her real hard. He was used to being a hero on the store porch and in church affairs, and I can see how he must have felt to be always outdone around home. I know now that that is a griping thing to a man—not to be able to whip his woman mentally. Some women know how to give their man that conquesting feeling. My mother took her over-the-creek man and bare-knuckled him from brogans to broadcloth, and I am certain that he was proud of the change, in public. But in the house, he might have always felt over-the-creek, and because that was not the statue he had made for

himself to look at he resented it. But then, you cannot blame my mother too much if she did not see him as his entranced congregations did. The one who makes the idols never worships them, however tenderly he might have molded the clay. You cannot have knowledge and worship at the same time. Mystery is the essence of divinity. Gods must keep their distances from men.

33   Anyway, the next day, Sam Moseley's span of fine horses, hitched to our wagon, carried my mother to Macedonia Baptist Church for the last time. The finality of the thing came to me fully when the earth began to thud on the coffin.

34   That night, all of Mama's children were assembled together for the last time on earth. The next day, Bob and Sarah went back to Jacksonville to school. Papa was away from home a great deal, so two weeks later I was on my way to Jacksonville, too. I was under age, but the school had agreed to take me in under the circumstances. My sister was to look after me, in a way.

35   The midnight train had to be waved down at Maitland for me. That would put me into Jacksonville in the daytime.

36   As my brother Dick drove the mile with me that night, we approached the curve in the road that skirts Lake Catherine, and suddenly I saw the first picture of my visions. I had seen myself upon that curve at night leaving the village home, bowed down with grief that was more than common. As it all flashed back to me, I started violently for a minute, then I moved closer beside Dick as if he could shield me from those others that were to come. He asked me what was the matter, and I said I thought I heard something moving down by the lake. He laughed at that, and we rode on, the lantern showing the roadway, and me keeping as close to Dick as I could. A little, humped-up, shabby-backed trunk was behind us in the buckboard. I was on my way from the village, never to return to it as a real part of the town.

37   Jacksonville made me know that I was a little colored girl. Things were all about the town to point this out to me. Streetcars and stores and then talk I heard around the school. I was no longer among the white people whose homes I could barge into with a sure sense of welcome. These white people had funny ways. I could tell that even from a distance. I didn't get a piece of candy or a bag of crackers just for going into a store in Jacksonville as I did when I went into Galloway's or Hill's at Maitland, or Joe Clarke's in Eatonville.

38   Around the school I was an awful bother. The girls complained

that they couldn't get a chance to talk without me turning up somewhere to be in the way. I broke up many good "He said" conferences
just by showing up. It was not my intention to do so. What I wanted
was for it to go full steam ahead and let me listen. But that didn't
seem to please. I was not in the "he said" class, and they wished I
would kindly please stay out of the way. My underskirt was hanging
for instance. Why didn't I go some place and fix it? My head looked
like a hoo-raw's nest. Why didn't I go comb it? If I took time enough
to match my stockings, I wouldn't have time to be trying to listen
in on grown folk's business. These venerable old ladies were anywhere
from fifteen to eighteen.

39   In the classroom I got along splendidly. The only difficulty was
that I was rated as sassy. I just had to talk back at established authority
and that established authority hated backtalk worse than barbed-
wire pie. My brother was asked to speak to me in addition to a licking
or two. But on the whole, things went along all right. My immediate
teachers were enthusiastic about me. It was the guardians of study-
hour and prayer meetings who felt that their burden was extra hard
to bear.

40   School in Jacksonville was one of those twilight things. It was not
dark, but it lacked the bold sunlight that I craved. I worshipped two
of my teachers and loved gingersnaps with cheese, and sour pickles.
But I was deprived of the loving pine, the lakes, the wild violets in
the woods and the animals I used to know. No more holding down
first base on the team with my brothers and their friends. Just a
jagged hole where my home used to be.

41   At times, the girls of the school were lined up two and two and
taken for a walk. On one of these occasions, I had an experience
that set my heart to fluttering. I saw a woman sitting on a porch
who looked at a distance like Mama. Maybe it *was* Mama! Maybe
she was not dead at all. They had made some mistake. Mama had
gone off to Jacksonville and they thought that she was dead. The
woman was sitting in a rocking-chair just like Mama always did. It
must be Mama! But before I came abreast of the porch in my rigid
place in line, the woman got up and went inside. I wanted to stop
and go in. But I didn't even breathe my hope to anyone. I made up
my mind to run away someday and find the house and let Mama
know where I was. But before I did, the hope that the woman really
was my mother passed. I accepted my bereavement.

Growing into Manhood

ERNESTO GALARZA

Ernesto Galarza (1905–1984) was born in Jalcocotán, Nayarit, Mexico. He immigrated to Sacramento, California, in 1911. He earned a B.A. at Occidental College in 1927; an M.A. at Stanford University in 1929; and a Ph.D. at Columbia University in 1944. Galarza began his career with the Pan American Union, where for eleven years he wrote pamphlets and essays on Latin American labor policies. In 1947, he resigned and moved back to Sacramento to join the National Farm Labor Union in its fight to unionize the American and Mexican field laborers under the National Agricultural Workers Union. He met fierce opposition, but he persevered by writing, by lecturing at many universities, and by touring and reporting on conditions of the field workers. *Strangers in Our Fields* (1956) is one such report. *Merchants of Labor* (1964) is an exposé of secret agreements by Mexico and the United States in collusion with private companies to control migration and wages. *Spiders in the House and Workers in the Field* (1970) describes his 1947 struggle against the giant agribusinesses in California.

"Growing into Manhood" is an excerpt from Galarza'a autobiography, *Barrio Boy* (1971). Galarza describes the book in this way: "*Barrio Boy* is the story of a Mexican family, uprooted from its home in a mountain village, in continuous flight from the revolutionary wind that swept Mexico after 1910. The episodes of the journey were typical of those of hundreds of thousands of refugees. They settled permanently in California and other border states. The barrio of this tale is that of Sacramento, California."

1   Up to the time a boy was between five and six years old, Jalcocotán was for the most part an easy place in which to live. The neighbors and *compadres* and *comadres* who scolded you for your bad manners or sent you on errands did not interfere much if you were respectful and stayed out of the way. With my two cousins and other boys of my own age I always had something to watch or to do.

2   The near side of the pond was shallow and fringed with reeds and tall clumps of grass that blossomed with plumes of cream-colored fluff. Around them the pond was always muddy and cool. In your bare feet you sank up to the ankles and by wriggling your toes you could raise oozy, iridescent bubbles. Trampling and squishing the mud, we made plopping hollow sounds and pretended we had gas on our stomachs. Pulling your foot out of the soft gumbo while your friends listened closely made a noise remarkably like the mules in the corrals when they dropped manure.

3   Although we never collected polliwogs or frogs or lizards we chased them along the mud flat until they hopped into deep water or slithered away in the grass. Water snakes were everywhere, which we imagined were poisonous *viboras* or copperheads, like those the *jalcocotecanos* found in the forest. We spiced our play with a legend about an alligator that had crawled all the way up from Miramar and lay in wait for us somewhere in a deep pool of the arroyo—a monster no less real because he lived only in our imagination.

4   When the older boys of the village came to the pond on Sunday afternoons we watched them swim and dive. From a high branch of the big *nogal* they dropped a swing made of bush vines we called *liana*, braided like the women of the pueblo did their hair. The boy who was to dive next waited up in the *nogal*. Another handed him the end of the *liana*. The diver kicked off and let go as high as he could swing, his naked brown body twisting through the air like a split string bean. On our side of the swimming hole the smaller boys stripped and paddled while the divers yelled instructions on strokes and kicks.

5   Once in a great while the older boys would also allow us to join them in the bullfights they organized in one corner of the pasture. The bulls, the matadores, and the picadores were the ten- to twelve-year-olds, and the master of the fight was the oldest of the gang. We were permitted to take part only as fans or *aficionados*, to provide the yelling, the catcalls and the cheers. The master of the *corrida* directed us to sit on the ground on the upper slope of the bullring, which was entirely imaginary.

6   From behind a tree a trumpeter stepped to the edge of the ring. Blowing on a make-believe bugle he sounded a call and the bull rushed in—a boy with a plain sarape over his shoulders, holding with both hands in front of his chest the bleached skull of a steer complete with horns. Between the horns a large, thick cactus leaf from which the thorns had been removed, was tied. It was at the cactus pad that the matadores and picadores aimed their wooden swords and bamboo spears.

7   If the fight went according to the rules, the master declared the bull dead after a few rushes, by counting the stabs into the cactus, and the dead bull was replaced by a live one. Sometimes a sword or a spear missed the cactus pad and poked the bull in the stomach or some more sensitive spot. If the bull suspected that the miss was on purpose and dropped his skull to charge the torero with his fists, there was a free-for-all. We *aficionados* fell on one another with grunts and kicks, wrestling on the ground to increase the bedlam. If the commotion got out of the hands of the master of the *corrida*, there was always an adult watching from the village across the arroyo, who would walk over to the ring to scatter the rioters and send them home.

8   The girls of the village, needless to say, did not take part in the swimming parties or in the action of the bullfights. Neither did we, the boys who were under seven years of age.

9   This by no means put us in the same class. Up to his third year, a boy could still be led by the hand or undressed by an older sister. He was a *chilpayate*, a toddler who could play on the street naked without anybody noticing it. Little by little the *chilpayates* became men of sorts. They noticed that only girls had their earlobes pierced, wearing bits of string until their parents could afford genuine rings. They had to sit for hours to have their hair braided. At five years of age girls began to learn to carry water up from the arroyo in *ollas*, holding them on top of their heads with both hands, something that

no man in Jalco would think of doing. They played silly games like
La Ronda, hopping around and around, we thought, like *zopilotes*.
Boys did girls' chores only if, and everybody knew that it was only
if, there were no girls in the family—like shaking and sunning the
bed mats or sprinkling the street in front of your cottage.

10   Between five and six, the fact that girls belonged to a lower class
became even more obvious. Boys went into the forest to gather
firewood. If their father's *milpa* or banana patch was not too far
away they would be sent off before noon with a hot lunch in the
haversack. They picked coffee beans on the lower branches of the
bushes. They were taught to halter the burros and water them at
the arroyo. They cut and bundled weeds in the *milpa* to feed the
hens and the stock.

11   When a Jalco boy was passing six years of age and had become
used to such jobs, he spent more and more of his day with the men
and less time with the women. He was given more important tasks,
which had a great deal to do with his becoming a man: "para que
se vaya haciendo hombre." At six, a boy stood about as tall as a
machete, but he would not be able to use one for several years. By
the time he was fourteen he would be a man, complete with a machete
of his own, working the *milpa* or the coffee patch or the banana
stand by the side of his father, and able to do it by himself, if necessary.

12   Somewhere between seven and fourteen the village noticed other
signs of his coming manhood. The surest of these was his watching
the girls when they went to the arroyo to scrub clothes and bathe. We
under-sixers could do this anyway without anyone paying attention or
chasing us off. Sitting high on a boulder just above the pond I could
see them, with a white skirt pulled up and pinned over one shoulder,
slapping the clothes on the rocks, dipping them in the water and
wringing them. When the washing was over they slipped off the skirt
and slid into a pool, dunking themselves, chattering and laughing
above the noise of the current. That was how I found out, without
my folks making any particular fuss, that there were at least two
important differences between boys and girls besides the braids and
the perforated ears.

13   That was not, however, real girl watching. Around twelve years,
boys stood away, behind a tree or a bush. If someone noticed, they
pretended that they were going into the forest or to the *milpa* to
work.

14   After you picked out a girl you began watching her in the village,

coming closer step by step until everybody knew it. In this way the girl was staked out and every other young man in the pueblo was on notice. Any other watcher would have to fight for it sooner or later. All this took time; if you began watching when you were around twelve by the time you were sixteen you could propose, asking your parents to ask hers for permission to get married.

15   All this happened only if the parents of the girl liked you. If they didn't, her father would let you know. Jalco was a small, tight town and you could easily be caught shadowing the girl or even speaking to her. She would most likely get a beating, and you might be chased away by her father or brothers.

16   But you were not ready to take the risks of going steady in Jalco until you had proved yourself a man at work. At six years of age or thereabouts you stopped being a playmate and became an apprentice. Jacinto and his father were a good example of this.

17   Chinto, as we called him, became an apprentice *campesino* when he was only a little older than I. I saw them pass in front of our cottage in the early dawn, Chinto following his *jefe* to their cornpatch down the mountain. The man walked ahead, his cotton pants cinched tightly to his waist, one side of the fly crossed over the other and tucked into the waistband. The legs of the *calzones* were wound snug to the ankles, like puttees. At this time of the day the grass along the path to the *milpa* would be heavy with dew; the puttees soaked up less moisture than the bell-bottoms of the pants legs when they were loose. The soles and leather thongs of the huaraches the father wore were the soiled brown color of his ankles and toes. The hat was the usual ice cream cone of straw set on a wide brim curving down over the eyes and upward above the neck. He carried a machete in a sheath with the rawhide loop over one shoulder, and over the other the lunch bag.

18   Jacinto walked behind, dressed exactly like his father, except that he did not carry a machete. Several paces behind, he trotted to keep up with the steady gait of the man, learning the first lesson of his life as a *campesino:* that he would spend the rest of his life walking, walking, walking. "Ay va Jacinto con su papá," someone said in the gloom of our kitchen. It was the end of another boy and the beginning of another man.

19   They came back at nightfall in the same way, the man leading the boy. Both had rolled their pants legs above the knees, their white cotton shirts open in front, their hats tilted back. The man carried

his huaraches over his shoulder. When the trail had roughened and
calloused the feet of the boy, he would do the same.

20   The daily rounds that Jacinto and his father made were either to
the cornpatch, the *platanar* where they cultivated banana trees or
to the few rows of peppers and *jitomate* they tended. We knew the
day that Jacinto went to pick coffee berries with his father, because
they both carried wicker baskets, the man a large one, Jacinto a small
one. When they left the village for several days to herd cattle for a
patrón, father and son carried rawhide slings, the father a long sling,
the boy a short one. Rounding up heifers and calves, the father
taught the boy to whirl the sling and let one end go, timing it so
the pebble would strike the target. Jacinto showed us how, when he
was practicing in the pasture.

21   Jacinto and the other seven-year-olds who were growing into
manhood lost no time in making it clear to the rest of us that we
were nothing but stay-at-homes. As we felt more important than
girls, so Jacinto and his fellow apprentices felt more important than
us. It took courage to walk toward the *milpa* through the forest
where you could step on a rattler any moment, if you didn't see it
coiled in the path or hear its tail buzzing. It took stamina to weed
the corn hills and the banana trees under the broiling sun. Only a
boy with manstuff in him could walk down the mountain and up
the next ridge to spend the night tending heaps of burning wood
to make charcoal that the burros carried to Tepic and San Blas. At
night from Jalco we could see the orange bonfires high up on the
mountain to the east. We saw Jacinto come back with his father from
such work—jaunty *carboneros* with rolled-up pants legs, hats tilted
back, face and legs and arms smeared with charcoal, dust, and sweat.

22   It was in the cultivated patches in the forest that boys grew into
men. With machetes they cleared the steep slopes and the hollows,
setting fire to the brush and the stumps. In the ashes they planted
corn, beans, peppers, *jitomate*, and bananas. Under the shade of a
tall tree they grew coffee bushes. The forest provided the rest of
Jalcocotán's living—timber, charcoal, wild fruit, herbs, boars, deer,
and hides from alligators and cougars.

23   Out of the forest a man took out only what he and his family
could use. Not all the *campesinos* in Jalcocotán, or in all the pueblos
on the mountain together took out so much that the *monte* and the
arroyo could not replenish themselves. In the conversation of the
townspeople there were ancient sayings—*dichos*—that showed how

long the people and the forest had lived together: "Agua que no has de beber, déjala correr"—at the arroyo drink your fill, let the rest run down the hill. "El que a buen arbol se arrima buena sombra le da"—the shade beneath a goodly tree is good for you and good for me.

24 Other than the stone walls of their corrals, the *jalcocotecanos* did not build fences to separate one man's property from another's. When the soil wore out in a *milpa* and another one was cleared, there were no old fences to take down or new ones to put up.

25 The world of work into which Jacinto and the other seven-year-olds were apprenticed was within sight and sound of the pueblo. It was work under blazing suns, in rainstorms, in pitch-black nights. It was work that you were always walking to or walking from, work without wages and work without end. It was work that gave you a bone-tired feeling at the end of the day, so you learned to swing a machete, to tighten a cinch, and to walk without lost motion. Between seven and twelve you learned all this, each lesson driven home when your *jefe* said with a scowl: "Así no, hombre; así." And he showed you how.

26 But he knew that there was another world of work beyond Jalco. Over in Miramar, Los Cocos, Puga and such places there were haciendas where peasants from the pueblos could work for money. Some *jalcocotecanos* did this kind of hiring out. They cut sugarcane, herded cattle, butchered steers, tended the crops, gathered coconuts for the soap works, and cleared land *a puro machetazo*—with your bare hands and a machete.

27 Boys who went with their fathers to the haciendas soon learned the differences between making a living on the mountain and working for the *patrones*. One was that on the mountain you took home corn, bananas, peppers, coffee, and anything else you had raised, but never money. From the hacienda, when your contract ended, you never took anything to eat or wear except what you paid for at the *tienda de raya*, the company store. A peon could make as much as ten pesos a month at hard labor working from dawn to dusk, seven days a week, four weeks every month. It came to about two or three centavos per hour, plus your meals and a place to spread your straw sleeping mat.

28 The most important difference, however, was the *capataz*, the riding boss who watched the laborers all day long, just as the *guardia* watched them throughout the night. The business of the *capataz*

was to keep the *peonanda*, as the crews of field hands were called, hustling at the assigned tasks. He carried a machete slung from his saddle, a whip, and often a pistol: the equipment of a top sergeant of the hacienda. The captain was the *Administrador*, who in turn took his orders from the *patrón* who probably lived in Tepic or Guadalajara or perhaps even in La Capital, as everyone called Mexico City.

29   The men who had worked on haciendas knew of these matters. We heard snatches of firsthand reports from them but mostly we learned from Don Catarino, José, Don Cleofas, the muleteers who passed through Jalco. Whoever had been there came back cursing it. The riding boss was the Devil on horseback; in the company store every centavo you earned was taken back by a clerk who kept numbers in a book that proved you always owed him something. If a peon left the hacienda before his contract was over and his debts were paid, he became a fugitive. He either returned to his pueblo, his *compadres* and his *milpa* in some far-off place in the mountains, or he scratched for a living, lost in the forest. Old men in the village talked of the time they had worked on a hacienda as if they had served a sentence in prison or on a chain gang. They remembered *capataces* who had whipped them or cursed them fifty years before, and they still murmured a phrase: "Algún día me la pagan." There were a hundred blood debts of this kind in Jalcocotán, Doña Esther said, thousands of them in all the villages of the Sierra Madre, and millions in all the pueblos of Mexico.

30   "Algún día me la pagan."

31   "Tía, what does that mean?" I asked her more than once. She always sent me to my mother with the question. Her answer was: "It means that somebody owes him something."

32   "But what does somebody owe him?"

33   The anger and the foreboding in "algún día me la pagan" was in my mother's voice: "Something that hurts." She did not explain, just as she would not tell me why Catalino the bandit hated the *rurales* and shot so many of them.

34   Guessing at what people meant, I came to *feel* certain words rather than to *know* them. They were words which came from the lips of *jalcocotecanos* with an accent of suspicion, of fear, and of hatred. These words were *los rurales*, the *jefe político*, the *señor gobernador*, *las autoridades*, *el gobierno*. When a stranger rode into Jalco, people

stopped talking. Every detail about him and his horse was observed for a clue as to whether he was one of the *autoridades*.

35   It was the same with all outsiders. They always came asking questions, which the *jalcocotecanos* answered politely but roundabout. For me the world began to divide itself into two kinds of people—the men on horseback and the men who walked.

Pom's Engagement

VED MEHTA

Ved Mehta was born in 1934 in Lahore, India, which is now Pakistan. At the age of four, he lost his sight, which caused strife between his parents. His uneducated mother believed in faith healers and applied their magic to her son. His father, educated in medicine in England, took a more rational approach by sending the boy to Bombay's Dadar School for the Blind. At age fifteen, Mehta traveled to the Arkansas School for the Blind in Little Rock; from there he went on to earn his B.A. at Pomona College in California in 1956. He then published his autobiography, *Face to Face: An Autobiography* (1957), which addressed the ordeals of his blindness. He then earned another B.A. at Balliol College, Oxford, in 1959 and then returned to the United States to earn an M.A. at Harvard in 1961. That same year, he became a staff writer for *The New Yorker*. Most of his books since that time, both fiction and nonfiction, have appeared as installments in that magazine. Works such as *Portrait of India* (1970), *Walking the Indian Streets* (1975), and *Mahatma Gandhi and His Apostles* (1977) have introduced and clarified India for many American readers.

"Pom's Engagement" appeared in *The Ledge between the Streams* (1984), an autobiography that portrays Mehta's life from age nine to age fifteen. It is a memoir of a clumsy blind boy attempting to be normal—riding a bicycle or playing hide-and-seek—who is suddenly thrust into the political turmoil of the 1947 partition of the Indian subcontinent, which resulted in the separation of Pakistan from India.

1   Before we moved to Lahore, Daddyji had gone to Mussoorie, a hill station in the United Provinces, without telling us why he was going out of the Punjab. Now, several months after he made that trip, he gathered us around him in the drawing room at 11 Temple Road while Mamaji mysteriously hurried Sister Pom upstairs. He started talking as if we were all very small and he were conducting one of our "dinner-table-school" discussions. He said that by right and tradition the oldest daughter had to be given in marriage first, and that the ripe age for marriage was nineteen. He said that when a girl approached that age her parents, who had to take the initiative, made many inquiries and followed many leads. They investigated each young man and his family background, his relatives, his friends, his classmates, because it was important to know what kind of family the girl would be marrying into, what kind of company she would be expected to keep. If the girl's parents decided that a particular young man was suitable, then his people also had to make their investigations, but, however favorable their findings, their decision was unpredictable, because good, well-settled boys were in great demand and could afford to be choosy. All this took a lot of time. "That's why I said nothing to you children about why I went to Mussoorie," he concluded. "I went to see a young man for Pom. She's already nineteen."

2   We were stunned. We have never really faced the idea that Sister Pom might get married and suddenly leave, I thought.

3   "We won't lose Pom, we'll get a new family member," Daddyji said, as if reading my thoughts.

4   Then all of us started talking at once. We wanted to know if Sister Pom had been told; if she'd agreed; whom she'd be marrying.

5   "Your mother has just taken Pom up to tell her," Daddyji said. "But she's a good girl. She will agree." He added, "The young man in question is twenty-eight years old. He's a dentist, and so has a profession."

6   "Did you get a dentist because Sister Pom has bad teeth?" Usha

asked. Sister Pom had always been held up to us as an example of someone who, as a child, had spurned greens and had therefore grown up with a mouthful of poor teeth.

7   Daddyji laughed. "I confess I didn't think of anyone's teeth when I chose the young man in question."

8   "What is he like?" I asked. "What are we to call him?"

9   "He's a little bit on the short side, but he has a happy-go-lucky nature, like Nimi's. He doesn't drink, but, unfortunately, he does smoke. His father died at an early age of a heart attack, but he has a nice mother, who will not give Pom any trouble. It seems that everyone calls him Kakaji."

10   We all laughed. Kakaji, or "youngster," was what very small boys were called.

11   "That's what he must have been called when he was small, and the name stuck," Daddyji said.

12   In spite of myself, I pictured a boy smaller than I was and imagined him taking Sister Pom away, and then I imagined her having to keep his pocket money, to arrange his clothes in the cupboards, to comb his hair. My mouth felt dry.

13   "What will Kakaji call Sister Pom?" I asked.

14   "Pom, silly—what else?" Sister Umi said.

15   Mamaji and Sister Pom walked into the room. Daddyji made a place for Sister Pom next to him and said, "Now, now, now, no reason to cry. Is it to be yes?"

16   "Whatever you say," Sister Pom said in a small voice, between sobs.

17   "Pom, how can you say that? You've never seen him," Sister Umi said.

18   "Kakaji's uncle, Dr. Prakash Mehrotra, himself a dentist, has known our family from his student days in Lahore," Daddyji said. "As a student dentist, he used to be welcomed in Babuji's Shahalmi Gate house. He would come and go as he pleased. He has known for a long time what kind of people we are. He remembered seeing you, Pom, when we went to Mussoorie on holiday. He said yes immediately, and his approval seemed to be enough for Kakaji."

19   "You promised me you wouldn't cry again," Mamaji said to Sister Pom, patting her on the back, and then, to Daddyji, "She's agreed."

20   Daddyji said much else, sometimes talking just for the sake of talking, sometimes laughing at us because we were sniffling, and all

the time trying to make us believe that this was a happy occasion. First, Sister Umi took issue with him: parents had no business arranging marriages; if she were Pom she would run away. Then Sister Nimi: all her life she had heard him say to us children, "Think for yourself—be independent," and here he was not allowing Pom to think for herself. Brother Om took Daddyji's part: girls who didn't get married became a burden on their parents, and Daddyji had four daughters to marry off, and would be retiring in a few years. Sisters Nimi and Umi retorted: they hadn't gone to college to get married off, to have some young man following them around like a leech. Daddyji just laughed. I thought he was so wise, and right.

21   "Go and bless your big sister," Mamaji said, pushing me in the direction of Sister Pom.

22   "I don't want to," I said. "I don't know him."

23   "What'll happen to Sister Pom's room?" Usha asked. She and Ashok didn't have rooms of their own. They slept in Mamaji's room.

24   "Pom's room will remain empty, so that any time she likes she can come and stay in her room with Kakaji," Daddyji said.

25   The thought that a man I never met would sleep in Pom's room with Sister Pom there made my heart race. A sob shook me. I ran outside.

26   The whole house seemed to be in an uproar. Mamaji was shouting at Gian Chand, Gian Chand was shouting at the bearer, the bearer was shouting at the sweeper. There were the sounds of the kitchen fire being stoked, of the drain being washed out, of water running in bathrooms. From behind whichever door I passed came the rustle of saris, salwars, and kemises. The house smelled of fresh flowers, but it had a ghostly chill. I would climb to the landing of Sister Pom's room and thump down the stairs two at a time. Brother Om would shout up at me, "Stop it!" Sister Umi would shout down at me, "Don't you have anything better to do?" Sister Nimi would call to me from somewhere, "You're giving Pom a headache." I wouldn't heed any of them. As soon as I had thumped down, I would clatter to the top and thump my way down again.

27   Daddyji went past on the back veranda. "Who's coming with Kakaji?" I asked. Kakaji was in Lahore to buy some dental equipment, and in a few minutes he was expected for tea, to meet Sister Pom and the family.

28   "He's coming alone," Daddyji said, over his shoulder. "He's

come from very far away." I had somehow imagined that Kakaji
would come with at least as many people as we had in our family,
because I had started thinking of the tea as a kind of cricket match—
the elevens facing off.

29   I followed Daddyji into the drawing room. "Will he come alone
for his wedding, too?"

30   "No. Then he'll come with the bridegroom's party."

31   We were joined by everyone except Mamaji and Sister Pom, who
from the moment we got the news of Sister Pom's marriage had
become inseparable.

32   Gian Chand came in, the tea things rattling on his tray.

33   Later, I couldn't remember exactly how Kakaji had arrived, but
I remember noticing that his footfall was heavy, that his greeting
was affectionate, and that his voice seemed to float up with laughter.
I don't know what I'd expected, but I imagined that if I had been
in his place I would have skulked in the *gulli*, and perhaps changed
my mind and not entered at all.

34   "Better to have ventured and lost than never to have ventured at
all," Daddyji was saying to Kakaji about life's battles.

35   "Yes, Daddyji, just so," he said, with a little laugh. I had never
heard anybody outside our family call my father Daddyji. It sounded
odd.

36   Sister Pom was sent for, and she came in with Mamaji. Her footsteps were shy, and the rustle of her sari around her feet was slow,
as if she felt too conscious of the noise she was making just in walking.
Daddyji made some complimentary remark about the silver border
on her sari, and told her to sit next to Kakaji. Kakaji and Sister Pom
exchanged a few words about a family group photograph on the
mantelpiece, and about her studies. There was the clink of china as
Sister Pom served Kakaji tea.

37   "Won't you have some tea yourself?" Kakaji asked Sister Pom.

38   Sister Pom's sari rustled over her shoulder as she turned to Daddyji.

39   "Kakaji, none of my children have ever tasted tea or coffee,"
Daddyji said. "We consider both to be bad habits. My children have
been brought up on hot milk, and lately Pom has been taking a little
ghi in her milk at bedtime, for health reasons."

40   We all protested at Daddyji's broadcasting family matters.

41   Kakaji tactfully turned the conversation to a visit to Mussoorie
that our family was planning.

42   Mamaji offered him onion, potato, and cauliflower pakoras. He accepted, remarking how hot and crisp they were.

43   "Where will Sister Pom live?" Usha asked.

44   "In the summer, my practice is in Mussoorie," Kakaji said, "but in the winter it's in Dehra Dun."

45   It struck me for the first time that after Sister Pom got married people we didn't know, people she didn't know, would become more important to her than we were.

46   Kakaji had left without formally committing himself. Then, four days later, when we were all sitting in the drawing room, a servant brought a letter to Mamaji. She told us that it was from Kakaji's mother, and that it asked if Sister Pom might be engaged to Kakaji. "She even wants to know if Pom can be married in April or May," Mamaji said excitedly. "How propitious! That'll be the fifth wedding in the family in those two months." Cousins Prakash and Dev, Cousin Pushpa (Bhaji Ganga Ram's adopted daughter), and Auntie Vimla were all due to be married in Lahore then.

47   "You still have time to change your mind," Daddyji said to Sister Pom. "What do you really think of him?"

48   Sister Pom wouldn't say anything.

49   "How do you expect her to know what her mind is when all that the two talked about was a picture and her bachelor's exam in May?" Sister Umi demanded. "Could she have fallen in love already?"

50   "Love, Umi, means something very different from 'falling in love,'" Daddyji said. "It's not an act but a lifelong process. The best we can do as Pom's parents is to give her love every opportunity to grow."

51   "But doesn't your 'every opportunity' include knowing the person better than over a cup of tea, or whatever?" Sister Umi persisted.

52   "Yes, of course it does. But what we are discussing here is a simple matter of choice—not love," Daddyji said. "To know a person, to love a person, takes years of living together."

53   "Do you mean, then, that knowing a person and loving a person are the same thing?" Sister Umi asked.

54   "Not quite, but understanding and respect are essential to love, and that cannot come from talking together, even over a period of days or months. That can come only in good time, through years of experience. It is only when Pom and Kakaji learn to consider each other's problems as one and the same that they will find love."

55 "But, Daddyji, look at the risk you're taking, the risk you're making Pom take," Sister Nimi said.

56 "We are trying to minimize the risk as much as we can by finding Pom a family that is like ours," Daddyji said. "Kakaji is a dentist, I am a doctor. His life and way of thinking will be similar to mine. We are from the same caste, and Kakaji's family originally came from the Punjab. They eat meat and eggs, and they take religion in their stride, and don't pray every day and go to temples, like Brahmans. Kakaji knows how I walk into a club and how I am greeted there. The atmosphere in Pom's new home will be very much the same as the atmosphere here. Now, if I were to give Pom in marriage to a Brahman he'd expect Pom to live as he did. That would really be gambling."

57 "Then what you're doing is perpetuating the caste system," Sister Nimi said. She was the political rebel in the family. "You seem to presuppose that a Kshatriya should marry only a Kshatriya, that a Brahman should marry only a Brahman. I would just as soon marry a shopkeeper from the Bania caste or an Untouchable, and help to break down caste barriers."

58 "That day might come," Daddyji said. "But you will admit, Nimi, that by doing that you'd be increasing the odds."

59 "But for a cause I believe in," Sister Nimi said.

60 "Yes, but that's a whole other issue," Daddyji said.

61 "Daddyji, you say that understanding and respect are necessary for love," Sister Umi said. "I don't see why you would respect a person more because you lived with him and shared his problems."

62 "In our society, we think of understanding and respect as coming only through sacrifice," Daddyji said.

63 "Then you're advocating the subservience of women," Sister Nimi said, "because it's not Kakaji who will be expected to sacrifice—it's Pom. That's not fair."

64 "And why do you think that Pom will learn to respect Kakaji because she sacrifices for him?" Sister Umi said, pressing her point.

65 "No, Umi, it is the other way around," Daddyji said. "It is Kakaji who will respect Pom because she sacrifices for him."

66 "But that doesn't mean that Pom will respect Kakaji," Sister Umi persisted.

67 "But if Kakaji is moved by Pom's sacrifices he will show more consideration for her. He will grow to love her. I know in my own case I was moved to the depths to see Shanti suffer so because she

was so ill-prepared to be my wife. It took me long enough—too long, I believe—to reach that understanding, perhaps because I had broken away from the old traditions and had given in to Western influences."

68   "So you admit that Pom will have to suffer for years," Sister Umi said.

69   "Perhaps," Daddyji said. "But all that time she will be striving for ultimate happiness and love. Those are precious gifts that can only be cultivated in time."

70   "You haven't told us what this ultimate happiness is," Sister Umi said. "I don't really understand it."

71   "It is a uniting of ideals and purposes, and a merging of them. This is the tradition of our society, and it is the means we have adopted to make our marriages successful and beautiful. It works because we believe in the goodness of the individuals going into the marriage and rely on the strength of the sacred bond."

72   "But my ideal is to be independent," Sister Nimi said. "As you say, 'Think for yourself.' "

73   "But often you have to choose among ideals," Daddyji said. "You may have to choose between being independent and being married."

74   "But aren't you struck by the fact that all the suffering is going to be on Pom's part? Shouldn't Kakaji be required to sacrifice for their happiness, too?" Sister Nimi said, reverting to the old theme.

75   "There has to be a start," Daddyji said. "Remember, in our tradition it's her life that is joined with his; it is she who will forsake her past to build a new future with him. If both Pom and Kakaji were to be obstinate, were to compete with each other about who would sacrifice first, who would sacrifice more, what hope would there be of their ever getting on together, of their ever finding love?"

76   "Daddyji, you're evading the issue," Sister Nimi said. "Why shouldn't he take the initiative in this business of sacrifice?"

77   "He would perhaps be expected to if Pom were working, too, as in the West, and, though married, leading a whole different life from his. I suppose more than this I really can't say, and there may be some injustice in our system, at that. In the West, they go in for romantic love, which is unknown among us. I'm not sure that that method works any better than our method does."

78   Then Daddyji said to Sister Pom, "I have done my best. Even after you marry Kakaji, my responsibility for you will not be over. I will always be there in the background if you should need me."

79   "I respect your judgment, Daddyji," Sister Pom said obediently.
"I'll do what you say."

80   Mamaji consulted Shambu Pandit. He compared the horoscopes
of Sister Pom and Kakaji and set the date of the marriage for the
eleventh of May. . . . "That's just three days after she finishes her
B.A. finals!" we cried. "When will she study? You are sacrificing her
education to some silly superstition."

81   But Shambu Pandit would not be budged from the date. "I am
only going by the horoscopes of the couple," he said. "You might
as well protest to the stars."

82   We appealed to Daddyji, but he said he didn't want to interfere,
because such matters were up to Mamaji. That was as much as to
say that Shambu Pandit's date was a settled thing.

83   I recall that at about that time there was an engagement ceremony.
We all—Daddyji, Mamaji, Sister Pom, many of our Mehta and Mehra
relatives—sat cross-legged on the floor of the front veranda around
Shambu Pandit. He recited the Gayatri Mantra, the simple prayer
he used to tell us to say before we went to sleep, and made a thanks
offering of incense and ghi to a fire in a brazier, much as Mamaji
did—behind Daddyji's back—when one of us was going on a trip
or had recovered from a bout of illness. Servants passed around a
platter heaped up with crumbly sweet balls. I heard Kakaji's sister,
Billo, saying something to Sister Pom; she had just come from Dehra
Dun bearing a sari, a veil, and the engagement ring for Sister Pom,
after Romesh Chachaji, one of Daddyji's brothers, had gone to Dehra
Dun bearing some money, a silver platter and silver bowls, and
sweetmeats for Kakaji. It was the first time that I was able to think
of Kakaji both as a remote and frightening dentist who was going
to take Sister Pom away and as someone ordinary like us, who had
his own family. At some point, Mamaji prodded me, and I scooted
forward, crab fashion, to embrace Sister Pom. I felt her hand on my
neck. It had something cold and metallic on it, which sent a shiver
through me. I realized that she was wearing her engagement ring,
and that until then Mamaji was the only one in our family who had
worn a ring.

84   In the evening, the women relatives closeted themselves in the
drawing room with Sister Pom for the engagement singsong. I
crouched outside with my ear to the door. The door pulsated with
the beat of a barrel drum. The pulse in my forehead throbbed in

sympathy with the beat as I caught snatches of songs about bedsheets and henna, along with explosions of laughter, the songs themselves rising and falling like the cooing of the doves that nested under the eaves of the veranda. I thought that a couple of years earlier I would have been playing somewhere outside on such an occasion, without knowing what I was missing, or been in the drawing room clapping and singing, but now I was crouching by the door like a thief, and was feeling ashamed even as I was captivated.

Nigerian Childhood

WOLE SOYINKA

Wole Soyinka was born in 1934 in Isara, Nigeria. He was educated
in Ibadan, Nigeria, and then earned a B.A. at Leeds University in
England in 1959. He has worked as playwright, poet, and novelist
throughout his life. He has also served as professor and administrator
at various universities and colleges, such as University of Ife, Cambridge University, University of Ghana, and Cornell University. He
was awarded the Nobel Prize in Literature in 1986.

Soyinka's life and writings reflect Africa's political turmoil, especially the move from tribal order and folklore to a Christian civilization and a democratic government. Soyinka gained fame early with
his drama *The Invention* (1955), which was performed in London
at the Royal Court Theatre. It satirizes apartheid policies by showing
a sudden loss of pigment by the black population of South Africa,
a situation that causes chaos in the government. He wrote the play
A Dance of the Forests to celebrate Nigeria's independence and to
warn his people that they needed to step forward boldly into the
new world and not dwell with nostalgia on racial heroes of the
past. Soyinka lived his convictions, so when he helped Biafra during
Nigeria's civil war, he was arrested and spent two years in prison.
While there, he produced *The Man Died: Prison Notes of Wole Soyinka*, which is both an autobiography of his ordeals and a condemna-
tion of the insanity that had infected his country.

Aké: The Years of Childhood (1981) gives an account of Soyinka's
first ten years. It captures the changing images of the youth's maturity

and ends with his deep awareness of his parents' role in the beginnings of Nigerian independence. "Nigerian Childhood," an excerpt from *Aké,* reflects a period in Nigeria about twenty years before British rule ended. Soyinka lived with his father, headmaster of a girl's school, his mother, whom he called Wild Christian, and his sister Tinu. The reference to Bishop Crowther is to a man who became the first black African bishop of the Anglican Church. This narration describes the boy's fascination with the story of his Uncle Sanya, who was suspected of being an *òrò,* a spirit demon with supernatural powers.

1   If I lay across the lawn before our house, face upwards to the sky, my head towards BishopsCourt, each spread-out leg would point to the inner compounds of Lower Parsonage. Half of the Anglican Girls' School occupied one of these lower spaces, the other half had taken over BishopsCourt. The lower area contained the school's junior classrooms, a dormitory, a small fruit garden of pawpaws, guava, some bamboo, and wild undergrowth. There were always snails to be found in the rainy season. In the other lower compound was the mission bookseller, a shriveled man with a serene wife on whose ample back we all, at one time or the other slept, or reviewed the world. His compound became a short cut to the road that led to Ibarà, Lafenwá, or Igbèin and its Grammar School over which Ransome-Kuti presided and lived with his family. The bookseller's compound contained the only well in the parsonage; in the dry season, his place was never empty. And his soil appeared to produce the only coconut trees.

2   BishopsCourt, of Upper Parsonage, is no more. Bishop Ajayi Crowther would sometimes emerge from the cluster of hydrangea and bougainvillea, a gnomic face with popping eyes whose formal photograph had first stared at us from the frontispiece of his life history. He had lived, the teacher said, in BishopsCourt and from that moment, he peered out from among the creeping plants whenever I passed by the house on an errand to our Great Aunt, Mrs. Lijadu. BishopsCourt had become a boarding house for the girls' school

and an extra playground for us during the holidays. The Bishop sat, silently, on the bench beneath the wooden porch over the entrance, his robes twined through and through with the lengthening tendrils of the bougainvillea. I moved closer when his eyes turned to sockets. My mind wandered then to another photograph in which he wore a clerical suit with waistcoat and I wondered what he really kept at the end of the silver chain that vanished into the pocket. He grinned and said, Come nearer, I'll show you. As I moved towards the porch he drew on the chain until he had lifted out a wholly round pocket watch that gleamed of solid silver. He pressed a button and the lid opened, revealing, not the glass and the face dial but a deep cloud-filled space. Then, he winked one eye, and it fell from his face into the bowl of the watch. He snapped back the lid, nodded again and his head went bald, his teeth disappeared, and the skin pulled backward till the whitened cheekbones were exposed. Then he stood up and, tucking the watch back into the waistcoat pocket, moved a step towards me. I fled homewards.

3   BishopsCourt appeared sometimes to want to rival the Canon's house. It looked a houseboat despite its guard of whitewashed stones and luxuriant flowers, its wooden fretwork frontage almost wholly immersed in bougainvillea. And it was shadowed also by those omnipresent rocks from whose clefts tall, stout-boled trees miraculously grew. Clouds gathered and the rocks merged into their accustomed gray turbulence, then the trees were carried to and fro until they stayed suspended over BishopsCourt. This happened only in heavy storms. BishopsCourt, unlike the Canon's house, did not actually border the rocks or the woods. The girls' playing fields separated them and we knew that this buffer had always been there. Obviously bishops were not inclined to challenge the spirits. Only the vicars could. That Bishop Ajayi Crowther frightened me out of that compound by his strange transformations only confirmed that the Bishops, once they were dead, joined the world of spirits and ghosts. I could not see the Canon decaying like that in front of my eyes, nor the Rev. J. J. who had once occupied that house, many years before, when my mother was still like us. J. J. Ransome-Kuti had actually ordered back several ghommids[1] in his lifetime; my mother confirmed it. She was his grandniece and, before she came to live at our house,

---

[1]Wood spirits.

she had lived in the Rev. J. J.'s household. Her brother Sanya also lived there and he was acknowledged by all to be an *òrò*,[2] which made him at home in the woods, even at night. On one occasion, however, he must have gone too far.

4   "They had visited us before," she said, "to complain. Mind you, they wouldn't actually come into the compound, they stood far off at the edge, where the woods ended. Their leader, the one who spoke, emitted wild sparks from a head that seemed to be an entire ball of embers—no, I'm mixing up two occasions—that was the second time when he chased us home. The first time, they had merely sent an emissary. He was quite dark, short and swarthy. He came right to the backyard and stood there while he ordered us to call the Reverend.

5   "It was as if Uncle had been expecting the visit. He came out of the house and asked him what he wanted. We all huddled in the kitchen, peeping out."

6   "What was his voice like? Did he speak like an *egúngún?*"[3]

7   "I'm coming to it. This man, well, I suppose one should call him a man. He wasn't quite human, we could see that. Much too large a head, and he kept his eyes on the ground. So, he said he had come to report us. They didn't mind our coming to the woods, even at night, but we were to stay off any area beyond the rocks and that clump of bamboo by the stream."

8   "Well, what did Uncle say? And you haven't said what his voice was like."

9   Tinu turned her elder sister's eye on me. "Let Mama finish the story."

10   "You want to know everything. All right, he spoke just like your father. Are you satisfied?"

11   I did not believe that but I let it pass. "Go on. What did Grand Uncle do?"

12   "He called everyone together and wanted us to keep away from the place."

13   "And yet you went back!"

14   "Well, you know your Uncle Sanya. He was angry. For one thing the best snails are on the other side of that stream. So he continued

[2]A kind of tree demon.
[3]Spirit of a dead ancestor.

to complain that those *òrò* were just being selfish, and he was going
to show them who he was. Well, he did. About a week later he led
us back. And he was right you know. We gathered a full basket and
a half of the biggest snails you ever saw. Well, by this time we had
all forgotten about the warning, there was plenty of moonlight and
anyway, I've told you Sanya is an *òrò* himself. . . ."

15 "But why? He looks normal like you and us."

16 "You won't understand yet. Anyway, he is *òrò*. So with him we
felt quite safe. Until suddenly this sort of light, like a ball of fire
began to glow in the distance. Even while it was still far we kept
hearing voices, as if a lot of people around us were grumbling the
same words together. They were saying something like, 'You stubborn, stiff-necked children, we've warned you and warned you but
you just won't listen. . . .' "

17 Wild Christian looked above our heads, frowning to recollect the
better. "One can't even say, 'they.' It was only this figure of fire
that I saw and he was still very distant. Yet I heard him distinctly,
as if he had many mouths which were pressed against my ears. Every
moment, the fireball loomed larger and larger."

18 "What did Uncle Sanya do? Did he fight him?"

19 "*Sanya wo ni yen?* He was the first to break and run. *Bo o ló o yă
mi, o di kìtìpà kìtìpà!*[4] No one remembered all those fat snails. That
iwin[5] followed us all the way to the house. Our screams had arrived
long before us and the whole household was—well, you can imagine
the turmoil. Uncle had already dashed down the stairs and was in
the backyard. We ran past him while he went out to meet the creature.
This time that *iwin* actually passed the line of the woods, he continued
as if he meant to chase us right into the house, you know, he wasn't
running, just pursuing us steadily." We waited. This was it! Wild
Christian mused while we remained in suspense. Then she breathed
deeply and shook her head with a strange sadness.

20 "The period of faith is gone. There was faith among our early christians, real faith, not just church-going and hymn-singing. Faith.
Igbàgbó. And it is out of that faith that real power comes. Uncle stood
there like a rock, he held out his Bible and ordered, 'Go back! Go back
to that forest which is your home. Back I said, in the name of God.'

---

[4]If you aren't moving, get out of my way!
[5]A ghommid; a wood sprite which is also believed to live in the ground.

Hm. And that was it. The creature simply turned and fled, those sparks falling off faster and faster until there was just a faint glow receding into the woods." She sighed. "Of course, after prayers that evening, there was the price to be paid. Six of the best on every one's back. Sanya got twelve. And we all cut grass every day for the next week."

21   I could not help feeling that the fright should have sufficed as punishment. Her eyes gazing in the direction of the square house, Wild Christian nonetheless appeared to sense what was going on in my mind. She added, "Faith and—Discipline. That is what made those early believers. Psheeaw! God doesn't make them like that any more. When I think of that one who now occupies that house . . ."

22   Then she appeared to recall herself to our presence. "What are your both still sitting here for? Isn't it time for your evening bath? Lawanle!" "Auntie" Lawanle replied "Ma" from a distant part of the house. Before she appeared I reminded Wild Christian, "But you haven't told us why Uncle Sanya is *òrò*."

23   She shrugged, "He is. I saw it with my own eyes."

24   We both clamored, "When? When?"

25   She smiled, "You won't understand. But I'll tell you about it some other time. Or let him tell you himself next time he is here."

26   "You mean you saw him turn into an *òrò?*"

27   Lawanle came in just then and she prepared to hand us over, "Isn't it time for these children's bath?"

28   I pleaded, "No, wait Auntie Lawanle," knowing it was a waste of time. She had already gripped us both, one arm each. I shouted back, "Was Bishop Crowther an *òrò?*"

29   Wild Christian laughed. "What next are you going to ask? Oh I see. They have taught you about him in Sunday school have they?"

30   "I saw him." I pulled back at the door, forcing Lawanle to stop. "I see him all the time. He comes and sits under the porch of the Girls' School. I've seen him when crossing the compound to Auntie Mrs. Lijadu."

31   "All right," sighed Wild Christian. "Go and have your bath."

32   "He hides among the bougainvillea. . . ." Lawanle dragged me out of hearing.

33   Later that evening, she told us the rest of the story. On that occasion, Rev. J. J. was away on one of his many mission tours. He traveled a lot, on foot and on bicycle, keeping in touch with all the branches of his diocese and spreading the Word of God. There was frequent opposition but nothing deterred him. One frightening

experience occurred in one of the villages in Ijebu. He had been warned not to preach on a particular day, which was the day for an *egúngún* outing, but he persisted and held a service. The *egúngún* procession passed while the service was in progress and, using his ancestral voice, called on the preacher to stop at once, disperse his people, and come out to pay obeisance. Rev. J. J. ignored him. The *egúngún* then left, taking his followers with him but, on passing the main door, he tapped on it with his wand, three times. Hardly had the last member of his procession left the church premises than the building collapsed. The walls simply fell down and the roof disintegrated. Miraculously however, the walls fell outwards while the roof supports fell among the aisles or flew outwards—anywhere but on the congregation itself. Rev. J. J. calmed the worshippers, paused in his preaching to render a thanksgiving prayer, then continued his sermon.

34   Perhaps this was what Wild Christian meant by Faith. And this tended to confuse things because, after all, the *egúngún* did make the church building collapse. Wild Christian made no attempt to explain how that happened, so the feat tended to be of the same order of Faith which moved mountains or enabled Wild Christian to pour ground-nut oil from a broad-rimmed bowl into an empty bottle without spilling a drop. She had the strange habit of sighing with a kind of rapture, crediting her steadiness of hand to Faith and thanking God. If however the basin slipped and she lost a drop to two, she murmured that her sins had become heavy and that she needed to pray more.

35   If Rev. J. J. had Faith, however, he also appeared to have Stubbornness in common with our Uncle Sanya. Stubbornness was one of the earliest sins we easily recognized, and no matter how much Wild Christian tried to explain the Rev. J. J. preaching on the *egúngún*'s outing day, despite warnings, it sounded much like stubbornness. As for Uncle Sanya there was no doubt about his own case; hardly did the Rev. J. J. pedal out of sight on his pastoral duties than he was off into the woods on one pretext or the other, and making for the very areas which the *òrò* had declared out of bounds. Mushrooms and snails were the real goals, with the gathering of firewood used as the dutiful excuse.

36   Even Sanya had however stopped venturing into the woods at night, accepting the fact that it was far too risky; daytime and early dusk carried little danger as most wood spirits only came out at night.

Mother told us that on this occasion she and Sanya had been picking mushrooms, separated by only a few clumps of bushes. She could hear his movements quite clearly, indeed, they took the precaution of staying very close together.

37   Suddenly, she said, she heard Sanya's voice talking animatedly with someone. After listening for some time she called out his name but he did not respond. There was no voice apart from his, yet he appeared to be chatting in friendly, excited tones with some other person. So she peeped through the bushes and there was Uncle Sanya seated on the ground chattering away to no one that she could see. She tried to penetrate the surrounding bushes with her gaze but the woods remained empty except for the two of them. And then her eyes came to rest on his basket.

38   It was something she had observed before, she said. It was the same, no matter how many of the children in the household went to gather snails, berries, or whatever, Sanya would spend most of the time playing and climbing rocks and trees. He would wander off by himself, leaving his basket anywhere. And yet, whenever they prepared to return home, his basket was always fuller than the others'. This time was no different. She came closer, startling our Uncle who snapped off his chatter and pretended to be hunting snails in the undergrowth.

39   Mother said that she was frightened. The basket was filled to the brim, impossibly bursting. She was also discouraged, so she picked up her near empty basket and insisted that they return home at once. She led the way but after some distance, when she looked back, Sanya appeared to be trying to follow her but was being prevented, as if he was being pulled back by invisible hands. From time to time he would snatch forward his arm and snap,

40   "Leave me alone. Can't you see I have to go home? I said I have to go."

41   She broke into a run and Sanya did the same. They ran all the way home.

42   That evening, Sanya took ill. He broke into a sweat, tossed on his mat all night and muttered to himself. By the following day the household was thoroughly frightened. His forehead was burning to the touch and no one could get a coherent word out of him. Finally, an elderly woman, one of J. J.'s converts, turned up at the house on a routine visit. When she learnt of Sanya's condition, she nodded wisely and acted like one who knew exactly what to do. Having first

found out what things he last did before his illness, she summoned my mother and questioned her. She told her everything while the old woman kept on nodding with understanding. Then she gave instructions:

43   "I want a basket of àgìdi, containing fifty wraps. Then prepare some èkuru in a large bowl. Make sure the èkuru stew is prepared with plenty of locust bean and crayfish. It must smell as appetizing as possible."

44   The children were dispersed in various directions, some to the market to obtain the àgìdi, others to begin grinding the beans for the amount of èkuru which was needed to accompany fifty wraps of àgìdi. The children's mouths watered, assuming at once that this was to be an appeasement feast, a sàarà[6] for some offended spirits.

45   When all was prepared, however, the old woman took everything to Sanya's sickroom, plus a pot of cold water and cups, locked the door on him, and ordered everybody away.

46   "Just go about your normal business and don't go anywhere near the room. If you want your brother to recover, do as I say. Don't attempt to speak to him and don't peep through the keyhole."

47   She locked the windows too and went herself to a distant end of the courtyard where she could monitor the movements of the children. She dozed off soon after, however, so that mother and the other children were able to glue their ears to the door and windows, even if they could not see the invalid himself. Uncle Sanya sounded as if he was no longer alone. They heard him saying things like:

48   "Behave yourself, there is enough for everybody. All right you take this, have an extra wrap . . . Open your mouth . . . here . . . you don't have to fight over that bit, here's another piece of crayfish . . . behave, I said . . ."

49   And they would hear what sounded like the slapping of wrists, a scrape of dishes on the ground, or water slopping into a cup.

50   When the woman judged it was time, which was well after dusk, nearly six hours after Sanya was first locked up, she went and opened the door. There was Sanya fast asleep but, this time, very peacefully. She touched his forehead and appeared to be satisfied by the change. The household who had crowded in with her had no interest in Sanya however. All they could see, with astonished faces, were the

[6]An offering, food shared out as offering.

scattered leaves of fifty wraps of *àgìdi*, with the contents gone, a large empty dish which was earlier filled with *èkuru*, and a water pot nearly empty.

51   No, there was no question about it, our Uncle Sanya was an *òrò;* Wild Christian had seen and heard proofs of it many times over. His companions were obviously the more benevolent type or he would have come to serious harm on more than one occasion, J. J.'s protecting Faith notwithstanding.

Aria: A Memoir of a Bilingual Childhood

RICHARD RODRIGUEZ

Richard Rodriguez was born in San Francisco in 1944. During his college days at Stanford University (B.A., 1967), at Columbia University (M.A., 1969), and as a Fulbright scholar, Rodriguez came to realize that his success depended in part not merely on his talents but on his ethnic background, which awarded him special favors. In 1973, he abruptly quit academic life. His revolt against affirmative action mandates resulted in his semi-seclusion for six years, during which time he wrote *Hunger of Memory* (1981), an autobiography.

Hunger of Memory opens with "Aria," which explores his childhood background and then discusses affirmative action policies and their effect on him. He insists that education should enforce a training in standard English, not bilingualism. He wants to take children out of the home, out of their private language, and thrust them into the public world.

1   I remember, to start with, that day in Sacramento, in a California now nearly thirty years past, when I first entered a classroom—able

to understand about fifty stray English words. The third of four children, I had been preceded by my older brother and sister to a neighborhood Roman Catholic school. But neither of them had revealed very much about their classroom experiences. They left each morning and returned each afternoon, always together, speaking Spanish as they climbed the five steps to the porch. And their mysterious books, wrapped in brown shopping-bag paper, remained on the table next to the door, closed firmly behind them.

2   An accident of geography sent me to a school where all my classmates were white and many were the children of doctors and lawyers and business executives. On that first day of school, my classmates must certainly have been uneasy to find themselves apart from their families, in the first institution of their lives. But I was astonished. I was fated to be the "problem student" in class.

3   The nun said, in a friendly but oddly impersonal voice: "Boys and girls, this is Richard Rodriguez." (I heard her sound it out: *Rich-heard Road-ree-guess.*) It was the first time I had heard anyone say my name in English. "Richard," the nun repeated more slowly, writing my name down in her book. Quickly I turned to see my mother's face dissolve in a watery blur behind the pebbled-glass door.

4   Now, many years later, I hear of something called "bilingual education"—a scheme proposed in the late 1960s by Hispanic-American social activists, later endorsed by a congressional vote. It is a program that seeks to permit non-English-speaking children (many from lower class homes) to use their "family language" as the language of school. Such, at least, is the aim its supporters announce. I hear them, and am forced to say no: It is not possible for a child, any child, ever to use his family's language in school. Not to understand this is to misunderstand the public uses of schooling and to trivialize the nature of intimate life.

5   Memory teaches me what I know of these matters. The boy reminds the adult. I was a bilingual child, but of a certain kind: "socially disadvantaged," the son of working-class parents, both Mexican immigrants.

6   In the early years of my boyhood, my parents coped very well in America. My father had steady work. My mother managed at home. They were nobody's victims. When we moved to a house many blocks from the Mexican-American section of town, they were not intimidated by those two or three neighbors who initially tried to

make us unwelcome. ("Keep your brats away from my sidewalk!") But despite all they achieved, or perhaps because they had so much to achieve, they lacked any deep feeling of ease, of belonging in public. They regarded the people at work or in crowds as being very distant from us. Those were the others, *los gringos*. That term was interchangeable in their speech with another, even more telling: *los americanos*.

7   I grew up in a house where the only regular guests were my relations. On a certain day, enormous families of relatives would visit us, and there would be so many people that the noise and the bodies would spill out to the backyard and onto the front porch. Then for weeks no one would come. (If the doorbell rang, it was usually a salesman.) Our house stood apart—gaudy yellow in a row of white bungalows. We were the people with the noisy dog, the people who raised chickens. We were the foreigners on the block. A few neighbors would smile and wave at us. We waved back. But until I was seven years old, I did not know the name of the old couple living next door or the names of the kids living across the street.

8   In public, my father and mother spoke a hesitant, accented, and not always grammatical English. And then they would have to strain, their bodies tense, to catch the sense of what was rapidly said by *los gringos*. At home, they returned to Spanish. The language of their Mexican past sounded in counterpoint to the English spoken in public. The words would come quickly, with ease. Conveyed through those sounds was the pleasing, soothing, consoling reminder that one was at home.

9   During those years when I was first learning to speak, my mother and father addressed me only in Spanish; in Spanish I learned to reply. By contrast, English (*inglés*) was the language I came to associate with gringos, rarely heard in the house. I learned my first words of English overhearing my parents speaking to strangers. At six years of age, I knew just enough words for my mother to trust me on errands to stores one block away—but no more.

10 I was then a listening child, careful to hear the very different sounds of Spanish and English. Wide-eyed with hearing, I'd listen to sounds more than to words. First, there were English (gringo) sounds. So many words still were unknown to me that when the butcher or the lady at the drugstore said something, exotic polysyllabic sounds would bloom in the midst of their sentences. Often the speech of people in public seemed to me very loud, booming with

confidence. The man behind the counter would literally ask, "What can I do for you?" But by being so firm and clear, the sound of his voice said that he was a gringo; he belonged in public society. There were also the high, nasal notes of middle-class American speech— which I rarely am conscious of hearing today because I hear them so often, but could not stop hearing when I was a boy. Crowds at Safeway or at bus stops were noisy with the birdlike sounds of *los gringos*. I'd move away from them all—all the chirping chatter above me.

11 My own sounds I was unable to hear, but I knew that I spoke English poorly. My words could not extend to form complete thoughts. And the words I did speak I didn't know well enough to make distinct sounds. (Listeners would usually lower their heads to hear better what I was trying to say.) But it was one thing for *me* to speak English with difficulty; it was more troubling to hear my parents speaking in public: their high-whining vowels and guttural consonants; their sentences that got stuck with "eh" and "ah" sounds; the confused syntax; the hesitant rhythm of sounds so different from the way gringos spoke. I'd notice, moreover, that my parents' voices were softer than those of gringos we would meet.

12 I am tempted to say now that none of this mattered. (In adulthood I am embarrassed by childhood fears.) And, in a way, it didn't matter very much that my parents could not speak English with ease. Their linguistic difficulties had no serious consequences. My mother and father made themselves understood at the county hospital clinic and at government offices. And yet, in another way, it mattered very much. It was unsettling to hear my parents struggle with English. Hearing them, I'd grow nervous, and my clutching trust in their protection and power would be weakened.

13 There were many times like the night at a brightly lit gasoline station (a blaring white memory) when I stood uneasily hearing my father talk to a teenage attendant. I do not recall what they were saying, but I cannot forget the sounds my father made as he spoke. At one point his words slid together to form one long word—sounds as confused as the threads of blue and green oil in the puddle next to my shoes. His voice rushed through what he had left to say. Toward the end, he reached falsetto notes, appealing to his listener's understanding. I looked away at the lights of passing automobiles. I tried not to hear any more. But I heard only too well the attendant's reply, his calm, easy tones. Shortly afterward, headed for home, I

shivered when my father put his hand on my shoulder. The very first chance that I got, I evaded his grasp and ran on ahead into the dark, skipping with feigned boyish exuberance.

14   But then there was Spanish: *español,* the language rarely heard away from the house; *español,* the language which seemed to me therefore a private language, my family's language. To hear its sounds was to feel myself specially recognized as one of the family, apart from *los otros.* A simple remark, an inconsequential comment could convey that assurance. My parents would say something to me and I would feel embraced by the sounds of their words. Those sounds said: *I am speaking with ease in Spanish. I am addressing you in words I never use with los gringos. I recognize you as someone special, close, like no one outside. You belong with us. In the family. Ricardo.*

15   At the age of six, well past the time when most middle-class children no longer notice the difference between sounds uttered at home and words spoken in public, I had a different experience. I lived in a world compounded of sounds. I was a child longer than most. I lived in a magical world, surrounded by sounds both pleasing and fearful. I shared with my family a language enchantingly private— different from that used in the city around us.

16   Just opening or closing the screen door behind me was an important experience. I'd rarely leave home all alone or without feeling reluctance. Walking down the sidewalk, under the canopy of tall trees, I'd warily notice the (suddenly) silent neighborhood kids who stood warily watching me. Nervously, I'd arrive at the grocery store to hear there the sounds of the gringo, reminding me that in this so-big world I was a foreigner. But if leaving home was never routine, neither was coming back. Walking toward our house, climbing the steps from the sidewalk, in summer when the front door was open, I'd hear voices beyond the screen door talking in Spanish. For a second or two I'd stay, linger there listening. Smiling, I'd hear my mother call out, saying in Spanish, "Is that you, Richard?" Those were her words, but all the while her sounds would assure me: *You are home now. Come closer inside. With us.* "*Sí,*" I'd reply.

17   Once more inside the house, I would resume my place in the family. The sounds would grow harder to hear. Once more at home, I would grow less conscious of them. It required, however, no more than the blurt of the doorbell to alert me all over again to listen to sounds. The house would turn instantly quiet while my mother went to the door. I'd hear her hard English sounds. I'd wait to hear her

voice turn to soft-sounding Spanish, which assured me, as surely as did the clicking tongue of the lock on the door, that the stranger was gone.

18 Plainly it is not healthy to hear such sounds so often. It is not healthy to distinguish public from private sounds so easily. I remained cloistered by sounds, timid and shy in public, too dependent on the voices at home. And yet I was a very happy child when I was at home. I remember many nights when my father would come back from work, and I'd hear him call out to my mother in Spanish, sounding relieved. In Spanish, his voice would sound the light and free notes that he never could manage in English. Some nights I'd jump up just hearing his voice. My brother and I would come running into the room where he was with our mother. Our laughing (so deep was the pleasure!) became screaming. Like others who feel the pain of public alienation, we transformed the knowledge of our public separateness into a consoling reminder of our intimacy. Excited, our voices joined in a celebration of sounds. *We are speaking now the way we never speak out in public—we are together,* the sounds told me. Some nights no one seemed willing to loosen the hold that sounds had on us. At dinner we invented new words that sounded Spanish, but made sense only to us. We pieced together new words by taking, say, an English verb and giving it Spanish endings. My mother's instructions at bedtime would be lacquered with mock-urgent tones. Or a word like *sí*, sounded in several notes, would convey added measures of feeling. Tongues lingered around the edges of words, especially fat vowels, and we happily sounded that military drum roll, the twirling roar of the Spanish *r*. Family language, my family's sounds: the voices of my parents and sisters and brother. Their voices insisting: *You belong here. We are family members. Related. Special to one another. Listen!* Voices singing and sighing, rising and straining, then surging, teeming with pleasure which burst syllables into fragments of laughter. At times it seemed there was steady quiet only when, from another room, the rustling whispers of my parents faded and I edged closer to sleep.

19 Supporters of bilingual education imply today that students like me miss a great deal by not being taught in their family's language. What they seem not to recognize is that, as a socially disadvantaged child, I regarded Spanish as a private language. It was a ghetto language that deepened and strengthened my feeling of public sepa-

rateness. What I needed to learn in school was that I had the right, and the obligation, to speak the public language. The odd truth is that my first-grade classmates could have become bilingual, in the conventional sense of the word, more easily than I. Had they been taught early (as upper-middle-class children often are taught) a "second language" like Spanish or French, they could have regarded it simply as another public language. In my case, such bilingualism could not have been so quickly achieved. What I did not believe was that I could speak a single public language.

20   Without question, it would have pleased me to have heard my teachers address me in Spanish when I entered the classroom. I would have felt much less afraid. I would have imagined that my instructors were somehow "related" to me; I would indeed have heard their Spanish as my family's language. I would have trusted them and responded with ease. But I would have delayed—postponed for how long?—having to learn the language of public society. I would have evaded—and for how long?—learning the great lesson of school: that I had a public identity.

21   Fortunately, my teachers were unsentimental about their responsibility. What they understood was that I needed to speak public English. So their voices would search me out, asking me questions. Each time I heard them I'd look up in surprise to see a nun's face frowning at me. I'd mumble, not really meaning to answer. The nun would persist. "Richard, stand up. Don't look at the floor. Speak up. Speak to the entire class, not just to me!" But I couldn't believe English could be my language to use. (In part, I did not want to believe it.) I continued to mumble. I resisted the teacher's demands. (Did I somehow suspect that once I learned this public language my family life would be changed?) Silent, waiting for the bell to sound, I remained dazed, diffident, afraid.

22   Because I wrongly imagined that English was intrinsically a public language and Spanish was intrinsically private, I easily noted the difference between classroom language and the language at home. At school, words were directed to a general audience of listeners. ("Boys and girls . . .") Words were meaningfully ordered. And the point was not self-expression alone, but to make oneself understood by many others. The teacher quizzed: "Boys and girls, why do we use that word in this sentence? Could we think of a better word to use there? Would the sentence change its meaning

if the words were differently arranged? Isn't there a better way of saying much the same thing?" (I couldn't say. I wouldn't try to say.)

23   Three months passed. Five. A half year. Unsmiling, ever watchful, my teachers noted my silence. They began to connect my behavior with the slow progress my brother and sisters were making. Until, one Saturday morning, three nuns arrived at the house to talk to our parents. Stiffly they sat on the blue livingroom sofa. From the doorway of another room, spying on the visitors, I noted the incongruity, the clash of two worlds, the faces and voices of school intruding upon the familiar setting of home. I overheard one voice gently wondering, "Do your children speak only Spanish at home, Mrs. Rodriguez?" While another voice added, "That Richard especially seems so timid and shy."

24   *That Rich-heard!*

25   With great tact, the visitors continued, "Is it possible for you and your husband to encourage your children to practice their English when they are home?" Of course my parents complied. What would they not do for their children's well-being? And how could they question the Church's authority which those women represented? In an instant they agreed to give up the language (the sounds) which had revealed and accentuated our family's closeness. The moment after the visitors left, the change was observed. "*Ahora,* speak to us only *en inglés,*" my father and mother told us.

26   At first, it seemed a kind of game. After dinner each night, the family gathered together to practice "our" English. It was still then *inglés*, a language foreign to us, so we felt drawn to it as strangers. Laughing, we would try to define words we could not pronounce. We played with strange English sounds, often over-anglicizing our pronunciations. And we filled the smiling gaps of our sentences with familiar Spanish sounds. But that was cheating, somebody shouted, and everyone laughed.

27   In school, meanwhile, like my brother and sisters, I was required to attend a daily tutoring session. I needed a full year of this special work. I also needed my teachers to keep my attention from straying in class by calling out "*Rich-heard*"—their English voices slowly loosening the ties to my other name, with its three notes, *Ri-car-do.* Most of all, I needed to hear my mother and father speak to me

in a moment of seriousness in "broken"—suddenly heartbreaking—
English. This scene was inevitable. One Saturday morning I entered
the kitchen where my parents were talking, but I did not realize that
they were talking in Spanish until, the moment they saw me, their
voices changed and they began speaking English. The gringo sounds
they uttered startled me. Pushed me away. In that moment of trivial
misunderstanding and profound insight, I felt my throat twisted by
unsounded grief. I simply turned and left the room. But I had no
place to escape to where I could grieve in Spanish. My brother and
sisters were speaking English in another part of the house.

28   Again and again in the days following, as I grew increasingly angry,
I was obliged to hear my mother and father encouraging me: "Speak
to us *en inglés.*" Only then did I determine to learn classroom English.
Thus, sometime afterward it happened: One day in school, I raised
my hand to volunteer an answer to a question. I spoke out in a
loud voice and I did not think it remarkable when the entire class
understood. That day I moved very far from being the disadvantaged
child I had been only days earlier. Taken hold at last was the belief,
the calming assurance, that I *belonged* in public.

29   Shortly after, I stopped hearing the high, troubling sounds of *los
gringos.* A more and more confident speaker of English, I didn't
listen to how strangers sounded when they talked to me. With so
many English-speaking people around me, I no longer heard American accents. Conversations quickened. Listening to persons whose
voices sounded eccentrically pitched, I might note their sounds for
a few seconds, but then I'd concentrate on what they were saying.
Now when I heard someone's tone of voice—angry or questioning
or sarcastic or happy or sad—I didn't distinguish it from the words
it expressed. Sound and word were thus tightly wedded. At the end
of each day I was often bemused, and always relieved, to realize how
"soundless," though crowded with words, my day in public had
been. An eight-year-old boy, I finally came to accept what had been
technically true since my birth: I was an American citizen.

30   But diminished by then was the special feeling of closeness at
home. Gone was the desperate, urgent, intense feeling of being at
home among those with whom I felt intimate. Our family remained
a loving family, but one greatly changed. We were no longer so
close, no longer bound tightly together by the knowledge of our
separateness from *los gringos.* Neither my older brother nor my sisters
rushed home after school any more. Nor did I. When I arrived home,

often there would be neighborhood kids in the house. Or the house would be empty of sounds.

31   Following the dramatic Americanization of their children, even my parents grew more publicly confident—especially my mother. First she learned the names of all the people on the block. Then she decided we needed to have a telephone in our house. My father, for his part, continued to use the word gringo, but it was not longer charged with bitterness or distrust. Stripped of any emotional content, the word simply became a name for those Americans not of Hispanic descent. Hearing him, sometimes, I wasn't sure if he was pronouncing the Spanish word *gringo*, or saying gringo in English.

32   There was a new silence at home. As we children learned more and more English, we shared fewer and fewer words with our parents. Sentences needed to be spoken slowly when one of us addressed our mother or father. Often the parent wouldn't understand. The child would need to repeat himself. Still the parent misunderstood. The young voice, frustrated, would end up saying, "Never mind"—the subject was closed. Dinners would be noisy with the clinking of knives and forks against dishes. My mother would smile softly between her remarks; my father, at the other end of the table, would chew and chew his food while he stared over the heads of his children.

33   My mother! My father! After English became my primary language, I no longer knew what words to use in addressing my parents. The old Spanish words (those tender accents of sound) I had earlier used—*mamá* and *papá*—I couldn't use any more. They would have been all-too-painful reminders of how much had changed in my life. On the other hand, the words I heard neighborhood kids call their parents seemed equally unsatisfactory. "Mother" and "father," "ma," "papa," "pa," "dad," "pop" (how I hated the all-American sound of that last word)—all these I felt were unsuitable terms of address for *my* parents. As a result, I never used them at home. Whenever I'd speak to my parents, I would try to get their attention by looking at them. In public conversations, I'd refer to them as my "parents" or my "mother" and "father."

34   My mother and father, for their part, responded differently, as their children spoke to them less. My mother grew restless, seemed troubled and anxious at the scarceness of words exchanged in the house. She would question me about my day when I came home from school. She smiled at my small talk. She pried at the edges of my sentences to get me to say something more. ("What . . . ?")

She'd join conversations she overheard, but her intrusions often stopped her children's talking. By contrast, my father seemed to grow reconciled to the new quiet. Though his English somewhat improved, he tended more and more to retire into silence. At dinner he spoke very little. One night his children and even his wife helplessly giggled at his garbled English pronunciation of the Catholic "Grace Before Meals." Thereafter he made his wife recite the prayer at the start of each meal, even on formal occasions when there were guests in the house.

35   Hers became the public voice of the family. On official business it was she, not my father, who would usually talk to strangers on the phone or in stores. We children grew so accustomed to his silence that years later we would routinely refer to his "shyness." (My mother often tried to explain: Both of his parents died when he was eight. He was raised by an uncle who treated him as little more than a menial servant. He was never encouraged to speak. He grew up alone—a man of few words.) But I realized my father was not shy whenever I'd watch him speaking Spanish with relatives. Using Spanish, he was quickly effusive. Especially when talking with other men, his voice would spark, flicker, flare alive with varied sounds. In Spanish he expressed ideas and feelings he rarely revealed when speaking English. With firm Spanish sounds he conveyed a confidence and authority that English would never allow him.

36   The silence at home, however, was not simply the result of fewer words passing between parents and children. More profound for me was the silence created by my inattention to sounds. At about the time I no longer bothered to listen with care to the sounds of English in public, I grew careless about listening to the sounds made by the family when they spoke. Most of the time I would hear someone speaking at home and didn't distinguish his sounds from the words people uttered in public. I didn't even pay much attention to my parents' accented and ungrammatical speech—at least not at home. Only when I was with them in public would I become alert to their accents. But even then their sounds caused me less and less concern. For I was growing increasingly confident of my own public identity.

37   I would have been happier about my public success had I not recalled, sometimes, what it had been like earlier, when my family conveyed its intimacy through a set of conveniently private sounds. Sometimes in public, hearing a stranger, I'd hark back to my lost past. A Mexican farm worker approached me one day downtown.

He wanted directions to some place. "*Hijito, . . .*" he said. And his voice stirred old longings. Another time I was standing beside my mother in the visiting room of a Carmelite convent, before the dense screen which rendered the nuns shadowy figures. I heard several of them speaking Spanish in their busy, singsong, overlapping voices, assuring my mother that, yes, yes, we were remembered, all our family was remembered, in their prayers. Those voices echoed faraway family sounds. Another day a dark-faced old woman touched my shoulder lightly to steady herself as she boarded a bus. She murmured something to me I couldn't quite comprehend. Her Spanish voice came near, like the face of a never-before-seen relative in the instant before I was kissed. That voice, like so many of the Spanish voices I'd hear in public, recalled the golden age of my childhood.

38   Bilingual educators say today that children lose a degree of "individuality" by becoming assimilated into public society. (Bilingual schooling is a program popularized in the seventies, that decade when middle-class "ethnics" began to resist the process of assimilation—the "American melting pot.") But the bilingualists oversimplify when they scorn the value and necessity of assimilation. They do not seem to realize that a person is individualized in two ways. So they do not realize that, while one suffers a diminished sense of *private* individuality by being assimilated into public society, such assimilation makes possible the achievement of *public* individuality.

39   Simplistically again, the bilingualists insist that a student should be reminded of his difference from others in mass society, of his "heritage." But they equate mere separateness with individuality. The fact is that only in private—with intimates—is separateness from the crowd a prerequisite for individuality; an intimate "tells" me that I am unique, unlike all others, apart from the crowd. In public, by contrast, full individuality is achieved, paradoxically, by those who are able to consider themselves members of the crowd. Thus it happened for me. Only when I was able to think of myself as an American, no longer an alien in gringo society, could I seek the rights and opportunities necessary for full public individuality. The social and political advantages I enjoy as a man began on the day I came to believe that my name is indeed *Rich-heard Road-ree-guess*. It is true that my public society today is often impersonal; in fact, my public society is usually mass society. But despite the anonymity of the crowd, and despite the fact that the individuality I achieve in public

is often tenuous—because it depends on my being one in a crowd—I celebrate the day I acquired my new name. Those middle-class ethnics who scorn assimilation seem to me filled with decadent self-pity, obsessed by the burden of public life. Dangerously, they romanticize public separateness and trivialize the dilemma of those who are truly socially disadvantaged.

40   If I rehearse here the changes in my private life after my Americanization, it is finally to emphasize a public gain. The loss implies the gain. The house I returned to each afternoon was quiet. Intimate sounds no longer greeted me at the door. Inside there were other noises. The telephone rang. Neighborhood kids ran past the door of the bedroom where I was reading my schoolbooks—covered with brown shopping-bag paper. Once I learned the public language, it would never again be easy for me to hear intimate family voices. More and more of my day was spent hearing words, not sounds. But that may only be a way of saying that on the day I raised my hand in class and spoke loudly to an entire roomful of faces, my childhood started to end.

from *Black Ice*

LORENE CARY

Lorene Cary was born and raised in Philadelphia. For the last two years of her high school studies, she attended St. Paul's School in Concord, New Hampshire. That experience at St. Paul's became the subject of her memoir, *Black Ice*, published in 1991. She earned her B.A. and M.A. at the University of Pennsylvania. She has served as an associate editor for *TV Guide*, as a writer for *Time*, and as a freelance writer who has published numerous short stories.

The essay reprinted here is one chapter of *Black Ice*. In it, she describes the manner in which she was recruited by St. Paul's School. During the recruitment process, she discovers the great love and affection of her family. They participated in the process because they wanted something good for her, and they wanted to protect her in that time of transition.

1   I had never heard of St. Paul's School until Mrs. Evans rang to tell me about it one fall night in 1971. I had just come home from Woolworth's, where I worked at the cheap-and-greasy fountain on Friday nights and Saturdays in a town my friends and I called "Tacky" Darby. I smelled as if I had scrubbed the grill with my uniform. My face shown with hamburger fat, and my Earth Shoes were spattered. At fourteen years old, I felt irritable and entitled to it, as adults seemed to be when they finished their work for the day.

2   Mrs. Evans's voice brimmed with excitement and fun. She was

our next-door neighbor, a retired kindergarten teacher married to a newspaper reporter who had been the first black man on staff at the *Philadelphia Bulletin*. Three years before, when I was eleven, he had given me my first typewriter, a straight-back, black Underwood. Mrs. Evans was witty and down-to-earth, firm but easygoing with children. Her eyesight was poor; she had a recurring tickle that caused her to clear her throat nearly to gagging; under her shiny skin her knuckles were gnarled—yet she glowed with health. My father said that she had better legs than most thirty-year-olds, and my mother asked her advice. My sister, Carole, ran away to the brick house where a plaster Venus arose from her seashell and dolphins leapt at half-moons in the cream-colored ceiling molding. It was a fairy-tale house, and Mrs. Evans was a fairy godmother to us, distant and charming. I forgot that at first. Instead, I cradled the receiver on my shoulder and counted my tips while she talked, laying the coins silently on the kitchen counter.

3   Mrs. Evans had been told about St. Paul's School by a "lovely woman"—I took that to mean someone white, but trustworthy. This "very exclusive boarding school" had recently gone coed, and they were interested in finding black girls, too, so they'd put out the word with alumni and friends. Mrs. Evans had never visited the school, but she knew that the campus would be beautiful, that there would be music and languages and the arts. She also knew that scholarships—generous scholarships—were available. Mrs. Evans gave me the phone number of an alumnus, a judge, to call for more information. I wrote it down, thanked her for thinking of me, and went upstairs. I didn't need another school, I thought. I needed a bath.

4   Later that night, despite my adolescent defiance, I could not help but think about what Mrs. Evans had said. This education was more than knowledge; it could mean credentials, self-confidence, power. I imagined living away from home, making a precocious launch into the wide world of competition.

5   On Monday after school, I hurried home to call the judge, but when I got there, all I could do was stand next to the telephone preparing statements. My mother watched me as she cooked dinner. "Did Mrs. Evans give you the number to his home or his chambers?" she asked.

6   I hadn't thought about "chambers." Did "chambers" have telephones? I imagined a Dickensian suite of rooms, wood-paneled and dark, and in the middle a big, florid man draped in black robes,

pondering important papers, a man who was not used to being interrupted by phone calls from strange fourteen-year-old black girls who wanted to go to his alma mater.

7   My mother laughed at me as I stood by the telephone in the kitchen staring at the number. "Just call him," she said.

8   Wherever I rang, the judge did not answer. A woman took the message and said that he would get back to me. We got on with dinner preparation. Our TV blared. Pots crackled, and dishes clattered; my parents talked over the TV; my eight-year-old sister talked over my parents; I talked over my sister. Then the telephone rang.

9   By the time I had motioned wildly for silence, the conversation was nearly finished. The judge said that he was pleased to hear of my interest. Then he gave me the name and address of another alumnus who would be hosting a meeting, and urged me to attend.

10   The meeting took place within a couple of weeks. We drove through West Philadelphia, past the squat row houses where I had been raised, past the city center and then north where Wissahickon Creek falls away from the road, and woods rise up behind it. We were headed toward Chestnut Hill, more a place name than a place for me until then, a symbol of money and social exclusiveness. My father steered us through Germantown, where wet leaves lay in treacherous layers over trolley tracks and cobblestones. Cars slipped on and off the rails and then swerved to avoid each other, making rubbery squeals and muffled thuds.

11   By the time we pulled into the stone driveway, I felt as if we were a long way from our home in the west end of Yeadon, an enclave of black professionals, paraprofessionals, wish-they-was-, look-like-, and might-as-well-be professionals, as we called ourselves. We were far away from the black suburb that, as a West Philly transplant, I disliked for its self-satisfied smugness. When we'd moved from our city apartment—from the living room with a convertible couch where my parents slept, from the bedroom where my sister and I slept (which was transformed into a dining room at Christmas), and from the kitchen where we normally ate, and where my mother pressed and curled women's hair in the evenings—Yeadon had impressed me with its leafy green grandeur and insularity. But now, as we stood in the Chestnut Hill driveway, I saw how modest our Tudors were, our semidetached Dutch colonials, our muddy driveways and the cyclone fences that held in our dogs. I saw it then, with eyes made keen by years of witnessing our merciless self-criticism: "What's

wrong with the colored race? I'll tell you what's wrong with the colored race. We don't *think*. That's what. And we do not stick together. And money? Forget it. Invest? Get outta here. Now you take a look at the Jews. Or you take the Chinese. . . ." I saw how consumed we'd been with ambition, and how modest had been our goals.

12   Inside the stone house, in a large living room, we joined a few other black people who had also come to learn about the School. A boy who was younger than I sat next to his mother. When I said hello, he did not turn his head to look at me, but only peeped out of the corner of his eyes and nodded, as if we might bolt out of the house together and go howling into the Chestnut Hill woods if we were to look too hard at each other. His mother, her hair done up like Coretta Scott King's, sat still like her son. She looked as dignified as a picture on the back of a church fan, and just as inanimate. If she kept any unauthorized verb forms from flying out from between her lips, she also held in any sign of life.

13   Jeremy Price (this name and a few others have been changed), a black teacher from St. Paul's, tried a few times to make small talk, but he was a Brahmin from another planet: cool, ironic, aloof. He was in his thirties, tweed-jacketed and bearded, with a round belly. He touched his body lightly with his fingers, as if he were not used to his own girth. In every other way he appeared absolutely smooth and easy to my adolescent eye, and assured to the point of arrogance.

14   Mr. Price made quick judgments of us; they showed in his eyes. Clearly, the pillar-of-the-church lady with the Southern coif (and Southern diffidence in the presence of white folks) wasn't his type. Mr. Price seemed about to say something brutal to her. My father stepped in to ask if he could join them. The look she gave Daddy went beyond grateful to adoring.

15   Women looked at my father that way. Their attention seemed to affect him as naturally as sunshine—and he never talked too much. "Still water runs deep," my great-grandmother had said about him when he came courting; she said so until she died. Men saw more ripples on the pond, which those of us who lived with him knew positively were caused by undertows.

16   For one thing, when men exchanged the inevitable sports conversation they discovered, as Mr. Price did, that my father was a student of judo. He'd spent three nights a week since his twenty-eighth birthday at the dojo. He had progressed from white belt to brown

to black. We'd gone to competitions throughout the mid-Atlantic region, and I'd watched three-minute dramas on the mat. Each time he had to beat or be beaten. In contest after contest he was a light-middleweight whose feet made the sound of rushing as they swept the dry mat and whose face turned purple when the last man, the one he finally could not beat, held him down, cutting into his wind-pipe with his bleached white *gi*. In those moments, when I prayed that he would not be killed in some fluke throw, I saw in his eyes a concentration and force that made life with us in the sparkling three-room apartment seem like some errant choice. He was, above all, a physical being, a wiry man who once tied our deluxe-size refrigerator to his back to move it, and would probably not object to being remembered that way. We three, two girls and a woman, surrounded him with doll babies and crisscross curtains. It was like watching a carnivore sit down to porridge each night.

17   Dad had first seen judo practiced in a 1945 film, *Blood on the Sun,* with James Cagney. Intended as anti-Japanese propaganda, the film showed an expansionist culture, arrogant and absolute. Daddy loved it. Judo: there was a vision of power—mental, physical, spiritual—beneath a placid exterior. It was nearly twenty years before my father stepped onto a mat. Now, he only needed to mention the word. People looked at him as if he had jumped out of a Samurai movie. Even Mr. Price lost his frost when the subject came up. As I watched the two of them chat, my fear of Mr. Price dissipated, but not my wariness. He did not quite seem one of us.

18   Mike Russell did. He was a St. Paul's senior recruiting black candidates as an independent-study project, and he had more poise than I'd ever seen in a teenager. His skin was chocolatey and fine-pored, and his bottom lip pouted like Sidney Poitier's. He was sleek and articulate. He paid attention to me.

19   I crossed my legs with what I hoped was lithe grace and stretched my neck until I nearly pitched forward onto the floor. I wanted to know the things he must know: about science and literature and language, living away from home, New England, white people, money, power, himself. I supposed that the other black students at St. Paul's must have had Russell's sophistication and charm, his commitment to the black progress.

20   I had to be part of that. With the force of religious conversion, the great God of education moved within me, an African Methodist God with a voice that boomed like thunder. It took all my strength

to hold myself inside my skin. This school—why, this was what I had been raised for, only I hadn't known it. They closed the curtains and turned off the lights for the slide show. I hoped that my face had not betrayed me.

21   Russell narrated the slide show. He told us about the Old Chapel, a steepled red-brick church, and towering behind it on the green lawn, the Chapel of St. Peter and St. Paul, built in 1886 to accommodate a larger student body, and enlarged in 1927. The New Chapel was massive. Its brick and stone walls were heavy and stolid; and yet its stained-glass windows seemed infinitely light, as if they could almost float up to the heavens.

22   We saw other buildings as well: the Schoolhouse, student houses (in keeping with the school's family-centered lexicon, they were not to be called dormitories), the Rectory, the funny circular post office, and special academic buildings for science, math, and art. The gray granite library with its white columns had been built by somebody famous. It sat at the edge of yet another pond, casting a wavering, silvery reflection on the water.

23   Over and over again we saw these buildings, draped with scenic young people, alone or in small groups, talking, laughing, bending their heads toward one another or running together on a green field in some pantomime of benevolent competition. I saw black boys. I saw girls, a few of them black, too. And I saw them all in a brilliant medley of New Hampshire seasons. At one point in the slide show, Russell flashed through the carousel to find a misplaced slide, creating an intoxicating display of colors—autumn red and gold, winter snowy blue-white, spring green and pink and blue—so sharp and bright that they seemed to originate not on the screen, but from deep inside my head, like music.

24   Mr. Price's voice, clear and insouciant, brought me back to myself. He was asking for someone to open the drapes.

25   My mother began with a question about the progress of coeducation. First there were tea dances, Mr. Price said, begun in the nineteenth century and carried forward into the 1960s as dance weekends. Girls were bused in, talked to, danced with, and then bused out again. He looked at Mike Russell and asked ironically, "How were they?"

26   Russell shook his head and laughed. "They were awful!"

27   Mr. Price went on. In 1969 and 1970, girls came, like foreigners, to participate in a winter-term exchange. The next winter, the first nineteen came to stay.

28   What was a tea dance? I wondered. Tea meant little girls with clean hands and faces sipping out of china cups, eating butter cookies with raspberry jam. Teas belonged in church or in childhood. A dance, to the contrary, meant teenagers in a basement: black lights, red bulbs, music jamming its way through our shoes and up into our feet. It meant arms in the air, whistles, a soul train down the middle of the room, whipping out new steps nice and casual as if we hadn't spent all week practicing. It meant sweat steaming out of the tops of our heads, shrinking Afros worthy of Angela Davis down to dreaded TWAs (teeny weeny Afros). A dance meant watching sharp so that no amorous brother spoiled our hot pants.

29   Tea had nothing to do with it.

30   Mr. Price acted as cultural interpreter for us, as if a bank of white and black computers stood on either side of him, bleeping away in incompatible languages. When my mother asked about the grading system, I heard her asking whether white teachers four hundred miles away would give her kid a fair grade. Hanging in the air was our fear that they'd let us survive, but never excel. Mr. Price answered by describing the system: High Honors for work that was truly outstanding; Honors for work that was very, very good; High Pass— he laughed and shook his head—was a great, gray, muddy area between the very good and the OK; Pass was just acceptable; and Unsatisfactory was "self-explanatory." Then he estimated how many students received which grades, and quite directly—said it right out in this white alumnus's house with the costly furnishings—told us how the black students were doing. He said most of them were working hard, but some were not, frankly, getting what the school had to offer. He did not answer the black mothers' fear of their children's powerlessness, their vulnerability to white adults who might equate sharpness of the mind with sharpness of features.

31   Mr. Price encouraged Russell to comment. Mike told a few stories about himself, portraying St. Paul's as a place where well-meaning, well-trained teachers tried hard to live up to their calling. Some, he added meaningfully, were more sensitive than others.

32   Then my mother told a story about a science award I had won in third grade. She started with the winning—the long, white staircase in the auditorium of the Franklin Institute, and how the announcer called my name twice because we were way at the back and it took me so long to get down those steps.

33   Mama's eyes glowed. She was a born raconteur, able to increase

the intensity of her own presence and fill the room. She was also a woman who seldom found new audiences for her anecdotes, so she made herself happy, she insisted, with us children, her mother, her sisters, her grandparents—an entire clan of storytellers competing for a turn on the family stage. This time all eyes were on my mother. Her body, brown and plump and smooth, was shot through with energy. This time the story had a purpose.

34   She told them how my science experiment almost did not get considered in the citywide competition. My third-grade teacher, angry that I'd forgotten to bring a large box for displaying and storing the experiment, made me pack it up to take home. (Our teacher had told us that the boxes were needed to carry the experiments from our class to the exhibition room, and she'd emphasized that she would not be responsible for finding thirty boxes on the day of the fair. Without a box, the experiment would have to go home. Other kids, white kids, had forgotten boxes during the week. They'd brought boxes the next day. I asked for the same dispensation, but was denied. The next day was the fair, she said. That was different.)

35   I came out of school carrying the pieces of the experiment my father had picked out for me from a textbook. This was a simple buoyancy experiment where I weighted each object in the air and then in water, to prove that they weighed less in water. I had with me the scale, a brick, a piece of wood, a bucket, and a carefully lettered poster.

36   Well, my mother marched me and my armload of buoyant materials right back into the school and caught the teacher before she left. The box was the only problem? Just the box? Nothing wrong with the experiment? An excited eight-year-old had forgotten a lousy, stinking box that you get from the supermarket, and for that, she was out of the running? The teacher said I had to learn to follow directions. My mother argued that I had followed directions by doing the experiment by myself, which was more than you could say for third graders who'd brought in dry-cell batteries that lit light bulbs and papier-mâché volcanoes that belched colored lava.

37   "Don't you ever put me in a position like that again," Mama said when we were out of earshot of the classroom. "You never know who is just waiting for an excuse to shut us out."

38   We got the box; my experiment went into the fair; I won the prize at school. I won third prize for my age group in the city.

39   My ears began to burn. I could not help but believe that they would see through this transparent plug, and before I had even laid hands on an application. They'd think we were forward and pushy. I forgot, for the moment, how relieved I'd felt when Mama had stood in front of that teacher defending me with a blinding righteousness, letting the teacher know that I was not as small and black and alone as I seemed, that I came from somewhere, and where I came from, she'd better believe, somebody was home.

40   The other mothers nodded approvingly. My father gave me a wide, clever-girl smile. Mr. Price and Russell looked at me deadpan. They seemed amused by my embarrassment.

41   The story was an answer, part rebuke and part condolence, to Mike Russell's stories, where no parents figured at all. It was a message to Mr. Price about her maternal concerns, and a way to prove that racism was not some vanquished enemy, but a real, live person, up in your face, ready, for no apparent reason, to mess with your kid. When I was in third grade, and her marriage to my father had looked like forever, when Martin Luther King was alive preaching love, and white flight had not yet sunk the real-estate values in West Philly, Mama could do her maternal duty, and face down a white teacher who would have deprived me of my award. Who at St. Paul's School would stand up for her child in her stead?

42   Mr. Price did not answer my mother's story. Instead he invited a few more questions. The Mama's boy asked about food and mosquitoes and telephones. He looked appalled to hear that there were no phones in the rooms, only public phone booths outside, and only a handful at that. I doubted that I'd see that child again.

43   If we wanted to be considered for candidacy, we were to write for an application, our own letters, composed in our own hand, and register to take standardized tests. In addition, Mr. Price said, it would be worth our while to visit the school in person.

44   Our host, Ralph Starr, who had slipped out of the room during the discussion, had slipped back in. Mr. Price thanked him for the use of his house. Mr. Starr took exception. He was glad to be able to help in the good work that Mr. Price and Mike were doing. In fact he thanked *us* for coming. The adults appeared pleased. They chatted with each other; I talked to Mike, and the session ended.

45   As we drove away, my mother could not get over how Mrs. Starr had given her barefoot toddler a spoonful of peanut butter to lick before she was spirited upstairs. Mama didn't feed us peanut butter.

It wasn't proper good food, she said. It was what PWTs—poor white trash—gave their kinds. For my lunch, Mom packed baked chicken on toast with lettuce and mayonnaise, ham, tuna, sliced tongue, or cheese.

46   I was as jolted by the sight as my mother, and not just the peanut butter, but the whole family scene. I had thought that rich white people would have been quieter, their children more tidy, their mothers less vibrant. I didn't like it that my mother, too, had been surprised. It made me nervous.

47   A week later, however, I did not think of the background kidbabble in Chestnut Hill, but of the wide drawing room and the slides. Mr. Price wrote promptly to inform us that he had indeed scheduled the visit we'd said we wanted to make to the school.

48   "They don't play, do they?" My parents took turns asking each other and answering back.

49   "Those people do not play."

CLASSIC MULTICULTURAL ESSAYS ABOUT

Issues of Identity

Custer Died for Your Sins

VINE DELORIA, JR.

Vine Deloria, Jr. was born in 1933 on the Pine Ridge Reservation in Martin, South Dakota, the son of an Indian Episcopalian clergyman. He earned a B. S. at the University of Iowa, an M.Th. at the Lutheran School of Theology, and a J.D. at the University of Colorado. As an educator and lawyer, Deloria stepped into the national limelight in 1969 with his first book, *Custer Died for Your Sins: An Indian Manifesto*. The book condemns white America's treatment of Indians and sets out goals for Indian activists. He boldly addresses the issues of termination and tribalism. *Termination,* he says, is the government policy to cut aid to Indians, close reservations, and assimilate the Indian population. *Tribalism* is the bonding of the people, the land, and their religion into a cohesive community. He advances tribalism but sees its liability—the tribes can form tight bonds but the white population and the government will not disappear and will continue to cut into and destroy tribal values. In his books and articles since writing *Custer Died for Your Sins*, Deloria has advanced his quest for a new treaty relationship between the tribes and the government, one that would give tribes quasi-international independence. His work continues.

1   One of the finest things about being an Indian is that people are always interested in you and your "plight." Other groups have

difficulties, predicaments, quandaries, problems, or troubles. Traditionally we Indians have had a "plight."

2 Our foremost plight is our transparency. People can tell just by looking at us what we want, what should be done to help us, how we feel, and what a "real" Indian is really like. Indian life, as it relates to the real world, is a continuous attempt not to disappoint people who know us. Unfulfilled expectations cause grief and we have already had our share.

3 Because people can see right through us, it becomes impossible to tell truth from fiction or fact from mythology. Experts paint us as they would like us to be. Often we paint ourselves as we wish we were or as we might have been.

4 The more we try to be ourselves the more we are forced to defend what we have never been. The American public feels most comfortable with the mythical Indians of stereotype-land who were always THERE. These Indians are fierce, they wear feathers and grunt. Most of us don't fit this idealized figure since we grunt only when overeating, which is seldom.

5 Indian reactions are sudden and surprising. One day at a conference we were singing "My Country 'Tis of Thee" and we came across the part that goes:

Land where our fathers died
Land of the Pilgrims' pride . . .

Some of us broke out laughing when we realized that our fathers undoubtedly died trying to keep those Pilgrims from stealing our land. In fact, many of our fathers died because the Pilgrims killed them as witches. We didn't feel much kinship with those Pilgrims, regardless of who they did in.

6 We often hear "give it back to the Indians" when a gadget fails to work. It's a terrible thing for a people to realize that society has set aside all nonworking gadgets for their exclusive use.

7 American blacks had become recognized as a species of human being by amendments to the Constitution shortly after the Civil War. Prior to emancipation they had been counted as three-fifths of a person in determining population for representation in the House of Representatives. Early Civil Rights bills nebulously state that other people shall have the same rights as "white people," indicating there *were* "other people." But Civil Rights bills passed during and after the Civil War systematically excluded Indian

people. For a long time an Indian was not presumed capable of initiating an action in a court of law, of owning property, or of giving testimony against whites in court. Nor could an Indian vote or leave his reservation. Indians were America's captive people without any defined rights whatsoever.

8   Then one day the white man discovered that the Indian tribes still owned some 135 million acres of land. To his horror he learned that much of it was very valuable. Some was good grazing land, some was farm land, some mining land, and some covered with timber.

9   Animals could be herded together on a piece of land, but they could not sell it. Therefore it took no time at all to discover that Indians were really people and should have the right to sell their lands. Land was the means of recognizing the Indian as a human being. It was the method whereby land could be stolen legally and not blatantly.

10   Once the Indian was thus acknowledged, it was fairly simple to determine what his goals were. If, thinking went, the Indian was just like the white, he must have the same outlook as the white. So the future was planned for the Indian people in public and private life. First in order was allotting them reservations so that they could sell their lands. God's foreordained plan to repopulate the continent fit exactly with the goals of the tribes as they were defined by their white friends.

11   It is fortunate that we were never slaves. We gave up land instead of life and labor. Because the Negro labored, he was considered a draft animal. Because the Indian occupied large areas of land, he was considered a wild animal. Had we given up anything else, or had anything else to give up, it is certain that we would have been considered some other thing.

12   Whites have had different attitudes toward the Indians and the blacks since the Republic was founded. Whites have always refused to give nonwhites the respect which they have been found to legally possess. Instead there has always been a contemptuous attitude that although the law says one thing, "we all know better."

13   Thus whites steadfastly refused to allow blacks to enjoy the fruits of full citizenship. They systematically closed schools, churches, stores, restaurants, and public places to blacks or made insulting provisions for them. For one hundred years every program of public and private white America was devoted to the exclusion of the black. It was,

perhaps, embarrassing to be rubbing shoulders with one who had not so long before been defined as a field animal.

14   The Indian suffered the reverse treatment. Law after law was passed requiring him to conform to white institutions. Indian children were kidnapped and forced into boarding schools thousands of miles from their homes to learn the white man's ways. Reservations were turned over to different Christian denominations for governing. Reservations were for a long time church operated. Everything possible was done to ensure that Indians were forced into American life. The wild animal was made into a household pet whether or not he wanted to be one.

America: The Multinational Society

ISHMAEL REED

Ishmael Reed was born in Chattanooga, Tennessee, in 1938. He attended the State University of New York at Buffalo from 1956 to 1960, where he developed his interest in and talent for writing. His first novel, *The Free Lance Pallbearers* (1967), attacks not only whites, whom he blames for world conditions, but also black leaders who exploit poor blacks. He also attacks the Christian Bible and the literature written by his fellow African Americans. His second novel, *Yellow Back Radio Broke-Down* (1969), introduces elements of Hoodoo (or Voodoo), which he would pursue in later works such as *Mumbo Jumbo* (1978). Reed combines the ideas, beliefs, and language of diverse cultures into a Hoodoo concept of time in which opposite meanings coexist. His language absorbs standard English into the dialect and slang of the street. In one sense, Reed builds his vision of the African American community by revising folklore, the oral traditions of his people, myth, art, and history.

"America: The Multinational Society" which appears in *Writin' is Fightin'* (1988), opens with a series of examples that demonstrate the vast cultural and racial richness of the United States. He uses those scenes to advance his thesis—that calling America a "Western civilization" is a misnomer. He reminds readers that the world has been arriving here not from Europe alone but from Africa and Asia

and more recently from South America and the Caribbean. He cele-
brates this place "where the cultures of the world crisscross."

> At the annual Lower East Side Jewish Festival yes-
> terday, a Chinese woman at a pizza slice in front of
> Ty Thuan Duc's Vietnamese grocery store. Beside
> her a Spanish-speaking family patronized a cart with
> two signs: "Italian Ices" and "Kosher by Rabbi
> Alper." And after the pastrami ran out, everybody
> ate knishes.
>
> (*New York Times*, 23 June 1983)

1   On the day before Memorial Day, 1983, a poet called me to
describe a city he had just visited. He said that one section included
mosques, built by the Islamic people who dwelled there. Attending
his reading, he said, were large numbers of Hispanic people, forty
thousand of whom lived in the same city. He was not talking about
a fabled city located in some mysterious region of the world. The
city he'd visited was Detroit.

2   A few months before, as I was leaving Houston, Texas, I heard
it announced on the radio that Texas's largest minority was Mexican
American, and though a foundation recently issued a report critical
of bilingual education, the taped voice used to guide the passengers
on the air trams connecting terminals in Dallas Airport is in both
Spanish and English. If the trend continues, a day will come when
it will be difficult to travel through some sections of the country
without hearing commands in both English and Spanish; after all,
for some western states, Spanish was the first written language and
the Spanish style lives on in the western way of life.

3   Shortly after my Texas trip, I sat in an auditorium located on the
campus of the University of Wisconsin at Milwaukee as a Yale professor—whose original work on the influence of African cultures upon
those of the Americas has led to his ostracism from some monocultural
intellectual circles—walked up and down the aisle, like an old-time

southern evangelist, dancing and drumming the top of the lectern, illustrating his points before some serious Afro-American intellectuals and artists who cheered and applauded his performance and his mastery of information. The professor was "white." After his lecture, he joined a group of Milwaukeeans in a conversation. All of the participants spoke Yoruban, though only the professor had ever traveled to Africa.

4 One of the artists told me that his paintings, which included African and Afro-American mythological symbols and imagery, were hanging in the local McDonald's restaurant. The next day I went to McDonald's and snapped pictures of smiling youngsters eating hamburgers below paintings that could grace the walls of any of the country's leading museums. The manager of the local McDonald's said, "I don't know what you boys are doing, but I like it," as he commissioned the local painters to exhibit in his restaurant.

5 Such blurring of cultural styles occurs in everyday life in the United States to a greater extent than anyone can imagine and is probably more prevalent than the sensational conflict between people of different backgrounds that is played up and often encouraged by the media. The result is what the Yale professor, Robert Thompson, referred to as a cultural bouillabaisse, yet members of the nation's present educational and cultural Elect still cling to the notion that the United States belongs to some vaguely defined entity they refer to as "Western civilization," by which they mean, presumably, a civilization created by the people of Europe, as if Europe can be viewed in monolithic terms. Is Beethoven's Ninth Symphony, which includes Turkish marches, a part of Western civilization, or the late nineteenth- and twentieth-century French paintings, whose creators were influenced by Japanese art? And what of the cubists, through whom the influence of African art changed modern painting, or the surrealists, who were so impressed with the art of the Pacific Northwest Indians that, in their map of North America, Alaska dwarfs the lower forty-eight in size?

6 Are the Russians, who are often criticized for their adoption of "Western" ways by Tsarist dissidents in exile, members of Western civilization? And what of the millions of Europeans who have black African and Asian ancestry, black Africans having occupied several countries for hundreds of years? Are these "Europeans" members of Western civilization, or the Hungarians, who originated across the Urals in a place called Greater Hungary, or the Irish, who came from the Iberian Peninsula?

7   Even the notion that North America is part of Western civilization because our "system of government" is derived from Europe
is being challenged by Native American historians who say that
the founding fathers, Benjamin Franklin especially, were actually
influenced by the system of government that had been adopted
by the Iroquois hundreds of years prior to the arrival of large
numbers of Europeans.

8   Western civilization, then, becomes another confusing category
like Third World, or Judeo-Christian culture, as man attempts to
impose his small-screen view of political and cultural reality upon
a complex world. Our most publicized novelist recently said that
Western civilization was the greatest achievement of mankind, an
attitude that flourishes on the street level as scribbles in public
restrooms: "White Power," "Niggers and Spics Suck," or "Hitler
was a prophet," the latter being the most telling, for wasn't
Adolph Hitler the archetypal monoculturalist who, in his pigheaded
arrogance, believed that one way and one blood was so pure that
it had to be protected from alien strains at all costs? Where did
such an attitude, which has caused so much misery and depression
in our national life, which has tainted even our noblest achievements
begin? An attitude that caused the incarceration of Japanese-
American citizens during World War II, the persecution of Chicanos
and Chinese Americans, the near-extermination of the Indians,
and the murder and lynchings of thousands of Afro-Americans.

9   Virtuous, hardworking, pious, even though they occasionally
would wander off after some fancy clothes, or rendezvous in the
woods with the town prostitute, the Puritans are idealized in our
schoolbooks as "a hardy band" of no-nonsense patriarchs whose
discipline razed the forest and brought order to the New World (a
term that annoys Native American historians). Industrious, responsible, it was their "Yankee ingenuity" and practicality that created the
work ethic. They were simple folk who produced a number of good
poets, and they set the tone for the American writing style, of lean
and spare lines, long before Hemingway. They worshipped in
churches whose colors blended in with the New England snow,
churches with simple structures and ornate lecterns.

10   The Puritans were a daring lot, but they had a mean streak. They
hated the theater and banned Christmas. They punished people in
a cruel and inhuman manner. They killed children who disobeyed
their parents. When they came in contact with those whom they

considered heathens or aliens, they behaved in such a bizarre and irrational manner that this chapter in the American history comes down to us as a late-movie horror film. They exterminated the Indians, who taught them how to survive in a world unknown to them, and their encounter with the calypso culture of Barbados resulted in what the tourist guide in Salem's Witches' House refers to as the Witchcraft Hysteria.

11   The Puritan legacy of hard work and meticulous accounting led to the establishment of a great industrial society; it is no wonder that the American industrial revolution began in Lowell, Massachusetts, but there was the other side, the strange and paranoid attitudes toward those different from the Elect.

12   The cultural attitudes of that early Elect continue to be voiced in everyday life in the United States: the president of a distinguished university, writing a letter to the *Times*, belittling the study of African civilizations; the television network that promoted its show on the Vatican art with the boast that this art represented "the finest achievements of the human spirit." A modern up-tempo state of complex rhythms that depends upon contacts with an international community can no longer behave as if it dwelled in a "Zion Wilderness" surrounded by beasts and pagans.

13   When I heard a schoolteacher warn the other night about the invasion of the American educational system by foreign curriculums, I wanted to yell at the television set, "Lady, they're already here." It has already begun because the world is here. The world has been arriving at these shores for at least ten thousand years from Europe, Africa, and Asia. In the late nineteenth and early twentieth centuries, large numbers of Europeans arrived, adding their cultures to those of the European, African, and Asian settlers who were already here, and recently millions have been entering the country from South America and the Caribbean, making Yale Professor Bob Thompson's bouillabaisse richer and thicker.

14   One of our most visionary politicians said that he envisioned a time when the United States could become the brain of the world, by which he meant the repository of all of the latest advanced information systems. I thought of that remark when an enterprising poet friend of mine called to say that he had just sold a poem to a computer magazine and that the editors were delighted to get it because they didn't carry fiction or poetry. Is that the kind of world we desire? A humdrum homogenous world of all brains but no heart, no fiction,

no poetry; a world of robots with human attendants bereft of imagination, of culture? Or does North America deserve a more exciting destiny? To become a place where the cultures of the world crisscross. This is possible because the United States is unique in the world: The world is here.

Where I Come from Is Like This

PAULA GUNN
ALLEN

Paula Gunn Allen, who was born in 1939, has roots in the Laguna Pueblo tribe of North America. She serves as professor of Native American and Ethnic Studies at the University of California, Berkeley. She edited *Studies in American Indian Literature* (1983) for the Modern Language Association. She has also won acclaim for several books of poetry, for a novel entitled *The Woman Who Owned the Shadows* (1983), and for numerous essays.

"Where I Come from Is Like This" is a featured essay in Allen's collection, *The Sacred Hoop*. She describes here the redefinition necessary for modern American Indian women, especially the balancing of tribal traditions with the demands of the modern culture. Allen notes that tribes ascribe various roles to women, but "they never portray women as mindless, helpless, simple, or oppressed." Within a tribe, women possess great power and demand respect. But today a "bicultural bind" restricts them; she says, "We vacillate between being dependent and strong, self-reliant and powerless, strongly motivated and hopelessly insecure."

I

1   Modern American Indian women, like their non-Indian sisters, are deeply engaged in the struggle to redefine themselves. In their

struggle they must reconcile traditional tribal definitions of women
with industrial and postindustrial non-Indian definitions. Yet while
these definitions seem to be more or less mutually exclusive, Indian
women must somehow harmonize and integrate both in their own
lives.

2   An American Indian woman is primarily defined by her tribal
identity. In her eyes, her destiny is necessarily that of her people,
and her sense of herself as a woman is first and foremost prescribed
by her tribe. The definitions of woman's roles are as diverse as tribal
cultures in the Americas. In some she is devalued, in others she wields
considerable power. In some she is a familial/clan adjunct, in some
she is as close to autonomous as her economic circumstances and
psychological traits permit. But in no tribal definitions is she perceived
in the same way as are women on western industrial and postindustrial
cultures.

3   In the west, few images of women form part of the cultural mythos,
and these are largely sexually charged. Among Christians, the
madonna is the female prototype, and she is portrayed as essentially
passive: her contribution is simply that of birthing. Little else is
attributed to her and she certainly possesses few of the characteristics
that are attributed to mythic figures among Indian tribes. This image
is countered (rather than balanced) by the witch-goddess/whore
characteristics designed to reinforce cultural beliefs about women,
as well as western adversarial and dualistic perceptions of reality.

4   The tribes see women variously, but they do not question the
power of femininity. Sometimes they see women as fearful, sometimes
peaceful, sometimes omnipotent and omniscient, but they never
portray women as mindless, helpless, simple, or oppressed. And while
the women in a given tribe, clan, or band may be all these things,
the individual woman is provided with a variety of images of women
from the interconnected supernatural, natural, and social worlds she
lives in.

5   As a half-breed American Indian woman, I cast about in my mind
for negative images of Indian women, and I find none that are
directed to Indian women alone. The negative images I do have are
of Indians in general and in fact are more often of males than of
females. All these images come to me from non-Indian sources, and
they are always balanced by a positive image. My ideas of womanhood, passed on largely by my mother and grandmothers, Laguna
Pueblo women, are about practicality, strength, reasonableness, intel-

ligence, wit, and competence. I also remember vividly the women who came to my father's store, the women who held me and sang to me, the women at Feast Day, at Grab Days,[1] the women in the kitchen of my Cubero home, the women I grew up with; none of them appeared weak or helpless, none of them presented herself tentatively. I remember a certain reserve on those lovely brown faces; I remember the direct gaze of eyes framed by bright-colored shawls draped over their heads and cascading down their backs. I remember the clean cotton dresses and carefully pressed hand-embroidered aprons they always wore; I remember laughter and good food, especially the sweet bread and the oven bread they gave us. Nowhere in my mind is there a foolish woman, a dumb woman, a vain woman, or a plastic woman, though the Indian women I have known have shown a wide range of personal style and demeanor.

6   My memory includes the Navajo woman who was badly beaten by her Sioux husband; but I also remember that my grandmother abandoned her Sioux husband long ago. I recall the stories about the Laguna woman beaten regularly by her husband in the presence of her children so that the children would not believe in the strength and power of femininity. And I remember the women who drank, who got into fights with other women and with the men, and who often won those battles. I have memories of tired women, partying women, stubborn women, sullen women, amicable women, selfish women, shy women, and aggressive women. Most of all I remember the women who laugh and scold and sit uncomplaining in the long sun on feast days and who cook wonderful food on wood stoves, in beehive mud ovens, and over open fires outdoors.

7   Among the images of women that come to me from various tribes as well as my own are White Buffalo Woman, who came to the Lakota long ago and brought them the religion of the Sacred Pipe which they still practice; Tinotzin the goddess who came to Juan Diego to remind him that she still walked the hills of her people and sent him with her message, her demand and her proof to the Catholic bishop in the city nearby. And from Laguna I take the images of Yellow Woman, Coyote Woman, Grandmother Spider (Spider Old Woman), who brought the light, who gave us weaving and medicine,

---

[1]Laguna ritual in which women throw food and small items (like pieces of cloth) to those attending.

who gave us life. Among the Keres she is known as Thought Woman who created us all and who keeps us in creation even now. I remember Iyatiku, Earth Woman, Corn Woman, who guides and counsels the people to peace and who welcomes us home when we cast off this coils of flesh as huskers cast off the leaves that wrap the corn. I remember Iyatiku's sister, Sun Woman, who held metals and cattle, pigs and sheep, highways and engines and so many things in her bundle, who went away to the east saying that one day she would return.

II

8   Since the coming of the Anglo-Europeans beginning in the fifteenth century, the fragile web of identity that long held tribal people secure has gradually been weakened and torn. But the oral tradition has prevented the complete destruction of the web, the ultimate disruption of tribal ways. The oral tradition is vital; it heals itself and the tribal web by adapting to the flow of the present while never relinquishing its connection to the past. Its adaptability has always been required, as many generations have experienced. Certainly the modern American Indian woman bears slight resemblance to her forebears—at least on superficial examination—but she is still a tribal woman in her deepest being. Her tribal sense of relationship to all that is continues to flourish. And though she is at times beset by her knowledge of the enormous gap between the life she lives and the life she was raised to live, and while she adapts her mind and being to the circumstances of her present life, she does so in tribal ways, mending the tears in the web of being from which she takes her existence as she goes.

9   My mother told me stories all the time, though I often did not recognize them as that. My mother told me stories about cooking and childbearing; she told me stories about menstruation and pregnancy; she told me stories about gods and heroes, about fairies and elves, about goddesses and spirits; she told me stories about the land and the sky, about cats and dogs, about snakes and spiders; she told me stories about climbing trees and exploring the mesas; she told me stories about going to dances and getting married; she told me stories about dressing and undressing, about sleeping and waking;

she told me stories about herself, about her mother, about her grand-mother. She told me stories about grieving and laughing, about thinking and doing; she told me stories about school and about people; about darning and mending; she told me stories about tur-quoise and about gold; she told me European stories and Laguna stories; she told me Catholic stories and Presbyterian stories; she told me city stories and country stories; she told me political stories and religious stories. She told me stories about living and stories about dying. And in all of those stories she told me who I was, who I was supposed to be, whom I came from, and who would follow me. In this way she taught me the meaning of the words she said, that all life is a circle and everything has a place within it. That's what she said and what she showed me in the things she did and the way she lives.

10   Of course, through my formal, white, Christian education, I dis-covered that other people had stories of their own—about women, about Indians, about fact, about reality—and I was amazed by a number of startling suppositions that others made about tribal cus-toms and beliefs. According to the un-Indian, non-Indian view, for instance, Indians barred menstruating women from ceremonies and indeed segregated them from the rest of the people, consigning them to some space specially designed for them. This showed that Indians considered menstruating women unclean and not fit to enjoy the company of decent (nonmenstruating) people, that is, men. I was surprised and confused to hear this because my mother had taught me that white people had strange attitudes toward menstruation: they thought something was bad about it, that it meant you were sick, cursed, sinful, and weak and that you had to be very careful during that time. She taught me that menstruation was a normal occurrence, that I could go swimming or hiking or whatever else I wanted to do during my period. She actively scorned women who took to their beds, who were incapacitated by cramps, who "got the blues."

11   As I struggled to reconcile these very contradictory interpretations of American Indians' traditional beliefs concerning menstruation, I realized that the menstrual taboos were about power, not about sin or filth. My conclusion was later borne out by some tribes' own explanations, which, as you may well imagine, came as quite a relief to me.

12   The truth of the matter as many Indians see it is that women who

are at the peak of their fecundity are believed to possess power that throws male power totally out of kilter. They emit such force that, in their presence, any male-owned or -dominated ritual or sacred object cannot do its usual task. For instance, the Lakota say that a menstruating woman anywhere near a yuwipi man, who is a special sort of psychic, spirit-empowered healer, for a day or so before he is to do his ceremony will effectively disempower him. Conversely, among many if not most tribes, important ceremonies cannot be held without the presence of women. Sometimes the ritual woman who empowers the ceremony must be unmarried and virginal so that the power she channels is unalloyed, unweakened by sexual arousal and penetration by a male. Other ceremonies require tumescent women, others the presence of mature women who have borne children, and still others depend for empowerment on post-menopausal women. Women may be segregated from the company of the whole band or village on certain occasions, but on certain occasions men are also segregated. In short, each ritual depends on a certain balance of power, and the positions of women within the phases of womanhood are used by tribal people to empower certain rites. This does not derive from a male-dominant view; it is not a ritual observance imposed on women by men. It derives from a tribal view of reality that distinguishes tribal people from feudal and industrial people.

13   Among the tribes, the occult power of women, inextricably bound to our hormonal life, is thought to be very great; many hold that we possess innately the blood-given power to kill—with a glance, with a step, or with a judicious mixing of menstrual blood into somebody's soup. Medicine women among the Pomo of California cannot practice until they are sufficiently mature; when they are immature, their power is diffuse and is likely to interfere with their practice until time and experience have it under control. So women of the tribes are not especially inclined to see themselves as poor helpless victims of male domination. Even in those tribes where something akin to male domination was present, women are perceived as powerful, socially, physically, and metaphysically. In times past, as in times present, women carried enormous burdens with aplomb. We were far indeed from the "weaker sex," the designation that white aristocratic sisters unhappily earned for us all.

14   I remember my mother moving furniture all over the house when she wanted it changed. She didn't wait for my father to come home

and help—she just went ahead and moved the piano, a huge upright from the old days, the couch, the refrigerator. Nobody had told her she was too weak to do such things. In imitation of her, I would delight in loading trucks at my father's store with cases of pop or fifty-pound sacks of flour. Even when I was quite small I could do it, and it gave me a belief in my own physical strength that advancing middle age can't quite erase. My mother used to tell me about the Acoma Pueblo women she had seen as a child carrying huge ollas (water pots) on their heads as they wound their way up the tortuous stairwell carved into the face of the "Sky City" mesa, a feat I tried to imitate with books and tin buckets. ("Sky City" is the term used by the Chamber of Commerce for the mother village of Acoma, which is situated atop a high sandstone table mountain.) I was never very successful, but even the attempt reminded me that I was supposed to be strong and balanced to be a proper girl.

15   Of course, my mother's Laguna people are Keres Indian, reputed to be the last extreme mother-right people on earth. So it is no wonder that I got notably nonwhite notions about the natural strength and prowess of women. Indeed, it is only when I am trying to get non-Indian approval, recognition, or acknowledgment that my "weak sister" emotional and intellectual ploys get the better of my tribal woman's good sense. At such times I forget that I just moved the piano or just wrote a competent paper or just completed a financial transaction satisfactorily or have supported myself and my children for most of my adult life.

16   Nor is my contradictory behavior atypical. Most Indian women I know are in the same bicultural bind: we vacillate between being dependent and strong, self-reliant and powerless, strongly motivated and hopelessly insecure. We resolve the dilemma in various ways: some of us party all the time; some of us drink to excess; some of us travel and move around a lot; some of us land good jobs and then quit them; some of us engage in violent exchanges; some of us blow our brains out. We act in these destructive ways because we suffer from the societal conflicts caused by having to identify with two hopelessly opposed cultural definitions of women. Through this destructive dissonance we are unhappy prey to the self-disparagement common to, indeed demanded of, Indians living in the United States today. Our situation is caused by the exigencies of a history of invasion, conquest, and colonization whose searing marks are probably ineradicable. A popular bumper sticker on many Indian cars pro-

claims: "If You're Indian You're In," to which I always find myself adding under my breath, "Trouble."

III

17   No Indian can grow to any age without being informed that her people were "savages" who interfered with the march of progress pursued by respectable, loving, civilized white people. We are the villains of the scenario when we are mentioned at all. We are absent from much of white history except when we are calmly, rationally, succinctly, and systematically dehumanized. On the few occasions we are noticed in any way other than as howling, bloodthirsty beings, we are acclaimed for our noble quaintness. In this definition, we are exotic curios. Our ancient arts and customs are used to draw tourist money to state coffers, into the pocketbooks and bank accounts of scholars, and into support of the American-in-Disneyland promoters' dream.

18   As a Roman Catholic child I was treated to bloody tales of how the savage Indians martyred the hapless priests and missionaries who went among them in an attempt to lead them to the one true path. By the time I was through high school I had the idea that Indians were people who had benefited mightily from the advanced knowledge and superior morality of the Anglo-Europeans. At least I had, perforce, that idea to lay beside the other one that derived from my daily experience of Indian life, an idea less dehumanizing and more accurate because it came from my mother and the other Indian people who raised me. That idea was that Indians are a people who don't tell lies, who care for their children and their old people. You never see an Indian orphan, they said. You always know when you're old that someone will take care of you—one of your children will. Then they'd list the old folks who were being taken care of by this child or that. No child is ever considered illegitimate among the Indians, they said. If a girl gets pregnant, the baby is still part of the family, and the mother is too. That's what they said, and they showed me real people who lived according to those principles.

19   Of course the ravages of colonization have taken their toll; there are orphans in Indian country now, and abandoned, brutalized old folks; there are even illegitimate children, though the very concept

still strikes me as absurd. There are battered children and neglected children, and there are battered wives and women who have been raped by Indian men. Proximity to the "civilizing" effects of white Christians has not improved the moral quality of life in Indian country, though each group, Indian and white, explains the situation differently. Nor is there much yet in the oral tradition that can enable us to adapt to these inhuman changes. But a force is growing in that direction, and it is helping Indian women reclaim their lives. Their power, their sense of direction and of self will soon be visible. It is the force of the women who speak and work and write, and it is formidable.

20   Through all the centuries of war and death and cultural and psychic destruction have endured the women who raise the children and tend the fires, who pass along the tales and the traditions, who weep and bury the dead, who are the dead, and who never forget. There are always the women, who make pots and weave baskets, who fashion clothes and cheer their children on at powwow, who make fry bread and piki bread, and corn soup and chili stew, who dance and sing and remember and hold within their hearts the dream of their ancient peoples—that one day the woman who thinks will speak to us again, and everywhere there will be peace. Meanwhile we tell the stories and write the books and trade tales of anger and woe and stories of fun and scandal and laugh over all manner of things that happen every day. We watch and we wait.

21   My great-grandmother told my mother: Never forget you are Indian. And my mother told me the same thing. This, then, is how I have gone about remembering, so that my children will remember too.

Life Stories

MICHAEL DORRIS

Michael Dorris was born into the Modoc Indian tribe in Dayton, Washington, in 1945. He earned a B.A. at Georgetown University and an M.Phil. at Yale University. He has served as instructor at several colleges and universities, including University of New Hampshire, University of Redland, University of Auckland, New Zealand, and most recently at Dartmouth College. He has also served on the Native American Council. He won critical acclaim in 1975 with his book *Native Americans: Five Hundred Years After*, which examines the economic and social conditions of the tribes in the modern era. He awoke the national consciousness in 1987 with *The Broken Cord*, a nonfiction account of the effects of fetal alcohol syndrome on his adopted son.

"Life Stories" is an essay about an Indian male's solo venture into the wilderness to find an epiphany that would signal his advance into adulthood and membership into the tribe of warriors. However, that adventure no longer exists, so youngsters today must find enlightenment in a different way—perhaps through various summer jobs that may or may not offer foresight into the future. He describes his jobs tending lawns, counselling young people, delivering mail, selling theater tickets, and counting money in a French bank. Even though he had no illuminating moment of enlightenment, the various summer jobs, collectively, carried him forward into maturity "like overlapping stairs, unfolding a particular pattern at once haphazard and inevitable."

1   In most cultures, adulthood is equated with self-reliance and responsibility, yet often Americans do not achieve this status until we are in our late twenties or early thirties—virtually the entire average lifespan of a person in a traditional non-Western society. We tend to treat prolonged adolescence as a warm-up for real life, as a wobbly suspension bridge between childhood and legal maturity. Whereas a nineteenth-century Cheyenne or Lakota teenager was expected to alter self-conception in a split-second vision, we often meander through an analogous rite of passage for more than a decade—through high school, college, graduate school.

2   Though he had never before traveled alone outside his village, the Plains Indian male was expected at puberty to venture solo into the wilderness. There he had to fend for and sustain himself while avoiding the menace of unknown dangers, and there he had absolutely to remain until something happened that would transform him. Every human being, these tribes believed, was entitled to at least one moment of personal, enabling insight.

3   Anthropology proposes feasible psychological explanations for why this flash was eventually triggered: Fear, fatigue, reliance on strange foods, the anguish of loneliness, stress, and the expectation of ultimate success all contributed to a state of receptivity. Every sense was quickened, alerted to perceive deep meaning, until at last the interpretation of an unusual event—a dream, a chance encounter, or an unexpected vista—reverberated with metaphor. Through this unique prism, abstractly preserved in a vivid memory or song, a boy caught foresight of both his adult persona and of his vocation, the two inextricably entwined.

4   Today the best approximations that many of us get to such a heady sense of eventuality come in the performance of our school vacation jobs. Summers are intermissions, and once we hit our teens it is during these breaks in our structured regimen that we initially taste the satisfaction of remuneration that is earned, not merely doled. Tasks defined as *work* are not only graded, they are compensated; they have a worth that is unarguable because it translates into hard currency. Wage labor—and in the beginning, this generally means a

confining, repetitive chore for which we are quickly over-qualified—
paradoxically brings a sense of blooming freedom. At the outset, the
complaint to a peer that business supersedes fun is oddly liberating—
no matter what drudgery requires your attention, it is by its very
required nature serious and adult.

5   At least that's how it seemed to me. I come from a line of people
hard hit by the Great Depression. My mother and her sisters went
to work early in their teens—my mother operated a kind of calculator
known as a comptometer while her sisters spent their days, respec-
tively, at a peanut factory and at Western Union. My grandmother
did piecework sewing. Their efforts, and the Democratic Party, saw
them through, and to this day they never look back without appreciation for their later solvency. They take nothing for granted. Accom-
plishments are celebrated, possessions are valuable, in direct
proportion to the labor entailed to acquire them; anything easily
won or bought on credit is suspect. When I was growing up we were
far from wealthy, but what money we had was correlated to the
hours some one of us had logged. My eagerness to contribute to,
or at least not diminish, the coffer was countered by arguments of
those whose salaries kept me in school: My higher education was a
sound group investment. The whole family was adamant that I have
the opportunities they had missed, and no matter how much I
objected, they stinted themselves to provide for me.

6   Summer jobs were therefore a relief, an opportunity to pull a share
of the load. As soon as the days turned warm I began to peruse the
classifieds, and when the spring semester was done, I was ready to
punch a clock. It even felt right. Work in June, July, and August
had an almost Biblical aspect: In the hot, canicular weather your
brow sweated, just as God had ordained. Moreover, summer jobs
had the luxury of being temporary. No matter how bizarre, how
onerous, how off my supposed track, employment terminated with
the falling leaves and I was back on neutral ground. So, during each
annual three-month leave from secondary school and later from the
university, I compiled an eclectic résumé: lawn cutter, hair sweeper
in a barber shop, lifeguard, delivery boy, temporary mail carrier,
file clerk, youth program coordinator on my Montana reservation,
ballroom dance instructor, theater party promoter, night-shift hospital records keeper, human adding machine in a Paris bank, encyclopedia salesman, newspaper stringer, recreation bus manager, salmon
fisherman.

7   The reasonable titles disguise the madness of some of these occupations. For instance, I seemed inevitably to be hired to trim the yards of the unconventional. One woman followed beside me, step by step, as I traversed her yard in ever tighter squares, and called my attention to each missed blade of grass. Another client never had the "change" to pay me, and so reimbursed my weekly pruning with an offering culled from his library. I could have done without the *Guide to Artificial Respiration* (1942) or the many well-worn copies of Reader's Digest Condensed Books, but sometimes the selection merited the wait. Like a rat lured repeatedly back to the danger of mild electric shock by the mystique of intermittent reenforcement, I kept mowing by day in hopes of turning pages all night.

8   The summer I was eighteen a possibility arose for a rotation at the post office, and I grabbed it. There was something casually sophisticated about work that required a uniform, about having a federal ranking, even if it was GS-1 (Temp/Sub), and it was flattering to be entrusted with a leather bag containing who knew what important correspondence. Every day I was assigned a new beat, usually in a rough neighborhood avoided whenever possible by regular carriers, and I proved quite capable of complicating what would normally be fairly routine missions. The low point came on the first of August when I diligently delivered four blocks' worth of welfare checks to the right numbers on the wrong streets. It is no fun to snatch unexpected wealth from the hands of those who have but moments previously opened their mailboxes and received a bonus.

9   After my first year of college, I lived with relatives on an Indian reservation in eastern Montana and filled the only post available: Coordinator of Tribal Youth Programs. I was seduced by the language of the announcement into assuming that there existed Youth Programs to be coordinated. In fact, the Youth consisted of a dozen bored, disgruntled kids—most of them my cousins—who had nothing better to do each day than to show up at what was euphemistically called "the gym" and hate whatever Program I had planned for them. The Youth ranged in age from fifteen to five and seemed to have as their sole common ambition the determination to smoke cigarettes. This put them at immediate and on-going odds with the Coordinator, who on his first day naively encouraged them to sing the "Doe, a deer, a female deer" song from *The Sound of Music*. They looked at me, that bleak morning, and I looked at them, each boy and girl equipped with a Pall Mall behind an ear, and we all

knew it would be a long, struggle-charged battle. It was to be a contest of wills, the hearty and wholesome vs. prohibited vice. I stood for dodge ball, for collecting bugs in glass jars, for arts and crafts; they had pledged a preternatural allegiance to sloth. The odds were not in my favor and each waking dawn I experienced the light-headedness of anticipated exhaustion, that thrill of giddy dissociation in which nothing seems real or of great significance. I went with the flow and learned to inhale.

10   The next summer, I decided to find work in an urban setting for a change, and was hired as a general office assistant in the Elsa Hoppenfeld Theatre Party Agency, located above Sardi's restaurant in New York City. The Agency consisted of Elsa Hoppenfeld herself, Rita Frank, her regular deputy, and me. Elsa was a gregarious Viennese woman who established contacts through personal charm, and she spent much of the time courting trade away from the building. Rita was therefore both my immediate supervisor and constant companion; she had the most incredible fingernails I had ever seen—long, carefully shaped pegs lacquered in cruel primary colors and hard as stone—and an attitude about her that could only be described as zeal.

11   The goal of a theater party agent is to sell blocks of tickets to imminent Broadway productions, and the likely buyers are charities, B'nai Briths, Hadassahs, and assorted other fund-raising organizations. We received commissions on volume, and so it was necessary to convince a prospect that a play—preferably an expensive musical—for which we had reserved the rights to seats would be a boffo smash hit.

12   The object of our greatest expectation that season was an extravaganza called *Chu Chem*, a saga that aspired to ride the coattails of *Fiddler on the Roof* into entertainment history. It starred the estimable Molly Picon and told the story of a family who had centuries ago gone from Israel to China during the diaspora, yet had, despite isolation in an alien environment, retained orthodox culture and habits. The crux of the plot revolved around a man with several marriageable daughters and nary a kosher suitor within 5,000 miles. For three months Rita and I waxed eloquent in singing the show's praises. We sat in our little office, behind facing desks, and every noon while she redid her nails I ordered out from a deli that offered such exotic (to me) delicacies as fried egg sandwiches, lox and cream cheese, pastrami, *tongue*. I developed of necessity and habit a tele-

phone voice laced with a distinctly Yiddish accent. It could have been a great career. However, come November, *Chu Chem* bombed. Its closing was such a financial catastrophe for all concerned that when the following January one Monsieur Dupont advertised on the Placement Board at my college, I decided to put an ocean between me and my former trusting clientele.

13   M. Dupont came to campus with the stated purpose of interviewing candidates for teller positions in a French bank. Successful applicants, required to be fluent in *français*, would be rewarded with three well-paid months and a rent-free apartment in Paris. I headed for the language lab and registered for an appointment.

14   The only French in the interview was *Bonjour, ça va?*, after which M. Dupont switched into English and described the wonderful deal on charter air flights that would be available to those who got the nod. Round-trip to Amsterdam, via Reykjavik, leaving the day after exams and returning in mid-September, no changes or substitutions. I signed up on the spot. I was to be a *banquier*, with *pied-à-terre* in Montparnasse!

15   Unfortunately, when I arrived with only $50 in travelers' checks in my pocket—the flight had cleaned me out, but who needed money since my paycheck started right away—no one in Paris had ever heard of M. Dupont.

16   *Alors.*

17   I stood in the Gare du Nord and considered my options. There weren't any. I scanned a listing of Paris hotels and headed for the cheapest one: the Hotel Villedo, $10 a night. The place had an ambiance that I persuaded myself was antique, despite the red light above the sign. The only accommodation available was "the bridal suite," a steal at $20. The glass door to my room didn't lock and there was a rather continual floor show, but at some point I must have dozed off. When I awoke the church bells were ringing, the sky was pink, and I felt renewed. No little setback was going to spoil my adventure. I stood and stretched, then walked to a mirror that hung above the sink next to the bed. I leaned forward to punctuate my resolve with a confident look in the eye.

18   The sink disengaged and fell to the floor. Water gushed. In panic I rummaged through my open suitcase, stuffed two pair of underwear into the pipe to quell the flow, and before the dam broke, I was out the door. I barreled through the lobby of the first bank I passed, asked to see the director, and told the startled man my sad story. For some

reason, whether from shock or pity, he hired me at $1.27 an hour to be a cross-checker of foreign currency transactions, and with two phone calls found me lodgings at a commercial school's dormitory.

19   From eight to five each weekday my duty was to sit in a windowless room with six impeccably dressed people, all of whom were totaling identical additions and subtractions. We were highly dignified with each other, very professional, no *tutoyer*ing.[1] Monsieur Saint presided, but the formidable Mademoiselle was the true power; she oversaw each of our columns and shook her head sadly at my American-shaped numbers.

20   My legacy from that summer, however, was more than an enduring penchant for crossed 7s. After I had worked for six weeks, M. Saint asked me during a coffee break why I didn't follow the example of other foreign students he had known and depart the office at noon in order to spend the afternoon touring the sights of Paris with the *Alliance Française*.

21   "Because," I replied in my halting French, "that costs money. I depend upon my full salary the same as any of you." M. Saint nodded gravely and said no more, but then on the next Friday he presented me with a white envelope along with my check.

22   "Do not open this until you have left the Société Générale," he said ominously. I thought I was fired for the time I had mixed up krøners and guilders, and, once on the sidewalk, I steeled myself to read the worst. I felt the quiet panic of blankness.

23   "Dear Sir," I translated the perfectly formed script. "You are a person of value. It is not correct that you should be in our beautiful city and not see it. Therefore we have amassed a modest sum to pay the tuition for a two-week afternoon program for you at the *Alliance Française*. Your wages will not suffer, for it is your assignment to appear each morning in this bureau and reacquaint us with the places you have visited. We shall see them afresh through your eyes." The letter had thirty signatures, from the Director to the janitor, and stuffed inside the envelope was a sheaf of franc notes in various denominations.

24   I rushed back to the tiny office. M. Saint and Mademoiselle had waited, and accepted my gratitude with their usual controlled smiles and precise handshakes. But they had blown their Gallic cover, and

[1]Addressing each other with informal pronouns and verb forms.

for the next ten days and then through all the days until I went home in September, our branch was awash with sightseeing paraphernalia. Everyone had advice, favorite haunts, criticisms of the *Alliance*'s choices or explanations. Paris passed through the bank's granite walls as sweetly as a June breeze through a window screen, and ever afterward the lilt of overheard French, a photograph of *Sacré Coeur* or the Louvre, even a monthly bank statement, recalls to me that best of all summers.

25   I didn't wind up in an occupation with any obvious connection to the careers I sampled during my school breaks, but I never altogether abandoned those brief professions either. They were jobs not so much to be held as to be weighed, absorbed, and incorporated, and, collectively, they carried me forward into adult life like overlapping stairs, unfolding a particular pattern at once haphazard and inevitable.

Growing Up Asian in America

KESAYA NODA

Kesaya E. Noda was born in 1950 in California, the American-born grandchild of Japanese immigrants to the United States. She grew up in New Hampshire, studied for a year and a half in Japan, and then earned a master's degree from Harvard Divinity School. Her 1981 book, *The Yamato Colony*, examines the social and cultural history of the California community where she grew up. She is currently a professor at Lesley College in Cambridge, Massachusetts.

"Growing Up Asian in America" first appeared in a collection published by Asian Women United of California, *Making Waves: An Anthology of Writings By and About Asian and American Women.* In this essay, Noda argues that her personality has been shaped from the outside by the heritage of the Japanese community and the influences of her parents and grandparents. Ethnic identity becomes something she must embrace or resist. She must accept the influence of both her Japanese-American heritage and her identity as a woman.

1   Sometimes when I was growing up, my identity seemed to hurtle toward me and paste itself right to my face. I felt that way, encoun-

tering the stereotypes of my race perpetuated by non-Japanese people (primarily white) who may or may not have had contact with other Japanese in America. "You don't like cheese, do you?" someone would ask. "I know your people don't like cheese." Sometimes questions came making allusions to history. That was another aspect of the identity. Events that had happened quite apart from the me who stood silent in that moment connected my face with an incomprehensible past. "Your parents were in California? Were they in those camps during the war?" And sometimes there were phrases or nicknames: "Lotus Blossom." I was sometimes addressed or referred to as racially Japanese, sometimes as Japanese American, and sometimes as an Asian woman. Confusions and distortions abounded.

2   How is one to know and define oneself? From the inside—within a context that is self defined, for a grounding in community and a connection with culture and history that are comfortably accepted? Or from the outside—in terms of messages received from the media and people who are often ignorant? Even as an adult I can still see two sides of my face and past. I can see from the inside out, in freedom. And I can see from the outside in, driven by the old voices of childhood and lost in anger and fear.

I Am Racially Japanese

3   A voice from my childhood says: "You are other. You are less than. You are unalterably alien." This voice has its own history. We have indeed been seen as other and alien since the early years of our arrival in the United States. The very first immigrants were welcomed and sought as laborers to replace the dwindling numbers of Chinese, whose influx had been cut off by the Chinese Exclusion Act of 1882. The Japanese fell natural heir to the same anti-Asian prejudice that had arisen against the Chinese. As soon as they began striking for better wages, they were no longer welcomed.

4   I can see myself today as a person historically defined by law and custom as being forever alien. Being neither "free white," nor "African," our people in California were deemed "aliens, ineligible for citizenship," no matter how long they intended to stay here. Aliens ineligible for citizenship were prohibited from owning, buying, or leasing land. They did not and could not belong here. The voice

in me remembers that I am always a *Japanese* American in the eyes
of many. A third-generation German American is an American. A
third-generation Japanese American is a Japanese American. Being
Japanese means being a danger to the country during the war and
knowing how to use chopsticks. I wear this history on my face.

5   I move to the other side. I see a different light and claim a different
context. My race is a line that stretches across ocean and time to link
me to the shrine where my grandmother was raised. Two high, white
banners lift in the wind at the top of the stone steps leading to the
shrine. It is time for the summer festival. Black characters are written
against the sky as boldly as the clouds, as lightly as kites, as sharply
as the big black crows I used to see above the fields in New Hampshire. At festival time there is liquor and food, ritual, discipline, and
abandonment. There is music and drunkenness and invocation. There
is hope. Another season has come. Another season has gone.

6   I am racially Japanese. I have a certain claim to this crazy place
where the prayers intoned by a neighboring Shinto priest (standing
in for my grandmother's nephew who is sick) are drowned out by
the rehearsals for the pop singing contest in which most of the
villagers will compete later that night. The village elders, the priest,
and I stand respectfully upon the immaculate, shining wooden floor
of the outer shrine, bowing our heads before the hidden powers.
During the patchy intervals when I can hear him, I notice the priest
has a stutter. His voice flutters up to my ears only occasionally because
two men and a woman are singing gustily into a microphone in the
compound, testing the sound system. A prerecorded tape of guitars,
samisens, and drums accompanies them. Rock music and Shinto
prayers. That night, to loud applause and cheers, a young man is given
the award for the most *netsuretsu*—passionate, burning—rendition of
a song. We roar our approval of the reward. Never mind that his
voice had wandered and slid, now slightly above, now slightly below
the given line of the melody. Netsuretsu. Netsuretsu.

7   In the morning, my grandmother's sister kneels at the foot of the
stone stairs to offer her morning prayers. She is too crippled to climb
the stairs, so each morning she kneels here upon the path. She shuts
her eyes for a few seconds, her motions as matter of fact as when
she washes rice. I linger longer than she does, so reluctant to leave,
savoring the connection I feel with my grandmother in America, the
past, and the power that lives and shines in the morning sun.

8   Our family has served this shrine for generations. The family's

need to protect this claim to identity and place outweighs any individual claim to any individual hope. I am Japanese.

I Am a Japanese American

9   "Weak." I hear the voice from my childhood years. "Passive," I hear. Our parents and grandparents were the ones who were put into those camps. They went without resistance; they offered cooperation as proof of loyalty to America. "Victim," I hear. And, "Silent."

10   Our parents are painted as hard workers who were socially uncomfortable and had difficulty expressing even the smallest opinion. Clean, quiet, motivated, and determined to match the American way; that is us, and that is the story of our time here.

11   "Why did you go into those camps," I raged at my parents, frightened by my own inner silence and timidity. "Why didn't you do anything to resist? Why didn't you name it the injustice it was?" Couldn't our parents even think? Couldn't they? Why were we so passive?

12   I shift my vision and my stance. I am in California. My uncle is in the midst of the sweet potato harvest. He is pressed, trying to get the harvesting crews onto the field as quickly as possible, worried about the flow of equipment and people. His big pickup is pulled off to the side, motor running, door ajar. I see two tractors in the yard in front of an old shed; the flat bed harvesting platform on which the workers will stand has already been brought over from the other field. It's early morning. The workers stand loosely grouped and at ease, but my uncle looks as harried and tense as a police officer trying to unsnarl a New York City traffic jam. Driving toward the shed, I pull my car off the road to make way for an approaching tractor. The front wheels of the car sink luxuriously into the soft, white sand by the roadside and the car slides to a dreamy halt, tail still on the road. I try to move forward. I try to move back. The front bites contentedly into the sand, the back lifts itself at a jaunty angle. My uncle sees me and storms down the road, running: He is shouting before he is even near me.

13   "What's the matter with you," he screams. "What the hell are you doing?" In his frenzy, he grabs his hat off his head and slashes it through the air across his knee. He is beside himself. "Don't you

know how to drive in sand? What's the matter with you? You've
blocked the whole roadway. How am I supposed to get my tractors
out of here? Can't you use your head? You've cut off the whole
roadway, and we've got to get out of here."

14   I stand on the road before him helplessly thinking. "No, I don't
know how to drive in sand. I've never driven in sand."

15   "I'm sorry, uncle," I say, burying a smile beneath a look of sincere
apology. I notice my deep amusement and my affection for him with
great curiosity. I am usually devastated by anger. Not this time.

16   During the several years that follow I learn about the people and
the place, and much more about what has happened in this California
village where my parents grew up. The issei, our grandparents, made
this settlement in the desert. Their first crops were eaten by rabbits
and ravaged by insects. The land was so barren that men walking
from house to house sometimes got lost. Women came here too.
They bore children in 114 degree heat, then carried the babies with
them into the fields to nurse when they reached the end of each row
of grapes or other truck farm crops.

17   I had had no idea what it meant to buy this kind of land and
make it grow green. Or how, when the war came, there was no space
at all for the subtlety of being who we were—Japanese Americans.
Either/or was the way. I hadn't understood that people were literally
afraid for their lives then, that their money had been frozen in banks;
that there was a five-mile travel limit; that when the early evening
curfew came and they were inside their houses, some of them watched
helplessly as people they knew went into their barns to steal their
belongings. The police were patrolling the road, interested only in
violators of curfew. There was no help for them in the face of thievery.
I had not been able to imagine before what it must have felt like to
be an American—to know absolutely that one is an American—and
yet to have almost everyone else deny it. Not only deny it, but
challenge that identity with machine guns and troops of white American soldiers. In those circumstances it was difficult to say, "I'm a
Japanese American." "American" had to do.

18   But now I can say that I am a Japanese American. It means I have
a place here in this country, too. I have a place here on the East
Coast, where our neighbor is so much a part of our family that my
mother never passes her house at night without glancing at the lights
to see if she is home and safe; where my parents have hauled hundreds
of pounds of rocks from fields and arduously planted Christmas trees

and blueberries, lilacs, asparagus, and crab apples; where my father still dreams of angling a stream to a new bed so that he can dig a pond in the field and fill it with water and fish. "The neighbors already came for their Christmas tree?" he asks in December. "Did they like it? Did they like it?"

19   I have a place on the West Coast where my relatives still farm, where I heard the stories of feuds and backbiting, and where I saw that people survived and flourished because fundamentally they trusted and relied upon one another. A death in the family is not just a death in a family, it is a death in the community. I saw people help each other with money, materials, labor, attention, and time. I saw men gather once a year, without fail, to clean the grounds of a ninety-year-old woman who had helped the community before, during, and after the war. I saw her remembering them with birthday cards sent to each of their children.

20   I come from a people with a long memory and a distinctive grace. We live our thanks. And we are Americans. Japanese Americans.

I Am a Japanese American Woman

21   Woman. The last piece of my identity. It has been easier by far for me to know myself in Japan and to see my place in America than it has been to accept my line of connection with my own mother. She was my dark self, a figure in whom I thought I saw all that I feared most in myself. Growing into womanhood and looking for some model of strength, I turned away from her. Of course, I could not find what I sought. I was looking for a black feminist or a white feminist. My mother is neither white nor black.

22   My mother is a woman who speaks with her life as much as with her tongue. I think of her with her own mother. Grandmother had Parkinson's disease and it had frozen her gait and set her fingers, tongue, and feet jerking and trembling in a terrible dance. My aunts and uncles wanted her to be able to live in her own home. They fed her, bathed her, dressed her, awoke at midnight to take her for one last trip to the bathroom. My aunts (her daughters-in-law) did most of the care, but my mother went from New Hampshire to California each summer to spend a month living with grandmother, because she wanted to and because she wanted to give my aunts at least a

small rest. During those hot summer days, mother lay on the couch watching the television or reading, cooking foods that grandmother liked, and speaking little. Grandmother thrived under her care.

23 The time finally came when it was too dangerous for grandmother to live alone. My relatives kept finding her on the floor beside her bed when they went to wake her in the morning. My mother flew to California to help clean the house and make arrangements for grandmother to enter a local nursing home. On her last day at home, while grandmother was sitting in her big, overstuffed armchair, hair combed and wearing a green summer dress, my mother went to her and knelt at her feet. "Here, Mamma," she said. "I've polished your shoes." She lifted grandmother's legs and helped her into the shiny black shoes. My grandmother looked down and smiled slightly. She left her house walking, supported by her children, carrying her pocket book, and wearing her polished black shoes. "Look, Mamma," my mom had said, kneeling. "I've polished your shoes."

24 Just the other day, my mother came to Boston to visit. She had recently lost a lot of weight and was pleased with her new shape and her feeling of good health. "Look at me, Kes," she exclaimed, turning toward me, front and back, as naked as the day she was born. I saw her small breasts and the wide, brown scar, belly button to pubic hair, that marked her because my brother and I were both born by Caesarean section. Her hips were small. I was not a large baby, but there was so little room for me in her that when she was carrying me she could not even begin to bend over toward the floor. She hated it, she said.

25 "Don't I look good? Don't you think I look good?"

26 I looked at my mother, smiling and as happy as she, thinking of all the times I have seen her naked. I have seen both my parents naked throughout my life, as they have seen me. From childhood through adulthood we've had our naked moments, sharing baths, idle conversations picked up as we moved between showers and closets, hurried moments as the beginning of days, quiet moments at the end of days.

27 I know this to be Japanese, this ease with the physical, and it makes me think of an old, Japanese folk song. A young nursemaid, a fifteen-year-old girl, is singing a lullaby to a baby who is strapped to her back. The nursemaid has been sent as a servant to a place far from her own home. "We're the beggars," she says, "and they are the nice people. Nice people wear fine sashes. Nice clothes."

If I should drop dead,
bury me by the roadside!
I'll give a flower
to everyone who passes.

What kind of flower?
The cam-cam-camellia [tsun-tsun-tsubaki]
watered by Heaven:
alms water.

28   The nursemaid is the intersection of heaven and earth, the intersection of the human, the natural world, the body, and the soul. In this song, with clear eyes, she looks steadily at life, which is sometimes so very terrible and sad. I think of her while looking at my mother, who is standing on the red and purple carpet before me, laughing, without any clothes.

29   I am my mother's daughter. And I am myself.

30   I am a Japanese American woman.

Epilogue

31   I recently heard a man from West Africa share some memories of his childhood. He was raised Muslim, but when he was a young man, he found himself deeply drawn to Christianity. He struggled against his inner impulse for years, trying to avoid the church yet feeling pushed to return to it again and again. "I would have done *anything* to avoid the change," he said. At last, he became Christian. Afterwards he was afraid to go home, fearing that he would not be accepted. The fear was groundless, he discovered, when at last he returned—he had separated himself, but his family and friends (all Muslim) had not separated themselves from him.

32   The man, who is now a professor of religion, said that in the Africa he knew as a child and a young man, pluralism was embraced rather than feared. There was "a kind of tolerance that did not deny your particularity," he said. He alluded to zestful, spontaneous debates that would sometimes loudly erupt between Muslims and Christians in the village's public spaces. His memories of an atheist who harangued the villagers when he came to visit them once a week

moved me deeply. Perhaps the man was an agricultural advisor or inspector. He harassed the women. He would say:

> "Don't go to the fields! Don't even bother to go to the fields. Let God take care of you. He'll send you the food. If you believe in God, why do you need to work? You don't need to work! Let God put the seeds in the ground. Stay home."

33   The professor said, "The women laughed, you know? They just laughed. Their attitude was, 'Here is a child of God. When will he come home?' "

34   The storyteller, the professor of religion, smiled a most fantastic, tender smile as he told this story. "In my country, there is a deep affirmation of the oneness of God," he said. "The atheist and the women were having quite different experiences in their encounter, though the atheist did not know this. He saw himself as quite separate from the women. But the women did not see themselves as being separate from him. 'Here is a child of God,' they said. 'When will he come home?' "

Straightening Our Hair

BELL HOOKS

bell hooks, born in 1952, contributes a regular column, "Sisters of the Yam," to *Z Magazine* and is an English professor at City University of New York. In choosing the pen name bell hooks, the author says that she chose the name of her great-grandmother in order to recognize the maternal wisdom passed down to children. She has published several books, including *Ain't I a Woman: Black Women and Feminism* (1981), *Feminist Theory from Margin to Center* (1984), *Talking Back: Thinking Feminist, Thinking Black* (1989), and *Yearning: Race, Gender, and Cultural Politics* (1990). In these works, she develops her black feminism as a defense against oppression by various forces of racism, sexism, and classism, and she speaks out against the domination of black women by all others. In *Breaking Bread: Insurgent Black Intellectual Life* (1991) and *Black Looks: Race and Representation* (1992), hooks examines the representation of blacks in the media and the meanings rendered in advertising.

The essay that follows, "Straightening Our Hair," first appeared in *Z Magazine*. In it, she opens with a description from her childhood experiences of women and children straightening each other's hair. She extends the boundaries of autobiography to expound upon more serious matters, such as the role of gender for her race, aspects of beauty, race relations, and one's confrontation and acceptance of one's natural being. She counsels, "Celebrating our bodies, we participate in a liberatory struggle that frees mind and heart."

1   On Saturday mornings we would gather in the kitchen to get our hair fixed, that is straightened. Smells of burning grease and hair, mingled with the scent of our freshly washed bodies, with collard greens cooking on the stove, with fried fish. We did not go to the hairdresser. Mama fixed our hair. Six daughters—there was no way we could have afforded hairdressers. In those days, this process of straightening black women's hair with a hot comb (invented by Madame C. J. Waler) was not connected in my mind with the effort to look white, to live out standards of beauty set by white supremacy. It was connected solely with rites of initiation into womanhood. To arrive at that point where one's hair could be straightened was to move from being perceived as child (whose hair could be neatly combed and braided) to being almost a woman. It was this moment of transition my sisters and I longed for.

2   Hair pressing was a ritual of black women's culture—of intimacy. It was an exclusive moment when black women (even those who did not know one another well) might meet at home or in the beauty parlor to talk with one another, to listen to the talk. It was as important a world as that of the male barber shop—mysterious, secret. It was a world where the images constructed as barriers between one's self and the world were briefly let go, before they were made again. It was a moment of creativity, a moment of change.

3   I wanted this change even though I had been told all my life that I was one of the "lucky" ones because I had been born with "good hair"—hair that was fine, almost straight—not good enough but still good. Hair that had no nappy edges, no "kitchen," that area close to the neck that the hot comb could not reach. This "good hair" meant nothing to me when it stood as a barrier to my entering this secret black woman world. I was overjoyed when mama finally agreed that I could join the Saturday ritual, no longer looking on but patiently waiting my turn. I have written of this ritual: "For each of us getting our hair pressed is an important ritual. It is not a sign of our longing to be white. There are no white people in our intimate

world. It is a sign of our desire to be women. It is a gesture that says we are approaching womanhood . . . Before we reach the appropriate age we wear braids, plaits that are symbols of our innocence, our youth, our childhood. Then, we are comforted by the parting hands that comb and braid, comforted by the intimacy and bliss. There is a deeper intimacy in the kitchen on Saturdays when hair is pressed, when fish is fried, when sodas are passed around, when soul music drifts over the talk. It is a time without men. It is a time when we work as women to meet each other's needs, to make each other feel good inside, a time of laughter and outrageous talk."

4   Since the world we lived in was racially segregated, it was easy to overlook the relationship between white supremacy and our obsession with hair. Even though black women with straight hair were perceived to be more beautiful than those with thick, frizzy hair, it was not overtly related to a notion that white women were a more appealing female group or that their straight hair set a beauty standard black women were struggling to live out. While this was probably the ideological framework from which the process of straightening black women's hair emerged, it was expanded so that it became a real space of black woman bonding through ritualized, shared experience. The beauty parlor was a space of consciousness raising, a space where black women shared life stories—hardship, trials, gossip; a place where one could be comforted and one's spirit renewed. It was for some women a place of rest where one did not need to meet the demands of children or men. It was the one hour some folk would spend "off their feet," a soothing, restful time of meditation and silence. These positive empowering implications of the ritual of hair pressing mediate but do not change negative implications. They exist alongside all that is negative.

5   Within white supremacist capitalist patriarchy, the social and political context in which the custom of black folks straightening our hair emerges, it represents an imitation of the dominant white group's appearance and often indicates internalized racism, self-hatred, and/or low self-esteem. During the 1960s black people who actively worked to critique, challenge, and change white racism pointed to the way in which black people's obsession with straight hair reflected a colonized mentality. It was at this time that the natural hairdo, the "afro," became fashionable as a sign of cultural resistance to racist oppression and as a celebration of blackness. Naturals were equated with political militancy. Many young black folks found just how

much political value was placed on straightened hair as a sign of respectability and conformity to societal expectations when they ceased to straighten their hair. When black liberation struggles did not lead to revolutionary change in society the focus on the political relationship between appearance and complicity with white racism ceased and folks who had once sported afros began to straighten their hair.

6   In keeping with the move to suppress black consciousness and efforts to be self-defining, white corporations began to acknowledge black people and most especially black women as potential consumers of products they could provide, including hair-care products. Permanents specially designed for black women eliminated the need for hair pressing and the hot comb. They not only cost more but they also took much of the economy and profit out of black communities, out of the pockets of black women who had previously reaped the material benefits (see Manning Marable's *How Capitalism Underdeveloped Black America*, South End Press). Gone was the context of ritual, of black woman bonding. Seated under noisy hair dryers black women lost a space for dialogue, for creative talk.

7   Stripped of the positive binding rituals that traditionally surrounded the experience, black women straightening our hair seemed more and more to be exclusively a signifier of white supremacist oppression and exploitation. It was clearly a process that was about black women changing their appearance to imitate white people's looks. This need to look as much like white people as possible, to look safe, is related to a desire to succeed in the white world. Before desegregation black people could worry less about what white folks thought about their hair. In a discussion with black women about beauty at Spelman College, students talked about the importance of wearing straight hair when seeking jobs. They were convinced and probably rightly so that their chances of finding good jobs would be enhanced if they had straight hair. When asked to elaborate they focused on the connection between radical politics and natural hairdos, whether natural or braided. One woman wearing a short natural told of purchasing a straight wig for her job search. No one in the discussion felt black women were free to wear our hair in natural styles without reflecting on the possible negative consequences. Often older black adults, especially parents, respond quite negatively to natural hairdos. I shared with the group that when I arrived home with my hair

in braids shortly after accepting my job at Yale my parents told me I looked disgusting.

8   Despite many changes in racial politics, black women continue to obsess about their hair, and straightening hair continues to be serious business. It continues to tap into the insecurity black women feel about our value in this white supremacist society. Talking with groups of women at various college campuses and with black women in our communities there seems to be general consensus that our obsession with hair in general reflects continued struggles with self-esteem and self-actualization. We talk about the extent to which black women perceive our hair as the enemy, as a problem we must solve, a territory we must conquer. Above all it is a part of our black female body that must be controlled. Most of us were not raised in environments where we learned to regard our hair as sensual or beautiful in an unprocessed state. Many of us talk about situations where white people ask to touch our hair when it is unprocessed then show surprise that the texture is soft or feels good. In the eyes of many white folks and other non-black folks, the natural afro looks like steel wool or a helmet. Responses to natural hairstyles worn by black women usually reveal the extent to which our natural hair is perceived in white supremacist culture as not only ugly but frightening. We also internalize that fear. The extent to which we are comfortable with our hair usually reflects on our overall feelings about our bodies. In our black women's support group, *Sisters of the Yam*, we talk about the ways we don't like our bodies, especially our hair. I suggested to the group that we regard our hair as though it is not part of our body but something quite separate—again a territory to be controlled. To me it was important for us to link this need to control with sexuality, with sexual repression. Curious about what black women who had hot-combed or had permanents felt about the relationship between straightened hair and sexual practice I asked whether people worried about their hairdo, whether they feared partners touching their hair. Straightened hair has always seemed to me to call attention to the desire for hair to stay in place. Not surprisingly many black women responded that they felt uncomfortable if too much attention was focused on their hair, if it seemed to be too messy. Those of us who have liberated our hair and let it go in whatever direction it seems fit often receive negative comments.

9   Looking at photographs of myself and my sisters when we had straightened hair in high school I noticed how much older we looked than when our hair was not processed. It is ironic that we live in a culture that places so much emphasis on women looking young, yet black women are encouraged to change our hair in ways that make us appear older. This past semester we read Toni Morrison's *The Bluest Eye* in a black women's fiction class. I ask students to write autobiographical statements which reflect their thoughts about the connection between race and physical beauty. A vast majority of black women wrote about their hair. When I asked individual women outside class why they continued to straighten their hair, many asserted that naturals don't look good on them, or that they required too much work. Emily, a favorite student with very short hair, always straightened it and I would tease and challenge her. She explained to me convincingly that a natural hairdo would look horrible with her face, that she did not have the appropriate forehead or bone structure. Later she shared that during spring break she had gone to the beauty parlor to have her perm and as she sat there waiting, thinking about class reading and discussion, it came to her that she was really frightened that no one else would think she was attractive if she did not straighten her hair. She acknowledged that this fear was rooted in feelings of low self-esteem. She decided to make a change. Her new look surprised her because it was so appealing. We talked afterwards about her earlier denial and justification for wearing straightened hair. We talked about the way it hurts to realize connection between racist oppression and the arguments we use to convince ourselves and others that we are not beautiful or acceptable as we are.

10   In numerous discussions with black women about hair one of the strongest factors that prevent black women from wearing unprocessed hairstyles is the fear of losing other people's approval and regard. Heterosexual black women talked about the extent to which black men respond more favorably to women with straight or straightened hair. Lesbian women point to the fact that many of them do not straighten their hair, raising the question of whether or not this gesture is fundamentally linked to heterosexism and a longing for male approval. I recall visiting a woman friend and her black male companion in New York years ago and having an intense discussion about hair. He took it upon himself to share with me that

I could be a fine sister if I would do something about my hair (secretly I thought mama must have hired him). What I remember is his shock when I calmly and happily asserted that I like the touch and feel of unprocessed hair.

11   When students read about race and physical beauty, several black women describe periods of childhood when they were overcome with longing for straight hair as it was so associated with desirability, with being loved. Few women had received affirmation from family, friends, or lovers when choosing not to straighten their hair and we have many stories to tell about advice we receive from everyone, including total strangers, urging to understand how much more attractive we would be if we would fix (straighten) our hair. When I interviewed for my job at Yale, white female advisers who had never before commented on my hair encouraged me not to wear braids or a large natural to the interview. Although they did not say straighten your hair, they were suggesting that I change my hairstyle so that it would most resemble theirs, so that it would indicate a certain conformity. I wore braids and no one seemed to notice. When I was offered the job I did not ask if it mattered whether or not I wore braids. I tell this story to my students so that they will know by this one experience that we do not always need to surrender our power to be self-defining to succeed in an endeavor. Yet I have found the issue of hairstyle comes up again and again with students when I give lectures. At one conference on black women and leadership I walked into a packed auditorium, my hair unprocessed wild and all over the place. The vast majority of black women seated there had straightened hair. Many of them looked at me with hostile contemptuous stares. I felt as though I was being judged on the spot as someone out on the fringe, an undesirable. Such judgments are made particularly about black women in the United States who choose to wear dreadlocks. They are seen and rightly so as the total antithesis of straightening one's hair, as a political statement. Often black women express contempt for those of us who choose this look.

12   Ironically, just as the natural unprocessed hair of black women is the subject of disregard and disdain we are witnessing return of the long dyed, blonde look. In their writing my black women students described wearing yellow mops on their heads as children to pretend they had long blonde hair. Recently black women singers who are working to appeal to white audiences, to be seen as crossovers, use

hair implanting and hair weaving to have long straight hair. There seems to be a definite connection between a black female entertainer's popularity with white audiences and the degree to which she works to appear white, or to embody aspects of white style. Tina Turner and Aretha Franklin were trend setters; both dyed their hair blonde. In everyday life we see more and more black women using chemicals to be blonde. At one of my talks focusing on the social construction of black female identity within a sexist and racist society, a black woman came to me at the end of the discussion and shared that her seven-year-old daughter was obsessed with blonde hair, so much so that she had made a wig to imitate long blonde curls. This mother wanted to know what she was doing wrong in her parenting. She asserted that their home was a place where blackness was affirmed and celebrated. Yet she had not considered that her processed straightened hair was a message to her daughter that black women are not acceptable unless we alter our appearance or hair texture. Recently I talked with one of my younger sisters about her hair. She uses bright colored dyes, various shades of red. Her skin is very dark. She has a broad nose and short hair. For her these choices of straightened dyed hair were directly related to feelings of low self-esteem. She does not like her features and feels that the hairstyle transforms her. My perception was that her choice of red straightened hair actually called attention to the features she was trying to mask. When she commented that this look receives more attention and compliments, I suggested that the positive feedback might be a direct response to her own projection of a higher level of self-satisfaction. Folk may be responding to that and not her altered looks. We talked about the messages she is sending her dark-skinned daughters—that they will be most attractive if they straighten their hair.

13   A number of black women have argued that straightened hair is not necessarily a signifier of low self-esteem. They argue that it is a survival strategy; it is easier to function in this society with straightened hair. There are fewer hassles. Or as some folk stated, straightened hair is easier to manage, takes less time. When I responded to this argument in our discussion at Spelman by suggesting that perhaps the unwillingness to spend time on ourselves, caring for our bodies, is also a reflection of a sense that this is not important or that we do not deserve such care. In this group and others, black women talked about being raised in households where spending too much time on appearance was ridiculed or considered vanity. Irrespective

of the way individual black women choose to do their hair, it is evident that the extent to which we suffer from racist and sexist oppression and exploitation affects the degree to which we feel capable of both self-love and asserting an autonomous presence that is acceptable and pleasing to ourselves. Individual preferences (whether rooted in self-hate or not) cannot negate the reality that our collective obsession with straightening black hair reflects the psychology of oppression and the impact of racist colonization. Together racism and sexism daily reinforce to all black females via the media, advertising, etc. that we will not be considered beautiful or desirable if we do not change ourselves, especially our hair. We cannot resist this socialization if we deny that white supremacy informs our efforts to construct self and identity.

14   Without organized struggles like the ones that happened in the 1960s and early 1970s, individual black women must struggle alone to acquire the critical consciousness that would enable us to examine issues of race and beauty, our personal choices, from a political standpoint. There are times when I think of straightening my hair just to change my style, just for fun. Then I remind myself that even though such a gesture could be simply playful on my part, an individual expression of desire, I know that such a gesture would carry other implications beyond my control. The reality is: straightened hair is linked historically and currently to a system of racial domination that impresses upon black people, and especially black women, that we are not acceptable as we are, that we are not beautiful. To make such a gesture as an expression of individual freedom and choice would make me complicit with a politic of domination that hurts us. It is easy to surrender this freedom. It is more important that black women resist racism and sexism in every way; that every aspect of our self-representation be a fierce resistance, a radical celebration of our care and respect for ourselves.

15   Even though I have not had straightened hair for a long time, this did not mean that I am able to really enjoy or appreciate my hair in its natural state. For years I still considered it a problem. (It wasn't naturally nappy enough to make a decent interesting afro. It was too thin.) These complaints expressed my continued dissatisfaction. True liberation of my hair came when I stopped trying to control it in any state and just accepted it as it is. It has been only in recent years that I have ceased to worry about what other people would say about my hair. It has been only in recent years that I could

feel consistent pleasure washing, combing, and caring for my hair. These feelings remind me of the pleasure and comfort I felt as a child sitting between my mother's legs feeling the warmth of her body and being as she combed and braided my hair. In a culture of domination, one that is essentially anti-intimacy, we must struggle daily to remain in touch with ourselves and our bodies, with one another. Especially black women and men, as it is our bodies that have been so often devalued, burdened, wounded in alienated labor. Celebrating our bodies, we participate in a liberatory struggle that frees mind and heart.

Back, but Not Home

MARIA L. MUNIZ

Maria L. Muniz was born in Cuba in 1958, a few months before Fidel Castro and his followers marched into Havana to establish his new communist regime. The dictator Batista fled the country with his supporters, and, in the years that followed, others, disillusioned with Castro's reign, also escaped the island. Her parents immigrated with Muniz to the United States when she was five years old. She received a good education and, in 1978, graduated from New York University. Thereafter, she worked for Catalyst, an association devoted to enlarging the career opportunities for women. In that role, she has written and edited books on careers for women and published many articles.

In "Back, but Not Home," published in 1979 in the *New York Times*, Muniz recalls when she left behind her large family in Cuba—the grandparents, cousins, aunts, uncles. Her cultural loss is reflected by her admission that, even though she is now a naturalized citizen, she still refers to herself as a "Cuban." As she puts it, "Outside American, inside Cuban." In addition, she wishes to return home "because the journey back will also mean a journey within."

1   With all the talk about resuming diplomatic relations with Cuba, and with the increasing number of Cuban exiles returning to visit

friends and relatives, I am constantly being asked, "Would you ever go back?" In turn, I have asked myself, "Is there any reason for me to go?" I have had to think long and hard before finding my answer. Yes.

2   I came to the United States with my parents when I was almost five years old. We left behind grandparents, aunts, uncles and several cousins. I grew up in a very middle-class neighborhood in Brooklyn. With one exception, all my friends were Americans. Outside of my family, I do not know many Cubans. I often feel awkward visiting relatives in Miami because it is such a different world. The way of life in Cuban Miami seems very strange to me and I am accused of being too "Americanized." Yet, although I am now an American citizen, whenever anyone has asked me my nationality, I have always and unhesitatingly replied, "Cuban."

3   Outside American, inside Cuban.

4   I recently had a conversation with a man who generally sympathizes with the Castro regime. We talked of Cuban politics and although the discussion was very casual, I felt an old anger welling inside. After sixteen years of living an "American" life, I am still unable to view the revolution with detachment or objectivity. I cannot interpret its results in social, political or economic terms. Too many memories stand in my way.

5   And as I listened to this man talk of the Cuban situation, I began to remember how as a little girl I would wake up crying because I had dreamed of my aunts and grandmothers and I missed them. I remembered my mother's trembling voice and the sad look on her face whenever she spoke to her mother over the phone. I thought of the many letters and photographs that somehow were always lost in transit. And as the conversation continued, I began to remember how difficult it often was to grow up Latina in an American world.

6   It meant going to kindergarten knowing little English. I'd been in this country only a few months and although I understood a good deal of what was said to me, I could not express myself very well. On the first day of school I remember one little girl's saying to the teacher: "But how can we play with her? She's so stupid she can't even talk!" I felt so helpless because inside I was crying, "Don't you know I can understand everything you're saying?" But I did not have words for my thoughts and my inability to communicate terrified me.

7   As I grew a little older, Latina meant being automatically relegated to the slowest reading classes in school. By now my English was fluent, but the teachers would always assume I was somewhat illiterate or slow. I recall one teacher's amazement at discovering I could read and write just as well as her American pupils. Her incredulity astounded me. As a child, I began to realize that Latina would always mean proving I was as good as the others. As I grew older, it became a matter of pride to prove I was better than the others.

8   As an adult I have come to terms with these memories and they don't hurt as much. I don't look or sound very Cuban. I don't speak with an accent and my English is far better than my Spanish. I am beginning my career and look forward to the many possibilities ahead of me.

9   But a persistent little voice is constantly saying, "There's something missing. It's not enough." And this is why when I am now asked, "Do you want to go back?" I say "yes" with conviction.

10   I do not say to Cubans, "It is time to lay aside the hurt and forgive and forget." It is impossible to forget an event that has altered and scarred all our lives so profoundly. But I find I am beginning to care less and less about politics. And I am beginning to remember and care more about the child (and how many others like her) who left her grandma behind. I have to return to Cuba one day because I want to know that little girl better.

11   When I try to review my life during the past sixteen years, I almost feel as if I've walked into a theater right in the middle of a movie. And I'm afraid I won't fully understand or enjoy the rest of the movie unless I can see and understand the beginning. And for me, the beginning is Cuba. I don't want to go "home" again; the life and home we all left behind are long gone. My home is here and I am happy. But I need to talk to my family still in Cuba.

12   Like all immigrants, my family and I have had to build a new life from almost nothing. It was often difficult, but I believe the struggle made us strong. Most of my memories are good ones.

13   But I want to preserve and renew my cultural heritage. I want to keep "la Cubana" within me alive. I want to return because the journey back will also mean a journey within. Only then will I see the missing piece.

CLASSIC MULTICULTURAL ESSAYS ABOUT

A Sense of Place

Why Kibbutzim?

BRUNO BETTELHEIM

Bruno Bettelheim (1903–1990) was born in Vienna, Austria. He earned his Ph.D. at the University of Vienna in 1938, but, as a Jew, he was targeted by the Nazis and incarcerated at Dachau and Buchenwald. Released the following year, he fled to the United States and became a naturalized citizen in 1944. He has written two significant works on the Nazi death camps: *The Informed Heart: Autonomy in a Mass Age* (1960) and *Surviving, and Other Essays* (1979), reprinted as *Surviving the Holocaust* (1986). In the United States, Bettelheim became an authority on the treatment of childhood autism and juvenile psychosis. He published *Love Is Not Enough: The Treatment of Emotionally Disturbed Children* (1950), *Truants from Life: The Rehabilitation of Emotionally Disturbed Children* (1955), and *The Empty Fortress: Infantile Autism and the Birth of the Self* (1962).

His 1969 book, *The Children of the Dream*, examines the ramifications of raising children in an Israeli kibbutz. "Why Kibbutzim?" is a part of that work. In this essay, Bettelheim compares the kibbutz parents to America's early Puritans in their devotion to their ideals: "Were it not for the kibbutz dream of a better society, there would be nothing unique left about Israel." He argues that the kibbutz ethos created a model for a noble life, one lived by personal sacrifice. Children raised in that environment would have unflinching dedication to the Jewish dream of a free nation.

1   From its very inception the purpose of the kibbutz movement, for both sexes, was first and foremost to create a new way of life in a very old and hostile land. True, the raising of a new generation to this new way of life was soon of crucial importance, but of necessity it took second place. Because unless the first generation created the society, how could it shelter any new generations? It was this older generation that subjected itself to great hardships and dangers, that first reclaimed the land, wresting harvests from a barren soil, and later fought the war that gained them statehood.

2   Today, apart from the still pervasive problem of making fast their new statehood, there is still the war for social ideals to be waged. But those ideals are harder to maintain when the problem is no longer one of creating a homeland, but of maintaining themselves as a splinter group in a land swept up in a booming economy. Such ideals are especially hard to preserve when the surrounding population is by now so largely concerned with acquiring the more convenient life that goes with a higher standard of living. The kibbutz parent, in his devotion to ideals, may be likened to our own early Puritans; except that these latter-day Puritans are not surrounded by a wilderness but by modern city life, which makes things a lot harder.

3   Kibbutzniks have never been more than a tiny minority in Israel. Nevertheless they have played a critical role there, both as idea and reality, out of all proportion to their numbers. For example, in 1944 Henrik Infield, in his book *Co-operative Living in Palestine,* places the total membership of all kibbutzim at about sixteen thousand. Twenty years later their numbers had grown to about eighty thousand, living in about 250 kibbutzim, but they were still only about 4 percent of the population of Israel. Yet this 4 percent accounted for some 15 percent of all members of the Knesset (Israeli parliament).

4   Even if the kibbutz stood for no more than a small sect, living by its esoteric convictions and trying to raise its children by these lights, their devotion to lofty ideals would command respect. But for Israel they do much more than that, since they still provide much

of the national ethos, and the best part of it. As many thoughtful Israelis told me: Were it not for the kibbutz dream of a better society, there would be nothing unique left about Israel. Having created a refuge where Jews can live free of persecution, Israel would be nothing more now than just a tiny new nation.

5   (Though written before the 1967 war, I see no reason to change this statement. The Arab-Israeli conflict is no longer a matter of the majority group persecuting a minority of its own citizens, but of two or more nation-states at odds over territorial rights. That one is smaller than the others does not make war and persecution the same thing, which they are not.)

6   It is also a nation with only one tenuous claim to the land: namely, that some two thousand years ago it was occupied by the spiritual ancestors of those who again hold possession now. This is not much of a claim compared to the uniqueness Jews felt, and which kept the Jews going during the two thousand years they were homeless.

7   All this has, in fact, led to many contradictions from which Kibbutz life still suffers: In reclaiming the land, as in creating the state of Israel, kibbutzniks displaced Arab neighbors and fought them though violence was contrary to their socialist convictions. Kibbutz founders wanted Israel to be an ideal state, free of all exploitation, where life would proceed in peace close to the biblical land. But the realities of the Middle East force Israel to be a garrison nation geared to defense, if not a war; a capitalist nation with many of the unpleasant features of a new nation trying to industrialize in a hurry.

8   I know that they also suffer from another contradiction, because they are keenly aware of it: Since they are atheists, they cannot base their claim to the land on the biblical promise that gave it to the Jews. The Jews needed a homestead. How desperately they needed it was made clear first by Hitler, and then by the plight of the Jews in Arab countries. But no other land was acceptable to the religious group, and no other land offered asylum to areligious Jews. So it had to be Israel, whether for political or emotional reasons.

9   In the face of all this contradiction and conflict, then, is where the kibbutz ethos makes a difference. It stands for utter devotion to the idea that once again Jews in Israel must not only create a new model of the good and just life, but actually live it—when need be at the cost of great personal hardship—or die for it if they must. Certainly the six-day war vindicated kibbutz child-rearing methods and made it once again a symbol of all that is best in Israel. Not

only did the kibbutz provide an inordinate percentage of the officer corps, it also suffered staggering losses. Some 4 percent of the Israeli population lives in the kibbutz, and kibbutzniks thus accounted for some 4 percent of the fighting force. But while about eight hundred soldiers fell in the war, two hundred of them came from the kibbutz (most of them born and raised there). Thus the 4 percent kibbutz segment of the Israeli army suffered 25 percent of all casualties. This was the true measure of their heroism, courage, and devotion to duty. Once more, as in the settling of the land and the war of liberation, the kibbutz ethos gives special meaning to the lives of Israelis today.

10   It is in this context of self-elected mission that the entire phenomenon of the kibbutz must be understood, and flowing from it, what the parents do or do not do in raising their children. . . .

11   How did the kibbutz way of raising children come about? First, it seems that kibbutz founders did not trust themselves to raise their own children in such a way as to become the carriers of a new society. To quote [Stanley] Diamond:

> The collective method of child rearing represents a rejection of the family, with particular reference to the parental roles. . . . It was felt that the family itself has to be banished, in order to rear the "new Jew.". . . [Kibbutz founders] were moved by the desire to create a new generation that would be "normal," "free," and "manly," unsullied by the exile. . . . They did not think themselves worthy of rearing such children within the confines of their own nuclear families, and they dared not trust themselves to the task.

12   Thus the realization of their larger dream depended on this new and uniquely brought up generation. But the new generation, and the unique way of bringing them up, were an afterthought, an accident. The kibbutz—a society that devotes its all to the future, and hence to its children, that has turned upside down all traditional modes of child rearing to realize its goals—started out as a society that had no interest in children whatsoever and no room for children in its life.

13   While this in no way invalidates the educational method, it

accounts for many contradictions that cannot be understood except from its unplanned inception. We are faced with the anomaly that what started as a nuisance, because it stood in the way of the founders' main purposes—to execute an idea—has become a central feature on which the idea's survival now depends.

14   As Joseph Baratz (1954) tells the story of Degania, the first kibbutz, the original kibbutzniks (of whom he was one) wanted no children in their community. Most of the settlers did not even want to marry, because "they were afraid that children would detach the family from the group, that . . . comradeship would be less steadfast." Therefore it was seriously proposed that all members should oblige themselves not to marry for at least five years after joining the kibbutz, because "living as we do . . . how can we have children?"

15   When the first child was born in the kibbutz "nobody knew what to do with him. Our women didn't know how to look after babies." But eventually "we saw it couldn't go on like this. . . . By the time there were four children in the settlement we decided something must be done. It was a difficult problem. How were the women both to work and look after their children? Should each mother look after her own family and do nothing else?" The men did not seem to feel strongly either way.

> But the women wouldn't hear of giving up their share of the communal work and life. . . . Somebody proposed that the kibbutz should hire a nurse . . . we didn't hire a nurse, but we chose one girl to look after the lot of them and we put aside a house were they could spend the day while the mothers were at work. And so this system developed and was afterwards adopted in all the kibbutzim, with the difference that in most of them the children sleep in the children's house, but with us [at Degania] they stay at night in their parents' quarters. . . . Only recently have we built a hostel for children over twelve where our own children live.

16   This is how the famous communal education of children began.

17   I myself questioned the founding generation: I wondered why the original group, so intent on creating a new way of life, had given no thought to their own continuity by planning for the next generation. The answer was always the same as the one given in

published accounts by the earliest settlers: "Founding the settlements, cultivating the land was so arduous, so much a grown-ups' task, that we could not think about children." I cannot help feeling that part of the original attraction of a thus-defined task might have been that it left no place for children. Because if one does not think of having children, it is because one has no wish for them at the time, and not because the task at hand is so arduous.

18   If my speculation is valid, one might carry it a step further and say that the founding generation knew they had no wish to replicate the family as they knew it, and of this they were entirely conscious. But despite their rejection they could not think of how else to raise children. Hence to them, the decision not to form families meant not to have children. If so, then kibbutz life was attractive to those who for this or other reasons did not wish to have children. My assumption seems supported by the incredibly low birthrate in the early days of kibbutz history, which contrasts sharply with other settings in which a people live in hardship and danger and nevertheless produce many children.

19   It would seem, then, that chance and a desire for quite other things dictated the child-caring arrangements made hastily, piecemeal, and with little plan or thought; arrangements that were later formalized into dogma, as is probably the origin of most dogmas.

Choosing a Dream: Italians in Hell's Kitchen

MARIO PUZO

Mario Puzo was born in New York City in 1920. He attended the
New School for Social Research and Columbia University. Primarily
a novelist, he has held various jobs with the New York Central
Railroad, the U.S. Civil Service, and Magazine Management. In the
mid-1960s, an editor at Putnam Publishing House overheard Puzo
telling stories about the Mafia, so he offered Puzo a $5,000 advance
for a novel based on Puzo's investigation and imagination. The
result—*The Godfather*—is literary and movie history. With Francis
Ford Coppola, he developed screenplays for three *Godfather* movies,
which won three Oscars and two Golden Globe awards. Puzo also
collaborated on other movies, including *Earthquake* and *Superman*.
One of his recent books , *The Fourth K*, is a political thriller set in
the twenty-first century, where terrorism is rampant and the president
of the United States, a fictional cousin of John F. Kennedy, has
trouble maintaining world peace.

"Choosing a Dream: Italians in Hell's Kitchen" is an essay that
Puzo contributed to a collection entitled *The Immigrant Experience:
The Anguish of Becoming an American* (1971). In this personal
essay, he describes his initial contempt for the Italian way of "always
shouting, always angry, quicker to quarrel than embrace." That
mood, however, changes to one of admiration. Without realizing it

in his youth, he had been surrounded by heroes: "Heroes all around me. I never saw them." He comes to admire their courage in leaving their native land, for "they, too, dreamed a dream."

1   As a child and in my adolescence, living in the heart of New York's Neapolitan ghetto, I never heard an Italian singing. None of the grown-ups I knew were charming or loving or understanding. Rather they seemed coarse, vulgar, and insulting. And so later in my life when I was exposed to all the clichés of lovable Italians, singing Italians, happy-go-lucky Italians, I wondered where the hell the moviemakers and story-writers got all their ideas from.

2   At a very early age I decided to escape these uncongenial folk by becoming an artist, a writer. It seemed then an impossible dream. My father and mother were illiterate, as were their parents before them. But practicing my art I tried to view the adults with a more charitable eye and so came to the conclusion that their only fault lay in their being foreigners; I was an American. This didn't really help because I was only half right. I was the foreigner. They were already more "American" than I could ever become.

3   But it did seem then that the Italian immigrants, all the fathers and mothers that I knew, were a grim lot; always shouting, always angry, quicker to quarrel than embrace. I did not understand that their lives were a long labor to earn their daily bread and that physical fatigue does not sweeten human natures.

4   And so even as a very small child I dreaded growing up to be like the adults around me. I heard them saying too many cruel things about their dearest friends, saw too many of their false embraces with those they had just maligned, observed with horror their paranoiac anger at some small slight or a fancied injury to their pride. They were, always, too unforgiving. In short, they did not have the careless magnanimity of children.

5   In my youth I was contemptuous of my elders, including a few under thirty. I thought my contempt special to their circumstances. Later when I wrote about these illiterate men and women, when I thought I understood them, I felt a condescending pity. After all, they had suffered, they had labored all the days of their lives. They

had never tasted luxury, knew little more economic security than those ancient Roman slaves who might have been their ancestors. And alas, I thought, with new-found artistic insight, they were cut off from their children because of the strange American tongue, alien to them, native to their sons and daughters.

6   Already an artist but not yet a husband or father, I pondered omnisciently on their tragedy, again thinking it special circumstance rather than a constant in the human condition. I did not yet understand why these men and women were willing to settle for less than they deserved in life and think that "less" quite a bargain. I did not understand that they simply could not afford to dream; I myself had a hundred dreams from which to choose. For I was already sure that I would make my escape, that I was one of the chosen. I would be rich, famous, happy. I would master my destiny. . . .

7   My family and I grew up together on Tenth Avenue, between Thirtieth and Thirty-first streets, part of the area called Hell's Kitchen. This particular neighborhood could have been a movie set for one of the Dead End Kid flicks or for the social drama of the East Side in which John Garfield played the hero. Our tenements were the western wall of the city. Beneath our windows were the vast black iron gardens of the New York Central Railroad, absolutely blooming with stinking boxcars freshly unloaded of cattle and pigs for the city slaughterhouse. Steers sometimes escaped and loped through the heart of the neighborhood followed by astonished young boys who had never seen a live cow.

8   The railroad yards stretched down to the Hudson River, beyond whose garbagey waters rose the rocky Palisades of New Jersey. There were railroad tracks running downtown on Tenth Avenue itself to another freight station called St. Johns Park. Because of this, because these trains cut off one side of the street from the other, there was a wooden bridge over Tenth Avenue, a romantic-looking bridge despite the fact that no sparkling water, no silver flying fish darted beneath it; only heavy dray carts drawn by tired horses, some flat-boarded trucks, tin lizzie automobiles and, of course, long strings of freight cars drawn by black, ugly engines. . . .

9   My father supported his wife and seven children by working as a trackman laborer for the New York Central Railroad. My oldest brother worked for the railroad as a brakeman, another brother was a railroad shipping clerk in the freight office. Eventually I spent some of the worst months of my life as the railroad's worst messenger boy.

10   My oldest sister was just as unhappy as a dressmaker in the garment industry. She wanted to be a school teacher. At one time or another my other two brothers also worked for the railroad—it got all six males in the family. The two girls and my mother escaped, though my mother felt it her duty to send all our bosses a gallon of homemade wine on Christmas. But everybody hated their jobs except my oldest brother who had a night shift and spent most of his working hours sleeping in freight cars. My father finally got fired because the foreman told him to get a bucket of water for the crew and not to take all day. My father took the bucket and disappeared forever.

11   Nearly all the Italian men living on Tenth Avenue supported their large families by working on the railroad. Their children also earned pocket money by stealing ice from the refrigerator cars in summer and coal from the open stoking cars in the winter. Sometimes an older lad would break the seal of a freight car and take a look inside. But this usually brought down the "Bulls," the special railroad police. And usually the freight was "heavy" stuff, too much work to cart away and sell, something like fresh produce or boxes of cheap candy that nobody would buy.

12   The older boys, the ones just approaching voting age, made their easy money by hijacking silk trucks that loaded up at the garment factory on Thirty-first Street. They would then sell the expensive dresses door to door, at bargain prices no discount house could match. From this some graduated into organized crime, whose talent scouts alertly tapped young boys versed in strongarm. Yet despite all this, most of the kids grew up honest, content with fifty bucks a week as truckdrivers, deliverymen, and white-collar clerks in the civil service.

13   I had every desire to go wrong but I never had a chance. The Italian family structure was too formidable.

14   I never came home to an empty house; there was always the smell of supper cooking. My mother was always there to greet me, sometimes with a policeman's club in her hand (nobody ever knew how she acquired it). But she was always there, or her authorized deputy, my older sister, who preferred throwing empty milk bottles at the heads of her little brothers when they got bad marks on their report cards. During the great Depression of the 1930s, though we were the poorest of the poor, I never remember not dining well. Many years later as a guest of a millionaire's club, I realized that our

poor family on home relief ate better than some of the richest people in America.

15   My mother would never dream of using anything but the finest imported olive oil, the best Italian cheeses. My father had access to the fruits coming off ships, the produce from railroad cars, all before it went through the stale process of middlemen; and my mother, like most Italian women, was a fine cook in the peasant style. . . .

16   I had to help support my family by working on the railroad. After school hours of course. This was the same railroad that had supplied free coal and free ice to the whole Tenth Avenue when I was young enough to steal with impunity. After school finished at 3 P.M. I went to work in the freight office as a messenger. I also worked Saturdays and Sundays when there was work available.

17   I hated it. One of my first short stories was about how I hated that job. But of course what I really hated was entering the adult world. To me the adult world was a dark enchantment, unnatural. As unnatural to the human dream as death. And as inevitable. . . .

18   Then why do I dream of those immigrant Italian peasants as having been happy? I remember how they spoke of their forebears, who spent all their lives farming the arid mountain slopes of Southern Italy. "He died in that house in which he was born," they say enviously. "He was never more than an hour from his village, not in all his life," they sigh. And what would they make of a phrase like "retrospective falsification"?

19   No, really, we are all happier now. It is a better life. And after all, as my mother always said, "Never mind about being happy. Be glad you're alive."

20   When I came to my "autobiographical novel," the one every writer does about himself, I planned to make myself the sensitive, misunderstood hero, much put upon by his mother and family. To my astonishment my mother took over the book and instead of my revenge I got another comeuppance. But it is, I think, my best book. And all those old-style grim conservative Italians whom I hated, then pitied so patronizingly, they also turned out to be heroes. Through no desire of mine. I was surprised. The thing that amazed me most was their courage. Where were their Congressional Medals of Honor? Their Distinguished Service Crosses? How did they ever have the balls to get married, have kids, go out to earn a living in a strange land, with no skills, not even knowing the language? They made it without tranquillizers, without sleeping pills, without psychiatrists,

without even a dream. Heroes. Heroes all around me. I never saw them.

21 But how could I? They wore lumpy work clothes and handlebar moustaches, they blew their noses on their fingers and they were so short that their high-school children towered over them. They spoke a laughable broken English and the furthest limit of their horizon was their daily bread. Brave men, brave women, they fought to live their lives without dreams. Bent on survival, they narrowed their minds to the thinnest line of existence.

22 It is no wonder that in my youth I found them contemptible. And yet they had left Italy and sailed the ocean to come to a new land and leave their sweated bones in America. Illiterate Colombos, they dared to seek the promised land. And so they, too, dreamed a dream.

The Way to Rainy Mountain

N. SCOTT MOMADAY

N. Scott Momaday was born in Lawton, Oklahoma, in 1934. He attended Augusta Military Academy; earned a B.A. at the University of New Mexico in 1958; and was awarded a Ph.D. at Stanford University in 1963. Momaday first gained fame with his novel *House Made of Dawn* (1968), which chronicles the life of an Indian boy who leaves the reservation but cannot find comfort in the outside world. The novel won a Pulitzer Prize and launched a series of writings firmly attached to his Kiowa roots. He made this observation: "When I was growing up on the reservation of the Southwest, I saw people who were deeply involved in their traditional life, in the memories of their blood. They had, as far as I could see, a certain strength and beauty that I find missing in the modern world at large. I like to celebrate the involvement in my writing."

Momaday followed the success of his novel with a nonfiction work, *The Way to Rainy Mountain* (1969), which chronicles Kiowa folktales, Indian history, and his own reminiscences about life among his ancestors and fellow Indians. In describing his grandmother, Momaday indirectly describes himself and his Indian heritage. Reminiscence, one kind of autobiography, often imbues the episode with nostalgic longing for a time that is gone forever. He uses the dignity of the old woman to symbolize pride in himself and all others of Indian ancestry, meanwhile touching the hearts of his readers, reminding them of lost tribes, lost religions, and lost hope.

1   A single knoll rises out of the plain in Oklahoma, north and west of the Wichita Range. For my people, the Kiowas, it is an old land-mark, and they gave it the name Rainy Mountain. The hardest weather in the world is there. Winter brings blizzards, hot tornadic winds arise in the spring, and in summer the prairie is an anvil's edge. The grass turns brittle and brown, and it cracks beneath your feet. There are green belts along the rivers and creeks, linear groves of hickory and pecan, willow and witch hazel. At a distance in July or August the steaming foliage seems almost to writhe in fire. Great green-and-yellow grasshoppers are everywhere in the tall grass, pop-ping up like corn to sting the flesh, and tortoises crawl about on the red earth, going nowhere in the plenty of time. Loneliness is an aspect of the land. All things in the plain are isolate; there is no confusion of objects in the eye, but *one* hill or *one* tree or *one* man. To look upon that landscape in the early morning, with the sun at your back, is to lose the sense of proportion. Your imagination comes to life, and this, you think, is where Creation was begun.

2   I returned to Rainy Mountain in July. My grandmother had died in the spring, and I wanted to be at her grave. She had lived to be very old and at last infirm. Her only living daughter was with her when she died, and I was told that in death her face was that of a child.

3   I like to think of her as a child. When she was born, the Kiowas were living that last great moment of their history. For more than a hundred years they had controlled the open range from the Smoky Hill River to the Red, from the headwaters of the Canadian to the fork of the Arkansas and Cimarron. In alliance with the Comanches, they had ruled the whole of the southern Plains. War was their sacred business, and they were among the finest horsemen the world had ever known. But warfare for the Kiowas was preeminently a matter of disposition rather than of survival, and they never understood the grim, unrelenting advance of the U.S. Cavalry. When at last, divided and ill-provisioned, they were driven onto the Staked Plains in the

cold rains of autumn, they fell into panic. In Palo Duro Canyon they abandoned their crucial stores to pillage and had nothing then but their lives. In order to save themselves, they surrendered to the soldiers at Fort Sill and were imprisoned in the old stone corral that now stands as a military museum. My grandmother was spared the humiliation of those high gray walls by eight or ten years, but she must have known from birth the affliction of defeat, the dark brooding of old warriors.

4 Her name was Aho, and she belonged to the last culture to evolve in North America. Her forebears came down from the high country in western Montana nearly three centuries ago. They were a mountain people, a mysterious tribe of hunters whose language has never been positively classified in any major group. In the late seventeenth century they began a long migration to the south and east. It was a long journey toward the dawn, and it led to a golden age. Along the way the Kiowas were befriended by the Crows, who gave them the culture and religion of the Plains. They acquired horses, and their ancient nomadic spirit was suddenly free of the ground. They acquired Tai-me, the sacred Sun Dance doll, from that moment the object and symbol of their worship, and so shared in the divinity of the sun. Not least, they acquired the sense of destiny, therefore courage and pride. When they entered upon the southern Plains, they had been transformed. No longer were they slaves to the simple necessity of survival; they were a lordly and dangerous society of fighters and thieves, hunters and priests of the sun. According to their origin myth, they entered the world through a hollow log. From one point of view, their migration was the fruit of an old prophecy, for indeed they emerged from a sunless world.

5 Although my grandmother lived out her long life in the shadow of Rainy Mountain, the immense landscape of the continental interior lay like memory in her blood. She could tell of the Crows, whom she had never seen, and of the Black Hills, where she had never been. I wanted to see in reality what she had seen more perfectly in the mind's eye, and traveled fifteen hundred miles to begin my pilgrimage.

6 Yellowstone, it seemed to me, was the top of the world, a region of deep lakes and dark timber, canyons and waterfalls. But, beautiful as it is, one might have the sense of confinement there. The skyline in all directions is close at hand, the high wall of the woods and deep cleavages of shade. There is a perfect freedom in the mountains, but

it belongs to the eagle and the elk, the badger and the bear. The Kiowas reckoned their stature by the distance they could see, and they were bent and blind in the wilderness.

7   Descending eastward, the highland meadows are a stairway to the plain. In July the inland slope of the Rockies is luxuriant with flax and buckwheat, stonecrop and larkspur. The earth unfolds and the limit of the land recedes. Clusters of trees and animals grazing far in the distance cause the vision to reach away and wonder to build upon the mind. The sun follows a longer course in the day, and the sky is immense beyond all comparison. The great billowing clouds that sail upon it are shadows that move upon the grain like water, dividing light. Farther down, in the land of the Crows and Blackfeet, the plain is yellow. Sweet clover takes hold of the hills and bends upon itself to cover and seal the soil. There the Kiowas paused on their way; they had come to the place where they must change their lives. The sun is at home on the plains. Precisely there does it have the certain character of a god. When the Kiowas came to the land of the Crows, they could see the dark lees of the hills at dawn across the Bighorn River, the profusion of light on the grain shelves, the oldest deity ranging after the solstices. Not yet would they veer southward to the caldron of the land that lay below; they must wean their blood from the northern winter and hold the mountains a while longer in their view. They bore Tai-me in procession to the east.

8   A dark mist lay over the Black Hills, and the land was like iron. At the top of a ridge I caught sight of Devil's Tower upthrust against the gray sky as if in the birth of time the core of the earth had broken through its crust and the motion of the world was begun. There are things in nature that engender an awful quiet in the heart of man; Devil's Tower is one of them. Two centuries ago, because they could not do otherwise, the Kiowas made a legend at the base of the rock. My grandmother said:

> "Eight children were there at play, seven sisters and their brother. Suddenly the boy was struck dumb; he trembled and began to run upon his hands and feet. His fingers became claws, and his body was covered with fur. Directly there was a bear where the boy had been. The sisters were terrified; they ran, and the bear after them. They came to the stump of a great tree, and the tree spoke to them.

It bade them climb upon it, and as they did so, it began to rise into the air. The bear came to kill them, but they were just beyond its reach. It reared against the tree and scored the bark all around with its claws. The seven sisters were borne into the sky, and they became the stars of the Big Dipper."

From that moment, and so long as the legend lives, the Kiowas have kinsmen in the night sky. Whatever they were in the mountains, they could be no more. However tenuous their well-being, however much they had suffered and would suffer again, they had found a way out of the wilderness.

9   My grandmother had a reverence for the sun, a holy regard that now is all but gone out of mankind. There was a wariness in her, and an ancient awe. She was a Christian in her later years, but she had come a long way about, and she never forgot her birthright. As a child she had been to the Sun Dances; she had taken part in those annual rites, and by them she had learned the restoration of her people in the presence of Tai-me. She was about seven when the last Kiowa Sun Dance was held in 1887 on the Washita River above Rainy Mountain Creek. The buffalo were gone. In order to consummate the ancient sacrifice—to impale the head of a buffalo bull upon the medicine tree—a delegation of old men journeyed into Texas, there to beg and barter for an animal from the Goodnight herd. She was ten when the Kiowas came together for the last time as a living Sun Dance culture. They could find no buffalo; they had to hang an old hide from the sacred tree. Before the dance could begin, a company of soldiers rode out from Fort Sill under orders to disperse the tribe. Forbidden without cause the essential act of their faith, having seen the wild herds slaughtered and left to rot upon the ground, the Kiowas backed away forever from the medicine tree. That was July 20, 1890, at the great bend of the Washita. My grandmother was there. Without bitterness, and for as long as she lived, she bore a vision of deicide.

10   Now that I can have her only in memory, I see my grandmother in the several postures that were peculiar to her: standing at the wood stove on a winter morning and turning meat in a great iron skillet; sitting at the south window, bent above her beadwork, and afterwards, when her vision had failed, looking down for a long time into the fold of her hands; going out upon a cane, very slowly as

she did when the weight of age came upon her; praying. I remember her most often at prayer. She made long, rambling prayers out of suffering and hope, having seen many things. I was never sure that I had the right to hear, so exclusive were they of all mere custom and company. The last time I saw her she prayed standing by the side of her bed at night, naked to the waist, the light of a kerosene lamp moving upon her dark skin. Her long, black hair, always drawn and braided in the day, lay upon her shoulders and against her breasts like a shawl. I do not speak Kiowa, and I never understood her prayers, but there was something inherently sad in the sound, some merest hesitation upon the syllables of sorrow. She began in a high and descending pitch, exhausting her breath to silence; then again and again—and always the same intensity of effort, of something that is, and is not, like urgency in the human voice. Transported so in the dancing light among the shadows of her room, she seemed beyond the reach of time. But that was illusion; I think I knew then that I should not see her again.

from *The Line of the Sun*

JUDITH ORTIZ COFER

Judith Ortiz Cofer was born in 1952 in Hormigueros, Puerto Rico, the daughter of a U.S. sailor and a Puerto Rican mother. She immigrated to the United States with her family in 1956. She earned a B.A. at Augusta College and an M.A. at Florida Atlantic University. She also attended Oxford University for a year. She has taught English and creative writing at a number of colleges and universities. Primarily a poet, she gained national attention in 1989 with the autobiographical work *The Line of the Sun*, which portrays the squalor of village life in Salud, Puerto Rico, and then shifts to Patterson, New Jersey, where the narrator must confront her heritage and try to stabilize the American and Puerto Rican features of her personality. Cofer said, "My family is one of the main topics of my poetry; the ones left behind on the island of Puerto Rico, and the ones who came to the United States. . . . The place of birth itself becomes a metaphor for the things we all must leave behind; the assimilation of a new culture is the coming into maturity by accepting the terms necessary for survival. My poetry is a study of this process of change, assimilation, and transformation."

1   It was a bitter winter in Paterson. The snow fell white and dry as coconut shavings, but as soon as it touched the dirty pavement it

turned into a muddy soup. Though we wore rubber boots, our feet stayed wet and cold all day. The bitter wind brought hot tears to our eyes, but it was so cold that we never felt them streaking our cheeks.

2   During Lent the nuns counted attendance at the seven o'clock mass and gave demerits if we did not take into our dry mouths Christ's warm body in the form of a wafer the priest held in his palm. The church was dark at that hour of the morning, and thick with the steaming garments of children dropped off by anxious mothers or, like us, numb from a seven-block walk.

3   In the hour of the mass, I thawed in the sweet unctuousness of the young Italian priest's voice chanting his prayers for the souls of these young children and their teachers, for their parents, for the dead and the living, for our deprived brothers and sisters, some of whom had not found comfort in Christ and were now in mortal danger of damning their souls to the raging fire of hell. He didn't really say hell, a word carefully avoided in our liturgy: it was all innuendo and Latin words that sounded like expletives. *Kyrie Eleison*, he would challenge; *Christe Eleison*, we would respond heartily, led by the strong voice of Sister Mary Beata, our beautiful homeroom teacher, whose slender body and perfect features were evident in spite of the layers of clothing she wore and the coif that surrounded her face. She was the envy of our freshman-class girls. In the classroom I sat in the back watching her graceful movements, admiring the translucent quality of her unblemished skin, wondering whether both her calm and her beauty were a gift from God, imagining myself in the medieval clothes of her nun's habit.

4   I sat in the last desk of the last row of the girl's side of the room, the smallest, darkest member of a class full of the strapping offspring of Irish immigrants with a few upstart Italians recently added to the roll. The blazing red hair of Jackie O'Connell drew my eyes like a flame to the center of the room, and the pattern of freckles on her nose fascinated me. She was a popular girl with the sisters; her father was a big-shot lawyer with political ambitions. Donna Finney was well developed for her age, her woman's body restrained within the angular lines of the green-and-white plaid uniform we would wear until our junior year, when we would be allowed to dress like young ladies in a pleated green skirt and white blouse. Donna sat in the row closest to the boys' side of the room.

5   The boys were taller and heavier than my friends at El Building; they wore their blue ties and opened doors for girls naturally, as if they did it at home too. At school we were segregated by sex: every classroom was divided into girlside and boyside, and even the play-ground had an imaginary line right down the middle, where the assigned nun of the day would stand guard at recess and lunchtime. There were some couples in the school, of course. Everyone knew Donna went with a junior boy, a basketball player named Mickey Salvatore, an Italian playing on our Fighting Irish team—and it was a known fact that they went out in his car. After school some girls met their boyfriends at Schulze's drugstore for a soda. I saw them go in on my way home. My mother, following Rafael's instructions, gave us thirty minutes to get home before she put on her coat and high heels and came looking for us. I had just enough time to round up my brother at the grammar-school building across the street and walk briskly the seven blocks home. No soda for me with friends at Schulze's.

6   Ramona had come looking for us one day when an afternoon assembly had held me up, and that episode had taught me a lesson. Her long black hair loose and wild from the wind, she was wearing black spiked shoes and was wrapped in a red coat and black shawl when she showed up outside the school building. The kids stared at her as if she were a circus freak, and the nuns looked doubtful, thinking perhaps they should ask the gypsy to leave the school grounds. One boy said something about her that made a hot blush of shame creep up my neck and burn my cheeks. They didn't know—couldn't know—that she was my mother, since Rafael made all our school arrangements every year, explaining that his wife could not speak English and therefore would not be attending PTA meetings and so forth. My mother looked like no other mother at the school, and I was glad she did not participate in school activities. Even on Sunday she went to the Spanish mass while we attended our separate service for children. My gypsy mother embarrassed me with her wild beauty. I wanted her to cut and spray her hair into a sculptured hairdo like the other ladies; I wanted her to wear tailored skirts and jackets like Jackie Kennedy; I even resented her youth, which made her look like my older sister. She was what I would have looked like if I hadn't worn my hair in a tight braid, if I had allowed myself to sway when I walked, and if I had worn loud colors and had spoken only Spanish.

7   I was beginning to understand why Rafael wanted to move us away from El Building. The older I got, the more embarrassed I felt about living in this crowded, noisy tenement, which the residents seemed intent on turning into a bizarre facsimile of an Island barrio. But for a while my fascination with Guzmán overpowered all other feelings, and when I came home from the organized, sanitized world of school, I felt drawn into his sickroom like an opium addict. I looked forward to the air thick with the smells of many cigarettes and of alcohol. More and more I took over the nursing duties which Ramona, with her impatient hands, relished little. She was used to fast-healing children and an absent husband. Guzmán's bleeding wound and his careful movements tried her patience.

8   And so it happened that my uncle and I began talking. Guzmán told me about his childhood on the Island in general terms, leaving out things he did not think I would understand, but his silences and omissions were fuel to my imagination and I filled in the details. I questioned him about his friend Rosa, whose name came up whenever he began to describe the Island. It was as if she were the embodiment of all that was beautiful, strange, and tempting about his homeland. He told me about her amazing knowledge of plants and herbs, how she knew what people needed just by talking to them. Once I asked him to describe her to me. His eyes had been closed as he spoke, seeing her, I suppose; but he opened them like one who slowly rises from a dream and looked at me, sitting by the side of his bed in my blue-and-white first Friday uniform, my hair pulled back in a tightly wound bun.

9   "Let your hair down," he said.

10 I reached back and pulled the long black pins out of my thick hair, letting it fall over my shoulders. It was quite long, and I never wore it loose.

11 "She had long black hair like yours," he said rising on his elbows to look intently into my face as if seeing me for the first time. I noticed his knuckles going white from the effort. "And she was light-complexioned like you." He fell back on the pillow, groaning a little. Ramona came in at that moment with fresh bandages and looked strangely at me sitting there with my hair undone, but did not say anything. Ordering Guzmán to shift to his side, she changed his bandage briskly.

12 "I need you to go to the bodega for me, Marisol," she said, not looking at me. I hated going into the gloomy little Spanish grocery

store with its fishy smell and loiterers who always had something smart to say to women.

13   "Why can't you send Gabriel?" I asked petulantly, feeling once again that strain developing between my mother and me which kept getting more in the way of all our attempts at communication. She refused to acknowledge the fact that I was fast becoming too old to order around.

14   "He is doing his homework." Tucking the sheet around her brother as if he were another child, she turned to me. "Just do what I tell you, niña, without arguments or back talk. It looks like we are going to have a serious discussion with your father when he comes home." She looked at me meaningfully.

15   When she left the room I braided my hair slowly. It was the new impasse we had reached. I would obey her but I would take my time doing so, pushing her to a steady burning anger which could no longer be relieved by the familiar routine of spanking, tears, reconciliation. It was a contest of wills that I knew no one could win, but Ramona was still hoping Rafael would know how to mediate. He was the absent disciplinarian—Solomon, the wise judge, the threat and the promise that hung over us day after day in her constant "when your father comes home."

16   I couldn't understand how she continued to treat me like a child when she had not been much older than I when she married Rafael. If I were on the Island I would be respected as a young woman of marriageable age. I had heard Ramona talking with her friends about a girl's fifteenth year, the *Quinceañera*, when everything changes for her. She no longer plays with children; she dresses like a woman and joins the women at coffee in the afternoon; she is no longer required to attend school if there is more pressing need for her at home, or if she is engaged. I was almost fifteen now—still in my silly uniform, bobby socks and all; still not allowed to socialize with my friends, living in a state of limbo, halfway between cultures. No one at school asked why I didn't participate in the myriad parish activities. They all understood that Marisol was *different*.

17   Talking with my uncle, listening to stories about his life on the Island, and hearing Ramona's constant rhapsodizing about that tropical paradise—all conspired to make me feel deprived. I should have grown up there. I should have been able to play in emerald-green pastures, to eat sweet bananas right off the trees, to learn about life from the women who were strong and wise like the fabled Mamá

Cielo. How could she be Ramona's mother? Ramona, who could not make a decision without invoking the name of our father, whose judgment we awaited like the Second Coming.

18   As I reached for the door to leave Guzmán's room, he stirred.

19   "Rosa," he said, groggy from medication.

20   "Do you need anything?" I was trembling.

21   Alert now, he pointed to the dresser against the wall. "Take my wallet from the top drawer and get me a carton of L&M's when you go to the bodega." He closed his eyes again, whispering, "Thanks, niña."

22   I took his wallet, unwilling to make more noise by looking through it for money. In the kitchen Ramona was washing dishes at the sink, her back to me, but she was aware of my presence, and her anger showed in the set of her shoulders. I suddenly remembered how much she used to laugh, and still did when she was around her women friends.

23   "The list and the money are on the table, Marisol. Don't take long. I need to start dinner soon."

24   I put my coat on and left the apartment. The smells of beans boiling in a dozen kitchens assailed my nostrils. Rice and beans, the unimaginative staple food of all these people who re-created every day the same routines they had followed in their mamá's houses so long ago. Except that here in Paterson, in the cold rooms stories about the frozen ground, the smells and sounds of a lost way of life could only be a parody.

25   Instead of heading out the front door and to the street, an impulse carried my feet down an extra flight of stairs to El Basement. It was usually deserted at this hour when everyone was preparing to eat. I sat on the bottom step and looked around me at the cavernous room. A yellow light hung over my head. I took Guzmán's wallet from my coat pocket. Bringing it close to my face, I smelled the old leather. Carefully I unfolded it flat on my lap. There were several photos in the plastic. On top was a dark Indian-looking woman whose features looked familiar. Her dark, almond-shaped eyes were just like Ramona's, but her dark skin and high cheekbones were Guzmán's. I guessed this was an early picture of my grandmother, Mamá Cielo. Behind that there was one of two teenage boys, one dark, one blond. They were smiling broadly, arms on each other's shoulders. There was a fake moon in the background like the ones they use in carnival photo booths. Though the picture was bent,

cutting the boys at the neck, and of poor quality, I recognized them: it was Guzmán and Rafael. I looked at it for a long time, especially at my father's face, almost unrecognizable to me with its unfamiliar look of innocent joy. Perhaps they had been drinking that night. I had often heard Ramona talking about the festivals dedicated to Our Lady of Salud, the famous smiling Virgin. Maybe they had the photo taken then. Was this the night that Guzmán had seen Rosa dressed like a gypsy at the fair? I had heard that story told late at night in my mother's kitchen, eavesdropping while I pretended to sleep. Did Rafael know Ramona then—was he happy because he was in love with the beautiful fourteen-year-old sister of his best friend?

26   In one of the plastic windows there was a newspaper clipping, yellow and torn, of a Spanish actress, wild black hair falling like a violent storm around a face made up to look glamorous, eyelashes thickened black, glossy lips parted in an open invitation. She was beautiful. I had seen her face often in the magazines my mother bought at the bodega, but why did Guzmán carry this woman's picture around? Was this what Rosa had looked like, or was she just his fantasy?

27   Deeply engrossed in my secret activity of going through my uncle's wallet, I was startled to hear men's voices approaching the top of the landing. I sat still waiting for them to go up the stairs, but they came down instead. There were four or five whose faces I recognized in the dim light as the working men of El Building, young husbands whose wives were Ramona's friends. I was not afraid, but I hid the wallet in my coat pocket and quickly got to my feet. My mind raced to come up with an excuse, though it was *their* presence in El Basement that was odd. The laundry room was used legitimately by women and otherwise by kids. The only other users, as I very well knew from my encounter with Joŝe and the woman, were people who wanted to hide what they were doing.

28   The voice I heard most clearly was that of Santiago, the only man from El Building ever to have been invited by Rafael into our apartment. After a severe winter week several years before, we had been left without heat until this man went down to city hall and got a judge to force the building superintendent to do something about the frozen heater pipes. Rafael had been in Europe at the time, but he obviously respected Santiago.

29   Coming down the steps, Santiago's voice directed the others. One man was to stand at the top and wait for the others, the rest were

to follow him into the basement. He nearly stumbled over me in the dim light, not seeing me wrapped in my gray coat.

30 "Niña, *por Dios*, what are you doing here at this hour?" His voice was gentle but I detected irritation.

31 "My mother lost something here earlier and sent me down to try to find it." I explained rather rapidly in my awkward formal Spanish.

32 He took my elbow in a fatherly way: "Marisol, I don't believe your mother would be so careless as to send you down here to this dark place at the dinner hour alone. But I won't mention that I saw you here, and you must do the same for me, for us. These men and I want to have a private conversation. Do you understand?"

33 "Yes," I said quickly, wanting to be released from his firm grasp, "I won't say anything." He let go of my arm and I ran up the stairs. Several other men had arrived and were talking in hushed tones at the top of the steps. I managed to catch a few sentences as I slipped by their surprised faces and into the streets. It was the factory they were discussing. Someone had said *huelga*, a strike. They were planning a strike.

34 Outside it was cold, but not bitter; a hint of spring in the breeze cooled my cheeks without biting into my skin. For once I felt a sense of pride in my father, who had managed to escape the horrible trap of factory work, though he was paying a high price for it. Tonight I'd have something to talk about with Guzmán. He would be interested in the secret basement meeting and the strike.

CLASSIC MULTICULTURAL ESSAYS ABOUT

The Importance of Language

Learning to Read and Write

FREDERICK DOUGLASS

Frederick Douglass (1817–1895) was born a slave in Tuckahoe, Maryland, and was sent at eight to work for his master's relatives in Baltimore. There, he secretly started a self-education program that continued into his adult life. In 1838, at age twenty-one, he escaped and fled to New Bedford, Massachusetts. To avoid bounty hunters, he changed his name (from Frederick Augustus Washington Bailey) and existed by working a variety of jobs—"saw wood, shovel coal, carry the hod, sweep the chimney, or roll oil casks."

The turning point of his life came in 1841 when he was invited to speak at a meeting of the Massachusetts Antislavery Society. His discourse, which explained what freedom meant to him, so influenced the audience that the society hired him for a lecture series. In 1845, he published *The Narrative of the Life of Frederick Douglass*, an autobiography that exposed his identity. He fled to Europe, continued his lectures, and raised enough money to buy his freedom. *My Bondage and My Freedom* (1855) and *Life and Times of Frederick Douglass* (1881) are expanded versions of his 1845 autobiography.

He returned to the United States in 1847 to found *North Star*, and antislavery newspaper in which he launched a campaign not only against slavery but against racism in northern businesses, churches, schools, and public facilities. During the Civil War, he recruited blacks for the Union Army. He even discussed the war effort with President Lincoln on several occasions. Later, during the administration of Benjamin Harrison, he served as U.S. minister to Haiti.

The portion of Douglass's *Narrative* reprinted below uncovers his wisdom, explores the conditions of bondage, and shows the human spirit searching with determination for its independence.

1   I lived in Master Hugh's family about seven years. During this time, I succeeded in learning to read and write. In accomplishing this, I was compelled to resort to various stratagems. I had no regular teacher. My mistress, who had kindly commenced to instruct me, had, in compliance with the advice and direction of her husband, not only ceased to instruct, but had set her face against my being instructed by any one else. It is due, however, to my mistress to say of her, that she did not adopt this course of treatment immediately. She at first lacked the depravity indispensable to shutting me up in mental darkness. I was at least necessary for her to have some training in the exercise of irresponsible power, to make her equal to the task of treating me as though I were a brute.

2   My mistress was, as I have said, a kind and tender-hearted woman; and in the simplicity of her soul she commenced, when I first went to live with her, to treat me as she supposed one human being ought to treat another. In entering upon the duties of a slaveholder, she did not seem to perceive that I sustained to her the relation of a mere chattel, and that for her to treat me as a human being was not only wrong, but dangerously so. Slavery proved as injurious to her as it did to me. When I went there, she was a pious, warm, and tender-hearted woman. There was no sorrow or suffering for which she had not a tear. She had bread for the hungry, clothes for the naked, and comfort for every mourner that came within her reach. Slavery soon proved its ability to divest her of these heavenly qualities. Under its influence, the tender heart became stone, and the lamblike disposition gave way to one of tiger-like fierceness. The first step in her downward course was in her ceasing to instruct me. She now commenced to practice her husband's precepts. She finally became even more violent in her opposition than her husband himself. She was not satisfied with simply doing as well as he had commanded; she seemed anxious to do better. Nothing seemed to make her more angry than to see me with a newspaper. She seemed to think that

here lay the danger. I have had her rush at me with a face made all up of fury, and snatch from me a newspaper, in a manner that fully revealed her apprehension. She was an apt woman; and a little experience soon demonstrated, to her satisfaction, that education and slavery were incompatible with each other.

3   From this time I was most narrowly watched. If I was in a separate room any considerable length of time, I was sure to be suspected of having a book, and was at once called to give an account of myself. All this, however, was too late. The first step had been taken. Mistress, in teaching me the alphabet, had given me the *inch*, and no precaution could prevent me from taking the *ell*.

4   The plan which I adopted, and the one by which I was most successful, was that of making friends of all the little white boys whom I met in the street. As many of these as I could, I converted into teachers. With their kindly aid, obtained at different times and in different places, I finally succeeded in learning to read. When I was sent on errands, I always took my book with me, and by going one part of my errand quickly, I found time to get a lesson before my return. I used also to carry bread with me, enough of which was always in the house, and to which I was always welcome; for I was much better off in this regard than many of the poor white children in our neighborhood. This bread I used to bestow upon the hungry little urchins, who, in return, would give me that more valuable bread of knowledge. I am strongly tempted to give the names of two or three of those little boys, as a testimonial of the gratitude and affection I bear them; but prudence forbids;—not that it would injure me, but it might embarrass them; for it is almost an unpardon- able offence to teach slaves to read in this Christian country. It is enough to say of the dear little fellows, that they lived on Philpot Street, very near Durgin and Bailey's ship-yard. I used to talk this matter of slavery over with them. I would sometimes say to them, I wished I could be as free as they would be when they got to be men. "You will be free as soon as you are twenty-one, *but I am a slave for life!* Have not I as good a right to be free as you have?" These words used to trouble them; they would express for me the liveliest sympathy, and console me with the hope that something would occur by which I might be free.

5   I was now about twelve years old, and the thought of being *a slave for life* began to bear heavily upon my heart. Just about this time, I got hold of a book entitled "The Columbian Orator." Every

opportunity I got, I used to read this book. Among much of other interesting matter, I found in it a dialogue between a master and his slave. The slave was represented as having run away from his master three times. The dialogue represented the conversation which took place between them, when the slave was retaken the third time. In this dialogue, the whole argument in behalf of slavery was brought forward by the master, all of which was disposed of by the slave. The slave was made to say some very smart as well as impressive things in reply to his master—things which had the desired though unexpected effect; for the conversation resulted in the voluntary emancipation of the slave on the part of the master.

6   In the same book, I met with one of Sheridan's mighty speeches on and in behalf of Catholic emancipation. These were choice documents to me. I read them over and over again with unabated interest. They gave tongue to interesting thoughts of my own soul, which had frequently flashed through my mind, and died away for want of utterance. The moral which I gained from the dialogue was the power of truth over the conscience of even a slaveholder. What I got from Sheridan was a bold denunciation of slavery, and a powerful vindication of human rights. The reading of these documents enabled me to utter my thoughts, and to meet the arguments brought forward to sustain slavery; but while they relieved me of one difficulty, they brought on another even more painful than the one of which I was relieved. The more I read, the more I was led to abhor and detest my enslavers. I could regard them in no other light than a band of successful robbers, who had left their homes, and gone to Africa, and stolen us from our homes, and in a strange land reduced us to slavery. I loathed them as being the meanest as well as the most wicked of men. As I read and contemplated the subject, behold! that very discontentment which Master Hugh had predicted would follow my learning to read had already come, to torment and sting my soul to unutterable anguish. As I writhed under it, I would at times feel that learning to read had been a curse rather than a blessing. It had given me a view of my wretched condition, without the remedy. It opened my eyes to the horrible pit, but to no ladder upon which to get out. In moments of agony, I envied my fellow-slaves for their stupidity. I have often wished myself a beast. I preferred the condition of the meanest reptile to my own. Any thing, no matter what, to get rid of thinking! It was this everlasting thinking of my condition that tormented me. There was no getting rid of it. It was pressed upon

me by every object within sight or hearing, animate or inanimate. The silver trump of freedom had roused my soul to eternal wakefulness. Freedom now appeared, to disappear no more forever. It was heard in every sound, and seen in every thing. It was ever present to torment me with a sense of my wretched condition. I saw nothing without seeing it, I heard nothing without hearing it, and felt nothing without feeling it. It looked from every star, it smiled in every calm, breathed in every wind, and moved in every storm.

7   I often found myself regretting my own existence, and wishing myself dead; and but for the hope of being free, I have no doubt but that I should have killed myself, or done something for which I should have been killed. While in this state of mind, I was eager to hear any one speak of slavery. I was a ready listener. Every little while, I could hear something about the abolitionists. It was some time before I found what the word meant. It was always used in such connections as to make it an interesting word to me. If a slave ran away and succeeded in getting clear, or if a slave killed his master, set fire to a barn, or did any thing very wrong in the mind of a slaveholder, it was spoken of as the fruit of *abolition*. Hearing the word in this connection very often, I set about learning what it meant. The dictionary afforded me little or no help. I found it was "the act of abolishing"; but then I did not know what was to be abolished. Here I was perplexed. I did not dare to ask any one about its meaning, for I was satisfied that it was something they wanted me to know very little about. After a patient waiting, I got one of our city papers, containing an account of the number of petitions from the north, praying for the abolition of slavery in the District of Columbia, and of the slave trade between the States. From this time I understood the words *abolition* and *abolitionist,* and always drew near when that word was spoken, expecting to hear something of importance to myself and fellow-slaves. The light broke in upon me by degrees. I went one day down on the wharf of Mr. Waters; and seeing two Irishmen unloading a scow of stone, I went, unasked, and helped them. When we had finished, one of them came to me and asked me if I were a slave. I told him I was. He asked, "Are ye a slave for life?" I told him that I was. The good Irishman seemed to be deeply affected by the statement. He said to the other that it was a pity so fine a little fellow as myself should be a slave for life. He said it was a shame to hold me. They both advised me to run away to the north; that I should find friends there, and that I should

be free. I pretended not to be interested in what they said, and treated them as if I did not understand them; for I feared they might be treacherous. White men have been known to encourage slaves to escape, and then, to get the reward, catch them and return them to their masters. I was afraid that these seemingly good men might use me so; but I nevertheless remembered their advice, and from that time I resolved to run away. I looked forward to time at which it would be safe for me to escape. I was too young to think of doing so immediately; besides, I wished to learn how to write, as I might have occasion to write my own pass. I consoled myself with the hope that I should one day find a good chance. Meanwhile, I would learn to write.

8   The idea as to how I might learn to write was suggested to me by being in Durgin and Bailey's ship-yard, and frequently seeing the ship carpenters, after hewing, and getting a piece of timber ready for use, write on the timber the name of that part of the ship for which it was intended. When a piece of timber was intended for the larboard side, it would be marked thus—"L." When a piece was for the starboard side, it would be marked thus—"S." A piece for the larboard side forward, would be marked thus—"L. F." When a piece was for starboard side forward, it would be marked thus—"S. F." For larboard aft, it would be marked thus—"L. A." For starboard aft, it would be marked thus—"S. A." I soon learned the names of these letters, and for what they were intended when placed upon a piece of timber in the ship-yard. I immediately commenced copying them, and in a short time was able to make the four letters named. After that, when I met with any boy who I knew could write, I would tell him I could write as well as he. The next word would be, "I don't believe you. Let me see you try it." I would then make the letters which I had been so fortunate as to learn, and ask him to beat that. In this way I got a good many lessons in writing, which it is quite possible I should never have gotten in any other way. During this time, my copy-book was the board fence, brick wall, and pavement; my pen and ink was a lump of chalk. With these, I learned mainly how to write. I then commenced and continued copying the Italics in Webster's Spelling Book, until I could make them all without looking on the book. By this time, my little Master Thomas had gone to school, and learned how to write, and had written over a number of copy-books. These had been brought home, and shown to some of our near neighbors, and then laid aside. My mistress used

to go to class meeting at the Wilk Street meetinghouse every Monday afternoon, and leave me to take care of the house. When left thus, I used to spend the time in writing in the spaces left in Master Thomas's copy-book, copying what he had written. I continued to do this until I could write a hand very similar to that of Master Thomas. Thus, after a long, tedious effort for years, I finally succeeded in learning how to write.

Discovering Books

RICHARD WRIGHT

Richard Wright (1906–1960) was born near Natchez, Mississippi. He was largely self-educated with the help of his mother, a teacher. He worked briefly in Memphis, then migrated to Chicago where he practiced his craft with writers' groups. He reached the national consciousness in 1938 with *Uncle Tom's Children*, a collection of stories that uncovered his view of racial hatred. He followed that work with *Native Son* (1940), which depicts the life of Bigger Thomas who, while a murderer of two women, becomes a victim of the system and a rare hero of the racial war.

Black Boy (1945) is Wright's autobiographical account of his childhood in Mississippi and Tennessee. Two primary themes run through the work: the racist environment that caused physical and mental pain and starvation and the complicity of blacks in passively accepting their position. The rebellion of young Richard Wright provided a wedge that drove him from family and friends in the south to the anticipated rewards of the north.

1   One morning I arrived early at work and went into the bank lobby where the Negro porter was mopping. I stood at a counter and picked up the Memphis *Commercial Appeal* and began my free reading of the press. I came finally to the editorial page and saw an article dealing with one H. L. Mencken. I knew by hearsay that he was the editor of the *American Mercury*, but aside from that I knew nothing

about him. The article was a furious denunciation of Mencken, con-
cluding with one, hot, short sentence: Mencken is a fool.

2   I wondered what on earth this Mencken had done to call down
upon him the scorn of the South. The only people I had ever heard
denounced in the South were Negroes, and this man was not a
Negro. Then what ideas did Mencken hold that made a newspaper
like the *Commercial Appeal* castigate him publicly? Undoubtedly he
must be advocating ideas that the South did not like. Were there,
then, people other than Negroes who criticized the South? I knew
that during the Civil War the South had hated northern whites, but
I had not encountered such hate during my life. Knowing no more
of Mencken than I did at that moment, I felt a vague sympathy for
him. Had not the South, which had assigned me the role of a nonman,
cast at him its hardest words?

3   Now, how could I find out about this Mencken? There was a
huge library near the riverfront, but I knew that Negroes were not
allowed to patronize its shelves any more than they were the parks
and playgrounds of the city. I had gone into the library several times
to get books for the white men on the job. Which of them would
now help me to get books? And how could I read them without
causing concern to the white men with whom I worked? I had so
far been successful in hiding my thoughts and feelings from them,
but I knew that I would create hostility if I went about this business
of reading in a clumsy way.

4   I weighed the personalities of the men on the job. There was
Don, a Jew; but I distrusted him. His position was not much better
than mine and I knew that he was uneasy and insecure; he had always
treated me in an offhand, bantering way that barely concealed his
contempt. I was afraid to ask him to help me to get books; his
frantic desire to demonstrate a racial solidarity with the whites against
Negroes might make him betray me.

5   Then how about the boss? No, he was a Baptist and I had the
suspicion that he would not be quite able to comprehend why a
black boy would want to read Mencken. There were other white
men on the job whose attitudes showed clearly that they were Kluxers
or sympathizers, and they were out of the question.

6   There remained only one man whose attitude did not fit into an
anti-Negro category, for I had heard the white men refer to him as
a "Pope lover." He was an Irish Catholic and was hated by the white
Southerners. I knew that he read books, because I had got him

volumes from the library several times. Since he, too, was an object of hatred, I felt that he might refuse me but would hardly betray me. I hesitated, weighing and balancing the imponderable realities.

7　One morning I paused before the Catholic fellow's desk.

8　"I want to ask you a favor," I whispered to him.

9　"What is it?"

10　"I want to read. I can't get books from the library. I wonder if you'd let me use your card?"

11　He looked at me suspiciously.

12　"My card is full most of the time," he said.

13　"I see," I said and waited, posing my question silently.

14　"You're not trying to get me into trouble, are you, boy?" he asked, staring at me.

15　"Oh, no, sir."

16　"What book do you want?"

17　"A book by H. L. Mencken."

18　"Which one?"

19　"I don't know. Has he written more than one?"

20　"He has written several."

21　"I didn't know that."

22　"What makes you want to read Mencken?"

23　"Oh, I just saw his name in the newspaper," I said.

24　"It's good of you to want to read," he said. "But you ought to read the right things."

25　I said nothing. Would he want to supervise my reading?

26　"Let me think," he said. "I'll figure out something."

27　I turned from him and he called me back. He stared at me quizzically.

28　"Richard, don't mention this to the other white men," he said.

29　"I understand," I said. "I won't say a word."

30　A few days later he called me to him.

31　"I've got a card in my wife's name," he said. "Here's mine."

32　"Thank you, sir."

33　"Do you think you can manage it?"

34　"I'll manage fine," I said.

35　"If they suspect you, you'll get in trouble," he said.

36　"I'll write the same kind of notes to the library that you wrote when you sent me for books," I told him. "I'll sign your name."

37　He laughed.

38　"Go ahead. Let me see what you get," he said.

39 That afternoon I addressed myself to forging a note. Now, what were the names of books written by H. L. Mencken? I did not know any of them. I finally wrote what I thought would be a foolproof note: *Dear Madam: Will you please let this nigger boy* —I used the word "nigger" to make the librarian feel that I could not possibly be the author of the note—*have some books by H. L. Mencken?* I forged the white man's name.

40 I entered the library as I had always done when on errands for whites, but I felt that I would somehow slip up and betray myself. I doffed my hat, stood a respectful distance from the desk, looked as unbookish as possible, and waited for the white patrons to be taken care of. When the desk was clear of people, I still waited. The white librarian looked at me.

41 "What do you want, boy?"

42 As though I did not possess the power of speech, I stepped forward and simply handed her the forged note, not parting my lips.

43 "What books by Mencken does he want?" she asked.

44 "I don't know, ma'am," I said, avoiding her eyes.

45 "Who gave you this card?"

46 "Mr. Falk," I said.

47 "Where is he?"

48 "He's at work, at the M—— Optical Company," I said. "I've been in here for him before."

49 "I remember," the woman said. "But he never wrote notes like this."

50 Oh, God, she's suspicious. Perhaps she would not let me have the books? If she had turned her back at that moment, I would have ducked out the door and never gone back. Then I thought of a bold idea.

51 "You can call him up, ma'am," I said, my heart pounding.

52 "You're not using these books, are you?" she asked pointedly.

53 "Oh, no, ma'am. I can't read."

54 "I don't know what he wants by Mencken," she said under her breath.

55 I knew now that I had won; she was thinking of other things and the race question had gone out of her mind. She went to the shelves. Once or twice she looked over her shoulder at me, as though she was still doubtful. Finally she came forward with two books in her hand.

56 "I'm sending him two books," she said. "But tell Mr. Falk to

come in next time, or send me the names of the books he wants. I
don't know what he wants to read."

57   I said nothing. She stamped the card and handed me the books.
Not daring to glance at them, I went out of the library, fearing that
the woman would call me back for further questioning. A block away
from the library I opened one of the books and read a title: *A Book
of Prefaces*. I was nearing my nineteenth birthday and I did not know
how to pronounce the word *preface*. I thumbed the pages and saw
strange words and strange names. I shook my head, disappointed. I
looked at the other book; it was called *Prejudices*. I knew what that
word meant; I had heard it all my life. And right off I was on guard
against Mencken's books. Why would a man want to call a book
Prejudices? The word was so stained with all my memories of racial
hate that I could not conceive of anybody using it for a title. Perhaps
I had made a mistake about Mencken? A man who had prejudices
must be wrong.

58   When I showed the books to Mr. Falk, he looked at me and
frowned.

59   "That librarian might telephone you," I warned him.

60   "That's all right," he said. "But when you're through reading
those books, I want you to tell me what you get out of them."

61   That night in my rented room, while letting the hot water run
over my can of pork and beans in the sink, I opened *A Book of
Prefaces* and began to read. I was jarred and shocked by the style,
the clear, clean, sweeping sentences. Why did he write like that? And
how did one write like that? I pictured the man as a raging demon,
slashing with his pen, consumed with hate, denouncing everything
American, extolling everything European or German, laughing at
the weaknesses of people, mocking God, authority. What was this?
I stood up, trying to realize what reality lay behind the meaning of
the words. . . . Yes, this man was fighting, fighting with words. He
was using words as a weapon, using them as one would use a club.
Could words be weapons? Well, yes, for here they were. Then, maybe,
perhaps, I could use them as a weapon? No. It frightened me. I read
on and what amazed me was not what he said, but how on earth
anybody had the courage to say it.

62   Occasionally I glanced up to reassure myself that I was alone in
the room. Who were these men about whom Mencken was talking
so passionately? Who was Anatole France? Joseph Conrad? Sinclair
Lewis, Sherwood Anderson, Dostoevski, George Moore, Gustave

Flaubert, Maupassant, Tolstoy, Frank Harris, Mark Twain, Thomas
Hardy, Arnold Bennett, Stephen Crane, Zola, Norris, Gorky, Berg-
son, Ibsen, Balzac, Bernard Shaw, Dumas, Poe, Thomas Mann, O.
Henry, Dreiser, H. G. Wells, Gogol, T. S. Eliot, Gide, Baudelaire,
Edgar Lee Masters, Stendhal, Turgenev, Huneker, Nietzsche, and
scores of others? Were these men real? Did they exist or had they
existed? And how did one pronounce their names?

63   I ran across many words whose meanings I did not know, and I
either looked them up in a dictionary or, before I had a chance to
do that, encountered the word in a context that made its meaning
clear. But what strange world was this? I concluded the book with
the conviction that I had somehow overlooked something terribly
important in life. I had once tried to write, had once reveled in
feeling, had let my crude imagination roam, but the impulse to dream
had been slowly beaten out of me by experience. Now it surged up
again and I hungered for books, new ways of looking and seeing. It
was not a matter of believing or disbelieving what I read, but of
feeling something new, of being affected by something that made
the look of the world different.

64   As dawn broke I ate my pork and beans, feeling dopey, sleepy. I
went to work, but the mood of the book would not die; it lingered,
coloring everything I saw, heard, did. I now felt that I knew what
the white men were feeling. Merely because I had read a book that
had spoken of how they lived and thought, I identified myself with
that book. I felt vaguely guilty. Would I, filled with bookish notions,
act in a manner that would make the whites dislike me?

65   I forged more notes and my trips to the library became more
frequent. Reading grew into a passion. My first serious novel was
Sinclair Lewis's *Main Street*. It made me see my boss, Mr. Gerald,
and identify him as an American type. I would smile when I saw
him lugging his golf bags into the office. I had always felt a vast
distance separating me from the boss, and now I felt closer to
him, though still distant. I felt now that I knew him, that I could
feel the very limits of his narrow life. And this had happened
because I had read a novel about a mythical man called George
F. Babbitt.

66   The plots and stories in the novels did not interest me so much
as the point of view revealed. I gave myself over to each novel without
reserve, without trying to criticize it; it was enough for me to see
and feel something different. And for me, everything was something

different. Reading was like a drug, a dope. The novels created moods in which I lived for days. But I could not conquer my sense of guilt, my feeling that the white men around me knew that I was changing, that I had begun to regard them differently.

67   Whenever I brought a book to the job, I wrapped it in newspaper—a habit that was to persist for years in other cities and under other circumstances. But some of the white men pried into my packages when I was absent and they questioned me.

68   "Boy, what are you reading those books for?"

69   "Oh, I don't know, sir."

70   "That's deep stuff you're reading, boy."

71   "I'm just killing time, sir."

72   "You'll addle your brains if you don't watch out."

73   I read Dreiser's *Jennie Gerhardt* and *Sister Carrie* and they revived in me a vivid sense of my mother's suffering; I was overwhelmed, I grew silent, wondering about the life around me. It would have been impossible for me to have told anyone what I derived from these novels, for it was nothing less than a sense of life itself. All my life had shaped me for the realism, the naturalism of the modern novel, and I could not read enough of them.

74   Steeped in new moods and ideas, I bought a ream of paper and tried to write; but nothing would come, or what did come was flat beyond telling. I discovered that more than desire and feeling were necessary to write and I dropped the idea. Yet I still wondered how it was possible to know people sufficiently to write about them? Could I ever learn about life and people? To me, with my vast ignorance, my Jim Crow station in life, it seemed a task impossible to achievement. I now knew what being a Negro meant. I could endure the hunger. I had learned to live with hate. But to feel that there were feelings denied me, that the very breath of life itself was beyond my reach, that more than anything else hurt, wounded me. I had a new hunger.

75   In buoying me up, reading also cast me down, made me see what was possible, what I had missed. My tension returned, new, terrible, bitter, surging, almost too great to be contained. I no longer *felt* that the world about me was hostile, killing; I *knew* it. A million times I asked myself what I could do to save myself, and there were no answers. I seemed forever condemned, ringed by walls.

76   I did not discuss my reading with Mr. Falk, who had lent me his library card; it would have meant talking about myself and

that would have been too painful. I smiled each day, fighting desperately to maintain my old behavior, to keep my disposition seemingly sunny. But some of the white men discerned that I had begun to brood.

77 "Wake up there, boy!" Mr. Olin said one day.

78 "Sir!" I answered for the lack of a better word.

79 "You act like you've stolen something," he said.

80 I laughed in the way I knew he expected me to laugh, but I resolved to be more conscious of myself, to watch my every act, to guard and hide the new knowledge that was dawning within me.

81 If I went north, would it be possible for me to build a new life then? But how could a man build a life upon vague, unformed yearnings? I wanted to write and I did not even know the English language. I bought English grammars and found them dull. I felt that I was getting a better sense of the language from novels than grammars. I read hard, discarding a writer as soon as I felt that I had grasped his point of view. At night the printed page stood before my eyes in sleep.

82 Mrs. Moss, my landlady, asked me one Sunday morning:

83 "Son, what is this you keep on reading?"

84 "Oh, nothing. Just novels."

85 "What you get out of 'em?"

86 "I'm just killing time," I said.

87 "I hope you know your own mind," she said in a tone which implied that she doubted if I had a mind.

88 I knew of no Negroes who read the books I liked and I wondered if any Negroes ever thought of them. I knew that there were Negro doctors, lawyers, newspapermen, but I never saw any of them. When I read a Negro newspaper I never caught the faintest echo of my preoccupation in its pages. I felt trapped and occasionally, for a few days, I would stop reading. But a vague hunger would come over me for books, books that opened up new avenues of feeling and seeing, and again I would forge another note to the white librarian. Again I would read and wonder as only the naive and unlettered can read and wonder, feeling that I carried a secret, criminal burden about with me each day.

89 That winter my mother and brother came and we set up housekeeping, buying furniture on the installment plan, being cheated and yet knowing no way to avoid it. I began to eat warm food and to my surprise found the regular meals enabled me to read

faster. I may have lived through many illnesses and survived them, never suspecting that I was ill. My brother obtained a job and we began to save toward the trip north, plotting our time, setting tentative dates for departure. I told none of the white men on the job that I was planning to go north; I knew that the moment they felt I was thinking of the North they would change toward me. It would have made them feel that I did not like the life I was living, and because my life was completely conditioned by what they said or did, it would have been tantamount to challenging them.

90 I could calculate my chances for life in the South as a Negro fairly clearly now.

91 I could fight the southern whites by organizing with other Negroes, as my grandfather had done. But I knew that I could never win that way; there were many whites and there were but few blacks. They were strong and we were weak. Outright black rebellion could never win. If I fought openly I would die and I did not want to die. News of lynchings were frequent.

92 I could submit and live the life of a genial slave, but that was impossible. All of my life had shaped me to live by my own feelings and thoughts. I could make up to Bess and marry her and inherit the house. But that, too, would be the life of a slave; if I did that, I would crush to death something within me, and I would hate myself as much as I knew the whites already hated those who had submitted. Neither could I ever willingly present myself to be kicked, as Shorty had done. I would rather have died than do that.

93 I could drain off my restlessness by fighting with Shorty and Harrison. I had seen many Negroes solve the problem of being black by transferring their hatred of themselves to others with a black skin and fighting them. I would have to be cold to do that, and I was not cold and I could never be.

94 I could, of course, forget what I had read, thrust the whites out of my mind, forget them; and find release from anxiety and longing in sex and alcohol. But the memory of how my father had conducted himself made that course repugnant. If I did not want others to violate my life, how could I voluntarily violate it myself?

95 I had no hope whatever of being a professional man. Not only had I been so conditioned that I did not desire it, but the fulfillment of such an ambition was beyond my capabilities. Well- to-do Negroes lived in a world that was almost as alien to me as the world inhabited by whites.

96   What, then, was there? I held my life in my mind, in my consciousness each day, feeling at times that I would stumble and drop it, spill
it forever. My reading had created a vast sense of distance between
me and the world in which I lived and tried to make a living, and
that sense of distance was increasing each day. My days and nights
were one long, quiet, continuously contained dream of terror, tension, and anxiety. I wondered how long I could bear it.

from Hidden Name and Complex Fate

RALPH ELLISON

Ralph Ellison (1914–1994) was born in Oklahoma City. He attended Tuskegee Institute from 1933 to 1936 and then moved to New York to serve as writer and researcher for the Federal Writers' Project. He became editor of the *Negro Quarterly* in 1942. In New York, he met Langston Hughes and Richard Wright, who was then writing *Native Son*. He served as lecturer and visiting professor at several universities and spent nine years as the Albert Schweitzer Professor of Humanities at New York University. Ellison's most well-known work is *Invisible Man* (1952), which he began in 1945. The book's protagonist, journeying through the underground wasteland of America, maintains his moral conscience to claim his freedom. The search for identity, says Ellison, is "*the* American dream."

"Hidden Name and Complex Fate" first appeared in *Shadow and Act* (1964). In it, he examines the language of names, including his own name. He explains how his father named him after Ralph Waldo Emerson but then died before he could explain to his son the reason for the name. He admits a certain magic may have provoked the naming, for he progressed into the arts, became a voracious reader, and eventually became a writer like his namesake.

1 Doubtlessly, writers begin their *conditioning* as manipulators of words long before they become aware of literature—certain Freudians would say at the breast. Perhaps, but if so that is far too early to be of use at this moment. Of this, though, I am certain: That despite the misconceptions of those educators who trace the reading difficulties experienced by large numbers of Negro children in northern schools to their southern background, these children are, in *their* familiar South, facile manipulators of words. I know, too, that the Negro community is deadly in its ability to create nicknames and to spot all that is ludicrous in an unlikely name or that which is incongruous in conduct. Names are not qualities, nor are words, in this particular sense, actions. To assume that they are could cost one his life many times a day. Language skills depend to a large extent upon a knowledge of the details, the manners, the objects, the folkways, the psychological patterns of a given environment. Humor and wit depend upon much of the same awareness, and so does the suggestive power of names.

2 "A small, brown, bow-legged Negro with the name 'Franklin D. Roosevelt Jones' might sound like a clown to someone who looks at him from the outside," said my friend Albert Murray, "but on the other hand he just might turn out to be a hell of a fireside operator. He might just lie back in all of that comic juxtaposition of names and manipulate you deaf, dumb, and blind—and you not even suspecting it, because you're thrown out of stance by his name! There you are, so dazzled by the F.D.R. image—which you *know* you can't see—and so delighted with your own superior position that you don't realize that it is *Jones* who must be confronted."

3 Well, as you must suspect, all of this speculation on the matter of names has a purpose, and now, because it is tied up so ironically with my own experience as a writer, I must turn to my own name.

4 For in the dim beginnings, before I ever thought consciously of writing, there was my own name, and there was, doubtlessly, a certain magic in it. From the start I was uncomfortable with it, and in

my earliest years it caused me much puzzlement. Neither could I understand what a poet was, nor why, exactly, my father had chosen one for my namesake. Perhaps I could have understood it perfectly well had he named me after his own father, but that name had been given to an older brother who died and thus was out of the question. But why hadn't he named me after a hero, such as Jack Johnson, or a soldier like Colonel Charles Young, or a great seaman like Admiral Dewey, or an educator like Booker T. Washington, or a great orator and abolitionist like Frederick Douglass? Or again, why hadn't he named me (as so many Negro parents had done) after President Theodore Roosevelt?

5   Instead, he named me after someone called Ralph Waldo Emerson, and then, when I was three, he died. It was too early for me to have understood his choice, although I'm sure he must have explained it many times, and it was also too soon for me to have made the connection between my name and my father's love for reading. Much later, after I began to write and work with words, I came to suspect that he was aware of the suggestive powers of names and of the magic involved in naming.

6   I recall an odd conversation with my mother during my early teens in which she mentioned their interest in, of all things, prenatal culture! But for a long time I actually knew only that my father read a lot, and that he admired this remote Mr. Emerson, who was something called a "poet and philosopher"—so much so, that he named his second son after him.

7   I knew also that, whatever his motives, the combination of names he'd given me caused me no end of trouble from the moment when I could talk well enough to respond to the ritualized question which grownups put to very young children. Emerson's name was quite familiar to Negroes in Oklahoma during those days when World War I was brewing, and adults, eager to show off their knowledge of literary figures and obviously amused by the joke implicit in such a small brown nubbin of a boy carrying around such a heavy moniker, would invariably repeat my first two names and then, to my great annoyance, they'd add "Emerson."

8   And I, in my confusion, would reply, "No, *no, I'm* not Emerson; he's the little boy who lives next door." Which only made them laugh all the louder. "Oh no," they'd say, "*you're* Ralph Waldo Emerson," while I had fantasies of blue murder.

9   For a while the presence next door of my little friend Emerson

made it unnecessary for me to puzzle too often over this peculiar adult confusion. And since there were other Negro boys named "Ralph" in the city, I came to suspect that there was something about the combination of names which produced their laughter. Even today I know of only one other "Ralph" who had as much comedy made out of his name, a campus politician and deep-voiced orator whom I knew at Tuskegee, who was called in friendly ribbing, "Ralph Waldo Emerson Edgar Allen Poe, spelled *Powe*." This must have been quite a trial for him, but I had been initiated much earlier.

10   During my early school years the name continued to puzzle me, for it constantly evoked in the faces of others some secret. It was as though I possessed some treasure or some defect, which was invisible to my own eyes and ears; something which I had but did not *possess,* like a piece of property in South Carolina, which was mine but which I would not have until some future time. I recall finding, about this time, while seeking adventure in back alleys—which possess, for boys, a superiority over playgrounds like that which kitchen utensils possess over toys designed for infants—a large photographic lens. I remember nothing of its optical qualities, nor of its speed or color correction, but it gleamed with crystal mystery and it was beautiful.

11   Mounted handsomely in a tube of shiny brass, it spoke to me of distant worlds of possibility. I played with it, looking through it with squinted eyes, holding it in shafts of sunlight, and tried to use it for a magic lantern. But most of this was as unrewarding as my attempts to make the music come from a phonograph record by holding the needle in my fingers.

12   I could burn holes through newspapers with it, or I could pretend that it was a telescope, the barrel of a cannon, or the third eye of a monster—*I* being the monster—but I could do nothing at all about its proper function of making images; nothing to make it yield its secret. But I would not discard it.

13   Older boys sought to get it away from me by offering knives or tops, agate marbles or whole zoos of grass snakes and horned toads in trade, but I held on to it. No one, not even the white boys I knew, had such a lens, and it was my own good luck to have found it. Thus I would hold on to it until such time as I could acquire the parts needed to make it function. Finally, I put it aside and it remained buried in my box of treasures, dusty and dull, to be lost and forgotten as I grew older and became interested in music.

14   I had reached by now the grades where it was necessary to learn

something about Mr. Emerson and what he had done, such as the *Concord Hymn* and the essay of *Self-Reliance,* and in following his advice, I reduced the "Waldo" to a simple and, I hoped, mysterious "W," and in my own reading I avoided his works like the plague. I could no more deal with my name—I shall never really master it—than I could find a creative use for my lens. Fortunately, there were other problems to occupy my mind. Not that I forgot my fascination with names, but more about that later.

15   Negro Oklahoma City was starkly lacking in writers. In fact, there was only Roscoe Dungee, the editor of the local Negro newspaper and a very fine editorialist in that valuable tradition of personal journalism which is now rapidly disappearing; a writer who, in his emphasis upon the possibilities for justice offered by the Constitution, anticipated the antisegregation struggle by decades. There were also a few reporters who drifted in and out, but these were about all. On the level of *conscious* culture, the Negro community was biased in the direction of music.

16   These were the middle and late twenties, remember, and the State was still a new "frontier" State. The capital city was one of the great centers for southwestern jazz, along with Dallas and Kansas City. Orchestras which were to become famous within a few years were constantly coming and going, as were the blues singers—Ma Rainey and Ida Cox—and the old bands like that of King Oliver. But best of all, thanks to Mrs. Zelia N. Breaux, there was an active and enthusiastic school music program through which any child who had the interest and the talent could learn to play an instrument and take part in the band, the orchestra, the brass quartet. And there was a yearly operetta and a chorus and a glee club. Harmony was taught for four years and the music appreciation program was imperative. European folk dances were taught throughout the Negro school system, and we were also taught complicated patterns of military drill.

17   I tell you this to point out that although there were no incentives to write, there was ample opportunity to receive an artistic discipline. Indeed, once one picked up an instrument it was difficult to escape. If you chafed at the many rehearsals of the school band or orchestra and were drawn to the many small jazz groups, you were likely to discover that the jazzmen were apt to rehearse far more than the school band; it was only that they seemed to enjoy themselves better and to possess a freedom of imagination which we were denied at

school. And one soon learned that the wild, transcendent moments which occurred at dances or "battles of music," moments in which memorable improvisations were ignited, depended upon a dedication to a discipline which was observed even when rehearsals had to take place in the crowded quarters of Halley Richardson's shoeshine parlor. It was not the place which counted, although a large hall with good acoustics was preferred, but what one did to perfect one's performance.

18   If this talk of musical discipline gives the impression that there were no forces working to nourish one who would one day blunder, after many a twist and turn, into writing, I am misleading you. And here I might give you a longish lecture on the "Ironies and Uses of Segregation." When I was a small child, there was no library for Negroes in our city; and not until a Negro minister invaded the main library did we get one. For it was discovered that there was no law, only custom, which held that we could not use these public facilities. The results were the quick renting of two large rooms in a Negro office building—the recent site of a pool hall—the hiring of a young Negro librarian, the installation of shelves, and a hurried stocking of the walls with any and every book possible. It was, in those first days, something of a literary chaos.

19   But how fortunate for a boy who loved to read! I started with the fairy tales and quickly went through the junior fiction; then through the Westerns and the detective novels, and very soon I was reading the classics—only I didn't know it. There were also the Haldeman-Julius Blue Books, which seem to have floated on the air down from Girard, Kansas; the syndicated columns of O. O. McIntyre, and the copies of *Vanity Fair* and the *Literary Digest* which my mother brought home from work—how in light of the effect of these on my own life could I ever join uncritically in the heavy-handed attacks on the so-called big media which have become so common today.

20   There were also the pulp magazines and, more important, that other library which I visited whenever I went to help my adopted grandfather, J. D. Randolph (my parents had lived in his rooming house when I was born), at his work as custodian of the Law Library of the Oklahoma State Capitol. Mr. Randolph had been one of the first teachers in what became Oklahoma City after having been one of the leaders of the group who walked from Gallatin, Tennessee, to the Oklahoma Territory. He was a tall man, as brown as smoked

leather, who looked like the Indians with whom he'd herded horses during the territory days. And while his status was merely that of custodian of the Law Library, I was to see the white legislators come down on many occasions to question him on points of law, and I was often to hear him answer without recourse to the uniform rows of books on the shelves. This was a thing to marvel at in itself, and the white lawmakers did so, but even more marvelous, ironic, intriguing, haunting—call it what you will—is the fact that the Negro who knew the answers was named after Jefferson Davis. What Tennessee lost, Oklahoma was to gain, and after gaining it (a gift of courage, intelligence, fortitude, and grace), used it only in concealment and, one hopes, with embarrassment.

21   *So let us, I say, make up our faces and our minds!*

If Black English Isn't a Language, Then Tell Me, What Is?

JAMES BALDWIN

James Baldwin (1924–1987) was a native of New York's Harlem and labeled himself as a native son of the black ghetto. He fought his way into the literary world after abandoning an interest in the ministry. Several scholarships and fellowships allowed him to work in Paris during his early career so that he could produce the novels *Go Tell It on the Mountain* (1953) and *Giovanni's Room* (1956). During that time, he also developed a collection of essays, *Notes of a Native Son* (1955). Additional fiction and essays followed, including *Nobody Knows My Name* (essays, 1961), *Another Country* (a novel, 1962), and *Going to Meet the Man* (a set of stories, 1965).

"If Black English Isn't a Language, Then Tell Me, What Is?" is a 1979 essay published in the *New York Times*. In it, he focuses on the *role* of language as a "political instrument" and a "proof of power." In particular, Baldwin argues, language gives one a sense of identity. He argues that blacks developed their own language from the days of slavery in order to survive. He states that his people have not "endured and transcended by means of what is patronizingly called a 'dialect.'" Ultimately, he says, the white people do not despise the language; they despise the experience behind the language.

1   The argument concerning the use, or the status, or the reality, of black English is rooted in American history and has absolutely nothing to do with the question the argument supposes itself to be posing. The argument has nothing to do with language itself but with the *role* of language. Language, incontestably, reveals the speaker. Language, also, far more dubiously, is meant to define the other—and, in this case, the other is refusing to be defined by a language that has never been able to recognize him.

2   People evolve a language in order to describe and thus control their circumstances, or in order not to be submerged by a reality that they cannot articulate. (And, if they cannot articulate it, they *are* submerged.) A Frenchman living in Paris speaks a subtly and crucially different language from that of the man living in Marseilles; neither sounds very much like a man living in Quebec; and they would all have great difficulty in apprehending what the man from Gaudeloupe, or Martinique, is saying, to say nothing of the man from Senegal—although the "common" language of all these areas is French. But each has paid, and is paying, a different price for this "common" language, in which, as it turns out, they are not saying, and cannot be saying, the same things: They each have very different realities to articulate, or control.

3   What joins all languages, and all men, is the necessity to confront life, in order, not inconceivably, to outwit death: The price for this is the acceptance, and achievement, of one's temporal identity. So that, for example, though it is not taught in the schools (and this has the potential of becoming a political issue) the south of France still clings to its ancient and musical Provençal, which resists being described as a "dialect." And much of the tension of the Basque countries, and in Wales, is due to the Basque and Welsh determination not to allow their languages to be destroyed. This determination also feeds the flames in Ireland for among the many indignities the Irish have been forced to undergo at English hands is the English contempt for their language.

4   It goes without saying, then, that language is also a political instrument, means, and proof of power. It is the most vivid and crucial key to identity: it reveals the private identity, and connects one with, or divorces one from, the larger, public, or communal identity. There have been, and are, times, and places, when to speak a certain language could be dangerous, even fatal. Or, one may speak the same language, but in such a way that one's antecedents are revealed, or (one hopes) hidden. This is true in France, and is absolutely true in England: The range (and reign) of accents on that damp little island make England coherent for the English and totally incomprehensible for everyone else. To open your mouth in England is (if I may use black English) to "put your business in the street": You have confessed your parents, your youth, your school, your salary, your self-esteem, and, alas, your future.

5   Now, I do not know what white Americans would sound like if there had never been any black people in the United States, but they would not sound the way they sound. *Jazz*, for example, is a very specific sexual term, as in *jazz me, baby*, but white people purified it into the Jazz Age. *Sock it to me*, which means, roughly, the same thing, has been adopted by Nathaniel Hawthorne's descendants with no qualms or hesitations at all, along with *let it all hang out* and *right on! Beat to his socks*, which was once the black's most total and despairing image of poverty, was transformed into a thing called the Beat Generation, which phenomenon was, largely, composed of *uptight*, middle-class white people, imitating poverty, trying to *get down*, to get *with it*, doing their *thing*, doing their despairing best to be *funky*, which we, the blacks, never dreamed of doing—we *were* funky, baby, like *funk* was going out of style.

6   Now, no one can eat his cake, and have it, too, and it is late in the day to attempt to penalize black people for having created a language that permits the nation its only glimpse of reality, a language without which the nation would be even more *whipped* than it is.

7   I say that this present skirmish is rooted in American history, and it is. Black English is the creation of the black diaspora. Blacks came to the United States chained to each other, but from different tribes: Neither could speak the other's language. If two black people, at that bitter hour of the world's history, had been able to speak to each other, the institution of chattel slavery could never have lasted as long as it did. Subsequently, the slave was given, under the eye, and the gun, of his master, Congo Square, and the Bible—or, in other

words, and under these conditions, the slave began the formation of the black church, and it is within this unprecedented tabernacle that black English began to be formed. This was not, merely, as in the European example, the adoption of a foreign tongue, but an alchemy that transformed ancient elements into a new language: *A language comes into existence by means of brutal necessity, and the rules of the language are dictated by what the language must convey.*

8   There was a moment, in time, and in this place, when my brother, or my mother, or my father, or my sister, had to convey to me, for example, the danger in which I was standing from the white man standing just behind me, and to convey this with a speed, and in a language, that the white man could not possibly understand, and that, indeed, he cannot understand, until today. He cannot afford to understand it. This understanding would reveal to him too much about himself, and smash that mirror before which he has been frozen for so long.

9   Now, if this passion, this skill, this (to quote Toni Morrison) "sheer intelligence," this incredible music, the mighty achievement of having brought a people utterly unknown to, or despised by "history"—to have brought this people to their present, troubled, troubling, and unassailable and unanswerable place—if this absolutely unprecedented journey does not indicate that black English is a language, I am curious to know what definition of language is to be trusted.

10   A people at the center of the Western world, and in the midst of so hostile a population, has not endured and transcended by means of what is patronizingly called a "dialect." We, the blacks, are in trouble, certainly, but we are not doomed, and we are not inarticulate because we are not compelled to defend a morality that we know to be a lie.

11   The brutal truth is that the bulk of the white people in America never had any interest in educating black people, except as this could serve white purposes. It is not the black child's language that is in question, it is not his language that is despised: It is his experience. A child cannot be taught by anyone who despises him, and a child cannot afford to be fooled. A child cannot be taught by anyone whose demand, essentially, is that the child repudiate his experience, and all that gives him sustenance, and enter a limbo in which he will no longer be black, and in which he knows that he can never become white. Black people have lost too many black children that way.

12   And, after all, finally, in a country with standards so untrustworthy, a country that makes heroes of so many criminal mediocrities, a country unable to face why so many of the nonwhite are in prison, or on the needle, or standing, futureless, in the streets—it may very well be that both the child, and his elder, have concluded that they have nothing whatever to learn from the people of a country that has managed to learn so little.

Learning to Read

MALCOLM X

Malcolm X (1925–1965) was born Malcolm Little in Omaha, Nebraska. As a young man, he was a street hustler until, at age twenty-one, he was convicted of robbery and sentenced to prison for seven years. In prison, as explained in the essay that follows, he copied the dictionary to improve his penmanship and his reading ability. Soon, his reading carried him to new levels—reading such philosophers as Schopenhauer, Kant, and Nietzsche. He left prison a self-taught man. He also studied the religious ideas of Black Muslim leader Elijah Muhammad and joined the sect under the name Malcolm X. In the 1950s and 1960s, he rose to prominence as a radical advocate of black separatism, preaching that the white race is evil and the black race is superior. In the mid-1960s, he became disenchanted with Elijah Muhammad's organization and formed his own. That divisive action may have triggered his assassination in 1965 as he prepared to speak at a Harlem ballroom.

"Learning to Read" is an excerpt from *The Autobiography of Malcolm X*, written by Malcolm X and Alex Haley. In it, Malcolm X describes how reading changed the course of his life forever: "As I see it today, the ability to read awoke inside me some long dormant craving to be mentally alive." It also awakened his sense of history and his anger, for he argues that the history of whites has perpetrated a fraud, one designed to "hide the black man's true role in history."

1 Many who today hear me somewhere in person, or on television, or those who read something I've said, will think I went to school far beyond the eighth grade. This impression is due entirely to my prison studies.

2 It had really begun back in the Charlestown Prison, when Bimbi first made me feel envy of his stock of knowledge. Bimbi had always taken charge of any conversation he was in, and I had tried to emulate him. But every book I picked up had few sentences which didn't contain anywhere from one to nearly all of the words that might as well have been in Chinese. When I just skipped those words, of course, I really ended up with little idea of what the book said. So I had come to the Norfolk Prison Colony still going through only book-reading motions. Pretty soon, I would have quit even these motions, unless I had received the motivation that I did.

3 I saw that the best thing I could do was get hold of a dictionary—to study, to learn some words. I was lucky enough to reason also that I should try to improve my penmanship. It was sad. I couldn't even write in a straight line. It was both ideas together that moved me to request a dictionary along with some tablets and pencils from the Norfolk Prison Colony school.

4 I spent two days just riffling uncertainly through the dictionary's pages. I'd never realized so many words existed! I didn't know *which* words I needed to learn. Finally, just to start some kind of action, I began copying.

5 In my slow, painstaking, ragged handwriting, I copied into my tablet everything printed on that first page, down to the punctuation marks.

6 I believe it took me a day. Then, aloud, I read back, to myself, everything I'd written on the tablet. Over and over, aloud, to myself, I read my own handwriting.

7 I woke up the next morning, thinking about those words—immensely proud to realize that not only had I written so much at one time, but I'd written words that I never new were in the world. Moreover, with a little effort, I also could remember what many of these words meant. I reviewed the words whose meanings I didn't remember. Funny thing, from the dictionary first page right now, that "aardvark" springs to my mind. The dictionary had a picture of it, a long-tailed, long-eared, burrowing African mammal, which lives off termites caught by sticking out its tongue as an anteater does for ants.

8   I was so fascinated that I went on—I copied the dictionary's next page. And the same experience came when I studied that. With every succeeding page, I also learned of people and places and events from history. Actually the dictionary is like a miniature encyclopedia. Finally the dictionary's A section had filled a whole tablet—and I went on into the B's. That was the way I started copying what eventually became the entire dictionary. It went a lot faster after so much practice helped me to pick up handwriting speed. Between what I wrote in my tablet, and writing letters, during the rest of my time in prison I would guess I wrote a million words.

9   I suppose it was inevitable that as my word-base broadened, I could for the first time pick up a book and read and now begin to understand what the book was saying. Anyone who has read a great deal can imagine the new world that opened. Let me tell you something: from then until I left that prison in every free moment I had, if I was not reading in the library, I was reading on my bunk. You couldn't have gotten me out of books with a wedge. Between Mr. Muhammad's teachings, my correspondence, my visitors—usually Ella and Reginald—and my reading of books, months passed without me even thinking about being imprisoned. In fact, up to then, I never had been so truly free in my life.

10   The Norfolk Prison Colony's library was in the school building. A variety of classes was taught there by instructors who came from such places as Harvard and Boston universities. The weekly debates between inmate teams were also held in the school building. You would be astonished to know how worked up convict debaters and audiences would get over subjects like "Should Babies Be Fed Milk?"

11   Available on the prison library's shelves were books on just about every general subject. Much of the big private collection that Parkhurst had willed to the prison was still in crates and boxes in the back of the library—thousands of old books. Some of them looked ancient: covers faded, old-time parchment-looking binding. Parkhurst, I've mentioned, seemed to have been principally interested in history and religion. He had the money and the special interest to have a lot of books that you wouldn't have in general circulation. Any college library would have been lucky to get that collection.

12   As you can imagine, especially in a prison where there was heavy emphasis on rehabilitation, an inmate was smiled upon if he demonstrated an unusually intense interest in books. There was a sizable number of well-read inmates, especially the popular debaters. Some

were said by many to be practically walking encyclopedias. They were almost celebrities. No university would ask any student to devour literature as I did when this new world opened to me, of being able to read and *understand*.

13   I read more in my room than in the library itself. An inmate who was known to read a lot could check out more than the permitted maximum number of books. I preferred reading in the total isolation of my own room.

14   When I had progressed to really serious reading, every night at about ten P.M. I would be outraged with the "lights out." It always seemed to catch me right in the middle of something engrossing.

15   Fortunately, right outside my door was a corridor light that cast a glow into my room. The glow was enough to read by, once my eyes adjusted to it. So when "lights out" came, I would sit on the floor where I could continue reading in that glow.

16   At one-hour intervals the night guards paced past every room. Each time I heard the approaching footsteps, I jumped into bed and feigned sleep. And as soon as the guard passed, I got back out of bed onto the floor area of that light-glow, where I would read for another fifty-eight minutes—until the guard approached again. That went on until three or four every morning. Three or four hours of sleep a night was enough for me. Often in the years in the streets I had slept less than that.

17   Mr. Muhammad, to whom I was writing daily, had no idea of what a new world had opened up to me through my efforts to document his teachings in books.

18   When I discovered philosophy, I tried to touch all the landmarks of philosophical development. Gradually, I read most of the old philosophers, Occidental and Oriental. The Oriental philosophers were the ones I came to prefer; finally, my impression was that most Occidental philosophy had largely been borrowed from the Oriental thinkers. Socrates, for instance, traveled in Egypt. Some sources even say that Socrates was initiated into some of the Egyptian mysteries. Obviously Socrates got some of his wisdom among the East's wise men.

19   I have often reflected upon the new vistas that reading opened to me. I knew right there in prison that reading had changed forever the course of my life. As I see it today, the ability to read awoke inside me some long dormant craving to be mentally alive. I certainly wasn't seeking any degree, the way a college confers a status symbol

upon its students. My homemade education gave me, with every additional book that I read, a little bit more sensitivity to the deafness, dumbness, and blindness that was afflicting the black race in America. Not long ago, an English writer telephoned me from London, asking questions. One was, "What's your alma mater?" I told him, "Books." You will never catch me with a free fifteen minutes in which I'm not studying something I feel might be able to help the black man.

20   Yesterday I spoke in London, and both ways on the plane across the Atlantic I was studying a document about how the United Nations proposes to insure the human rights of the oppressed minorities of the world. The American black man is the world's most shameful case of minority oppression. What makes the black man think of himself as only an internal United States issue is just a catchphrase, two words, "civil rights." How is the black man going to get "civil rights" before first he wins his *human* rights? If the American black man will start thinking about his *human* rights, and then start thinking of himself as part of one of the world's great peoples, he will see he has a case for the United Nations.

21   I can't think of a better case! Four hundred years of black blood and sweat invested here in America, and the white man still has the black man begging for what every immigrant fresh off the ship can take for granted the minute he walks down the gangplank.

22   But I'm digressing. I told the Englishman that my alma mater was books, a good library. Every time I catch a plane, I have with me a book that I want to read—and that's a lot of books these days. If I weren't out here every day battling the white man, I could spend the rest of my life reading, just satisfying my curiosity—because you can hardly mention anything I'm not curious about. I don't think anybody ever got more out of going to prison than I did. In fact, prison enabled me to study far more intensively than I would have if my life had gone differently and I had attended some college. I imagine that one of the biggest troubles with colleges is there are too many distractions, too much panty-raiding, fraternities, and boola-boola and all of that. Where else but in a prison could I have attacked my ignorance by being able to study intensely sometimes as much as fifteen hours a day?

23   Schopenhauer, Kant, Nietzsche, naturally, I read all of those. I don't respect them; I am just trying to remember some of those whose theories I soaked up in those years. These three, it's said, laid the groundwork on which the Fascist and Nazi philosophy was built.

I don't respect them because it seems to me that most of their time was spent arguing about things that are not really important. They remind me of so many of the Negro "intellectuals," so-called, with whom I have come in contact—they are always arguing about something useless.

24 Spinoza impressed me for a while when I found out that he was black. A black Spanish Jew. The Jews excommunicated him because he advocated a pantheistic doctrine, something like the "allness of God," or "God in everything." The Jews read their burial services for Spinoza, meaning that he was dead as far as they were concerned; his family was run out of Spain, they ended up in Holland, I think.

25 I'll tell you something. The whole stream of Western philosophy has now wound up in a cul-de-sac. The white man has perpetrated upon himself, as well as upon the black man, so gigantic a fraud that he has put himself into a crack. He did it through his elaborate, neurotic necessity to hide the black man's true role in history.

26 And today the white man is faced head on with what is happening on the Black Continent, Africa. Look at the artifacts being discovered there, that are proving over and over again, how the black man had great, fine, sensitive civilizations before the white man was out of the caves. Below the Sahara, in the places where most of America's Negroes' foreparents were kidnapped, there is being unearthed some of the finest craftsmanship, sculpture and other objects, that has ever been seen by modern man. Some of these things now are on view in such places as New York City's Museum of Modern Art. Gold work of such fine tolerance and workmanship that it has no rival. Ancient objects produced by black hands . . . refined by those black hands with results that no human hand today can equal.

27 History has been so "whitened" by the white man that even the black professors have known little more than the most ignorant black man about the talents and rich civilizations and cultures of the black man of millenniums ago. I have lectured in Negro colleges and some of these brainwashed black Ph.D.'s, with their suspenders dragging the ground with degrees, have run to the white man's newspapers calling me a "black fanatic." Why, a lot of them are fifty years behind the times. If I were president of one of these black colleges, I'd hock the campus if I had to, to send a bunch of black students off digging in Africa for more, more and more proof of the black race's historical greatness. The white man now is in Africa digging and searching. An African elephant can't stumble without falling on some white

man with a shovel. Practically every week, we read about some great new find from Africa's lost civilizations. All that's new is white science's attitude. The ancient civilizations of the black man have been buried on the Black Continent all the time.

28   Here is an example: A British anthropologist named Dr. Louis S. B. Leakey is displaying some fossil bones—a foot, part of a hand, some jaws, and skull fragments. On the basis of these, Dr. Leakey has said it's time to rewrite completely the history of man's origin.

29   This species of man lived 1,818,036 years before Christ. And these bones were found in Tanganyika. In the Black Continent.

30   It's a crime, the lie that has been told to generations of black men and white men both. Little innocent black children, born of parents who believed that their race had no history. Little black children seeing, before they could talk, that their parents considered themselves inferior. Innocent black children growing up, living out their lives, dying of old age—and all of their lives ashamed of being black. But the truth is pouring out of the bag now.

Nobody Mean More to Me Than You[1] and the Future Life of Willie Jordan

JUNE JORDAN

June Jordan was born in 1936 in New York City and educated at Barnard College and the University of Chicago. She is a poet, essayist, novelist, biographer, songwriter, and dramatist. She has served as visiting writer-in-residence at several colleges and universities and lectured at many schools. She is currently a professor of Afro-American studies and women's studies at the University of California, Berkeley.

"Nobody Mean More to Me Than You and the Future Life of Willie Jordan" is from *On Call* (1985), a collection of Jordan's essays. In it, she narrates her experiences in teaching a new course, "In Search of the Invisible Black Woman." She discovers black students who react negatively to the language used by Alice Walker

---

[1]Black English aphorisms crafted by Monica Morris, a junior at S.U.N.Y., Stony Brook, October 1984.

in *The Color Purple*. She was forced to switch her focus to Black English, and this essay is a catalog of techniques for learning it. But a second narration overlaps the first—the story of one of her students, Willie Jordan, whose twenty-five-year-old brother had been killed. The reaction of class members and the essay produced by Willie Jordan carry the message of Black English to another level, one laced with anger and pride and emerging power.

1   Black English is not exactly a linguistic buffalo; as children, most of the thirty-five million Afro-Americans living here depend on this language for our discovery of the world. But then we approach our maturity inside a larger social body that will not support our efforts to become anything other than the clones of those who are neither our mothers nor our fathers. We begin to grow up in a house where every true mirror shows us the face of somebody who does not belong there, whose walk and whose talk will never look or sound "right," because that house was meant to shelter a family that is alien and hostile to us. As we learn our way around this environment, either we hide our original word habits, or we completely surrender our own voice, hoping to please those who will never respect anyone different from themselves: Black English is not exactly a linguistic buffalo, but we should understand its status as an endangered species, as a perishing, irreplaceable system of community intelligence, or we should expect its extinction, and, along with that, the extinguishing of much that constitutes our own proud, and singular, identity.

2   What we casually call "English," less and less defers to England and its "gentlemen." "English" is no longer a specific matter of geography or an element of class privilege; more than thirty-three countries use this tool as a means of "intranational communication."[2] Countries as disparate as Zimbabwe and Malaysia, or Israel and Uganda, use it as their non-native currency of convenience. Obvi-

---

[2] *English Is Spreading, But What Is English?* A presentation by Professor S. N. Sridhar, Department of Linguistics, S.U.N.Y., Stony Brook, April 9, 1985: Dean's Convocation Among the Disciplines.

ously, this tool, this "English," cannot function inside thirty-three discrete societies on the basis of rules and values absolutely determined somewhere else, in a thirty-fourth other country, for example.

3   In addition to that staggering congeries of non-native users of English, there are five countries, or 333,746,000 people, for whom this thing called "English" serves as a native tongue.[3] Approximately 10 percent of these native speakers of "English" are Afro-American citizens of the U.S.A. I cite these numbers and varieties of human beings dependent on "English" in order, quickly, to suggest how strange and how tenuous is any concept of "Standard English." Obviously, numerous forms of English now operate inside a natural, an uncontrollable, continuum of development. I would suppose "the standard" for English in Malaysia is not the same as "the standard" in Zimbabwe. I know that standard forms of English for Black people in this country do not copy that of Whites. And, in fact, the structural differences between these two kinds of English have intensified, becoming more Black, or less White, despite the expected homogenizing effects of television[4] and other mass media.

4   Nonetheless, White standards of English persist, supreme and unquestioned, in these United States. Despite our multi-lingual population, and despite the deepening Black and White cleavage within that conglomerate, White standards control our official and popular judgments of verbal proficiency and correct, or incorrect, language skills, including speech. In contrast to India, where at least fourteen languages co-exist as legitimate Indian languages, in contrast to Nicaragua, where all citizens are legally entitled to formal school instruction in their regional or tribal languages, compulsory education in America compels accommodation to exclusively White forms of "English." White English, in America, is "Standard English."

5   This story begins two years ago. I was teaching a new course, "In Search of the Invisible Black Woman," and my rather large class seemed evenly divided among young Black women and men. Five or six White students also sat in attendance. With unexpected speed and enthusiasm we had moved through historical narration of the 19th century to literature by and about Black women, in the 20th.

---

[3] *English Is Spreading.*
[4] *New York Times,* March 15, 1985, Section One, p. 14: Report on Study by Linguists at the University of Pennsylvania.

I then assigned the first forty pages of Alice Walker's *The Color Purple,* and I came, eagerly, to class that morning:

6   "So!" I exclaimed, aloud. "What did you think? How did you like it?"

7   The students studied their hands, or the floor. There was no response. The tense, resistant feeling in the room fairly astounded me.

8   At last, one student, a young woman still not meeting my eyes, muttered something in my direction:

9   "What did you say?" I prompted her.

10   "Why she have them talk so funny. It don't sound right."

11   "You mean the language?"

12   Another student lifted his head: "It don't look right, neither. I couldn't hardly read it."

13   At this, several students dumped on the book. Just about unanimously, their criticisms targeted the language. I listened to what they wanted to say and silently marvelled at the similarities between their casual speech patterns and Alice Walker's written version of Black English.

14   But I decided against pointing to these identical traits of syntax, I wanted not to make them self-conscious about their own spoken language—not while they clearly felt it was "wrong." Instead I decided to swallow my astonishment. Here was a negative Black reaction to a prize-winning accomplishment of Black literature that White readers across the country had selected as a best seller. Black rejection was aimed at the one irreducibly Black element of Walker's work: the language—Celie's Black English. I wrote the opening lines of *The Color Purple* on the blackboard and asked the students to help me translate these sentences into Standard English:

> *You better not never tell nobody but God, It'd kill your mommy.*
>
> Dear God,
> I am fourteen years old. I have always been a good girl. Maybe you can give me a sign letting me know what is happening to me.
>   Last spring after Little Lucious come I heard them fussing. He was pulling on her arm. She say it too soon, Fonso. I aint well. Finally he leave her alone. A week go by, he pulling on her arm again.

She say, Naw, I ain't gonna. Can't you see I'm
already half dead, an all of the children.[5]

Our process of translation exploded with hilarity and even hysterical,
shocked laughter: The Black writer, Alice Walker, knew what she
was doing! If rudimentary criteria for good fiction include the manip-
ulation of language so that the syntax and diction of sentences will
tell you the identity of speakers, the probable age and sex and class
of speakers, and even the locale—urban/rural/southern/west-
ern—then Walker had written, perfectly. This is the translation into
Standard English that our class produced:

> *Absolutely, one should never confide in anybody besides
> God. Your secrets could prove devastating to your
> mother.*

> Dear God,
> I am fourteen years old. I have always been good.
> But now, could you help me to understand what is
> happening to me?
> Last spring, after my little brother, Lucious, was
> born, I heard my parents fighting. My father kept
> pulling at my mother's arm. But she told him, "It's
> too soon for sex, Alfonso. I am still not feeling
> well." Finally, my father left her alone. A week went
> by, and then he began bothering my mother, again:
> Pulling her arm. She told him, "No, I won't! Can't
> you see I'm already exhausted from all of these
> children?"

(Our favorite line was "It's too soon for sex, Alfonso.")

15   Once we could stop laughing, once we could stop our exponen-
tially wild improvisations on the theme of Translated Black English,
the students pushed to explain their own negative first reactions to
their spoken language on the printed page. I thought it was probably
akin to the shock of seeing yourself in a photograph for the first
time. Most of the students had never before seen a written facsimile
of the way they talk. None of the students had ever learned how to

[5]Alice Walker. *The Color Purple* (New York: Harcourt Brace Jovanovich, 1982),
p. 11.

read and write their own verbal system of communication: Black English. Alternatively, this fact began to baffle or else bemuse and then infuriate my students. Why not? Was it too late? Could they learn how to do it, now? And, ultimately, the final test question, the one testing my sincerity: Could I teach them? Because I had never taught anyone Black English and, as far as I knew, no one, anywhere in the United States, had ever offered such a course, the best I could say was "I'll try."

16   He looked like a wrestler.

17   He sat dead center in the packed room and, every time our eyes met, he quickly nodded his head as though anxious to reassure, and encourage me.

18   Short, with strikingly broad shoulders and long arms, he spoke with a surprisingly high, soft voice that matched the soft bright movement of his eyes. His name was Willie Jordan. He would have seemed even more unlikely in the context of Contemporary Women's Poetry, except that ten or twelve other Black men were taking the course, as well. Still, Willie was conspicuous. His extreme fitness, the muscular density of his presence underscored the riveted, gentle attention that he gave to anything anyone said. Generally, he did not join the loud and rowdy dialogue flying back and forth, but there could be no doubt about his interest in our discussions. And, when he stood to present an argument he'd prepared, overnight, that nervous smile of his vanished and an irregular stammering replaced it, as he spoke with visceral sincerity, word by word.

19   That was how I met Willie Jordan. It was in between "In Search of the Invisible Black Woman" and "The Art of Black English." I was waiting for departmental approval and I supposed that Willie might be, so to speak, killing time until he, too, could study Black English. But Willie really did want to explore contemporary women's poetry and, to that end, volunteered for extra research and never missed a class.

20   Towards the end of that semester, Willie approached me for an independent study project on South Africa. It would commence the next semester. I thought Willie's writing needed the kind of improvement only intense practice will yield. I knew his intelligence was outstanding. But he'd wholeheartedly opted for "Standard English" at a rather late age, and the results were stilted and frequently polysyllabic, simply for the sake of having more syllables.

Willie's unnatural formality of language seemed to me consistent with the formality of his research into South African apartheid. As he projected his studies, he would have little time, indeed, for newspapers. Instead, more than 90 percent of his research would mean saturation in strictly historical, if not archival, material. I was certainly interested. It would be tricky to guide him into a more confident and spontaneous relationship both with language and apartheid. It was going to be wonderful to see what happened when he could catch up with himself, entirely, and talk back to the world.

21   September, 1984: Breezy fall weather and much excitement! My class, "The Art of Black English," was full to the limit of the fire laws. And in Independent Study, Willie Jordan showed up weekly, fifteen minutes early for each of our sessions. I was pretty happy to be teaching, altogether!

22   I remember an early class when a young brother, replete with his ever-present porkpie hat, raised his hand and then told us that most of what he'd heard was "all right" except it was "too clean." "The brothers on the street," he continued, "they mix it up more. Life 'fuck' and 'motherfuck,' Or like 'shit.' " He waited. I waited. Then all of us laughed a good while, and we got into a brawl about "correct" and "realistic" Black English that led to Rule 1.

23   Rule 1: *Black English is about a whole lot more than mothafuckin.*

24   As a criterion, we decided, "realistic" could take you anywhere you want to go. Artful places. Angry places. Eloquent and sweetalkin places. Polemical places. Church. And the local Bar & Grill. We were checking out a language, not a mood or a scene or one guy's forgettable mouthing off.

25   It was hard. For most of the students, learning Black English required a fallback to patterns and rhythms of speech that many of their parents had beaten out of them. I mean *beaten.* And, in a majority of cases, correct Black English could be achieved only by striving for *incorrect* Standard English, something they were still pushing at, quite uncertainly. This state of affairs led to Rule 2.

26   Rule 2: *If it's wrong in Standard English it's probably right in Black English, or, at least, you're hot.*

27   It was hard. Roommates and family members ridiculed their studies, or remained incredulous, "You *studying* that shit? At school?" But we were beginning to feel the companionship of pioneers. And

we decided that we needed another rule that would establish each one of us as equally important to our success. This was Rule 3.

28   Rule 3: *If it don't sound like something that come out somebody mouth then it don't sound right. If it don't sound right then it ain't hardly right. Period.*

29   This rule produced two weeks of compositions in which the students agonizingly tried to spell the sound of the Black English sentence they wanted to convey. But Black English is, preeminently, an oral/spoken means of communication. *And spelling don't talk.* So we needed Rule 4.

30   Rule 4: *Forget about the spelling. Let the syntax carry you.*

31   Once we arrived at Rule 4 we started to fly, because syntax, the structure of an idea, leads you to the world view of the speaker and reveals her values. The syntax of a sentence equals the structure of your consciousness. If we insisted that the language of Black English adheres to a distinctive Black syntax, then we were postulating a profound difference between White and Black people, *per se*. Was it a difference to prize or to obliterate?

32   There are three qualities of Black English—the presence of life, voice, and clarity—that intensify to a distinctive Black value system that we became excited about and self-consciously tried to maintain.

1.   Black English has been produced by a pre-technocratic, if
     not anti-technological, culture. More, our culture has
     been constantly threatened by annihilation or, at least, the
     swallowed blurring of assimilation. Therefore, our lan-
     guage is a system constructed by people constantly needing
     to insist that we exist, that we are present. Our language
     devolves from a culture that abhors all abstraction, or any-
     thing tending to obscure or delete the fact of the human
     being who is here and now/the truth of the person who
     is speaking or listening. Consequently, *there is no passive
     voice construction possible in Black English.* For example,
     you cannot say, "Black English is being eliminated." You must
     say, instead, "White people eliminating Black English."
     The assumption of the presence of life governs all of
     Black English. Therefore, overwhelmingly, *all action takes*

place in the language of the present indicative. And every sentence assumes the living and active participation of at least two human beings, the speaker and the listener.

2. A primary consequence of the person-centered values of Black English is the delivery of voice. If you speak or write Black English, your ideas will necessarily possess that otherwise elusive attribute, *voice.*

3. One main benefit following from the person-centered values of Black English is that of *clarity.* If your idea, your sentence, assumes the presence of at least two living and active people, you will make it understandable, because the motivation behind every sentence is the wish to say something real to somebody real.

33 As the weeks piled up, translation from Standard English into Black English or vice versa occupied a hefty part of our course work.

34 Standard English (hereafter S.E.): "In considering the idea of studying Black English those questioned suggested—"

35 (What's the subject? Where's the person? Is anybody alive in here, in that idea?)

36 Black English (hereafter B.E.): "I been asking people what you think about somebody studying Black English and they answer me like this:"

37 But there were interesting limits. You cannot "translate" instances of Standard English preoccupied with abstraction or with nothing/ nobody evidently alive, into Black English. That would warp the language into uses antithetical to the guiding perspective of its community of users. Rather you must first change those Standard English sentences, themselves, into ideas consistent with the person-centered assumptions of Black English.

Guidelines for Black English

1. Minimal number of words for every idea: This is the source for the aphoristic and/or poetic force of the language; eliminate every possible word.

2. Clarity: If the sentence is not clear it's not Black English.

3. Eliminate use of the verb *to be* whenever possible. This leads to the deployment of more descriptive and, therefore, more precise verbs.

4. Use *be* and *been* only when you want to describe a chronic, ongoing state of things.

> He *be* at the office, by 9. (He is always at the office by 9.)

> He *been* with her since forever.

5. Zero copula: Always eliminate the verb *to be* whenever it would combine with another verb, in Standard English.

> S.E.: She is going out with him.

> B.E.: She going out with him.

6. Eliminate *do* as in:

> S.E.: What do you think? What do you want?

> B.E.: What you think? What you want?

Rules number 3, 4, 5, and 6 provide for the use of the minimal number of verbs per idea and, therefore, greater accuracy in the choice of verb.

7. In general, if you wish to say something really positive, try to formulate the idea using emphatic negative structure.

> S.E.: He's fabulous.

> B.E.: He bad.

8. Use double or triple negatives for dramatic emphasis.

> S.E.: Tina Turner sings out of this world.

> B.E.: Ain nobody sing like Tina.

9. Never use the *ed* suffix to indicate the past tense of a verb.

> S.E.: She closed the door.

> B.E.: She close the door. Or, she have close the door.

10. Regardless of intentional verb time, only use the third person singular, present indicative, for use of the verb *to have,* as an auxiliary.

> S.E.: He had his wallet then he lost it.

> B.E.: He have him wallet then he lose it.

> S.E.: We had seen that movie.

> B.E.: We seen that movie. Or, we have see that movie.

11. Observe a minimal inflection of verbs. Particularly, never change from the first person singular forms to the third person singular.

> S.E.: Present Tense Forms: He goes to the store.

> B.E.: He go to the store.

    S.E.: Past Tense Forms: He went to the store.
    B.E.: He go to the store. Or, he gone to the store. Or, he been to the store.

12. The possessive case scarcely ever appears in Black English. Never use an apostrophe ('s) construction. If you wander into a possessive case component of an idea, then keep logically consistent: *ours, his, theirs, mines.* But, most likely, if you bump into such a component, you have wandered outside the underlying world view of Black English.
    S.E.: He will take their car tomorrow.
    B.E.: He taking they car tomorrow.

13. Plurality: Logical consistency, continued: If the modifier indicates plurality then the noun remains in the singular case.
    S.E.: He ate twelve doughnuts.
    B.E.: He eat twelve doughnut.
    S.E.: She has many books.
    B.E.: She have many book.

14. Listen for, or invent, special Black English forms of the past tense, such as: "He losted it. That what she felted." If they are clear and readily understood, then use them.

15. Do not hesitate to play with words, sometimes inventing them: e.g., "astropotomous" means huge like a hippo plus astronomical and, therefore, signifies real big.

16. In Black English, unless you keenly want to underscore the past tense nature of an action, stay in the present tense and rely on the overall context of your ideas for the conveyance of time and sequence.

17. Never use the suffix -*ly* form of an adverb in Black English.
    S.E.: The rain came down rather quickly.
    B.E.: The rain come down pretty quick.

18. Never use the indefinite article *an* in Black English.
    S.E.: He wanted to ride an elephant.
    B.E.: He wanted to ride him a elephant.

19. Invariant syntax: in correct Black English it is possible to formulate an imperative, an interrogative, and a simple declarative idea with the same syntax.
    B.E.: You going to the store?
         You going to the store.
         You going to the store!

38   Where was Willie Jordan? We'd reached the mid-term of the
semester. Students had formulated Black English guidelines, by consensus, and they were now writing with remarkable beauty, purpose,
and enjoyment:

> *I ain hardly speakin for everybody but myself so*
> *understan that.*—Kim Parks

Samples from student writings:

> Janie have a great big ole hole inside her. Tea Cake
> the only thing that fit that hole. . . .

> That pear tree beautiful to Janie, especial when bees
> fiddlin with the blossomin pear there growin large
> and lovely. But personal speakin, the love she get
> from starin at that tree ain the love what starin back
> at her in them relationship. (Monica Morris)

> Love a big theme in, *They Eye Was Watching God.*
> Love show people new corners inside theyself. It
> pull out good stuff and stuff back bad stuff . . . Joe
> worship the doing uh his own hand and need other
> people to worship him too. But he ain't think about
> Janie that she a person and ought to live like any-
> body common do. Queen life not for Janie. (Monica
> Morris)

> In both life and writin, Black womens have varietous
> experience of love that be cold like a iceberg or fiery
> like a inferno. Passion got for the other partner
> involve, man or women, seem as shallow, ankle-
> deep water or the most profoundest abyss. (Con-
> stance Evans)

> Family love another bond that ain't never break
> under no pressure. (Constance Evans)

> You know it really cold/When the friend you/
> Always get out the fire/Act like they don't know
> you/When you in the beat. (Constance Evans)

> Big classroom discussion bout love at this time. I
> never take no class where us have any long arguin

for and against for two or three day. New to me and great. I find the class time talkin a million time more interestin than detail bout the book. (Kathy Esseks)

39　　As these examples suggest, Black English no longer limited the students, in any way. In fact, one of them, Philip Garfield, would shortly "translate" a pivotal scene from Ibsen's *A Doll's House,* as his final term paper.

> *Nora:* I didn't gived no shit. I thinked you a asshole back then, too, you make it so hard for me to save mines husband life.
> *Krogstad:* Girl, it clear you ain't any idea what you done. You done exact what I once done, and I losed my reputation over it.
> *Nora:* You asks me believe you once act brave save you wife life?
> *Krogstad:* Law care less why you done it.
> *Nora:* Law must suck.
> *Krogstad:* Suck or no, if I wants, judge screw you wid dis paper.
> *Nora:* No way, man. (Philip Garfield)

40　　But where was Willie? Compulsively punctual, and always thoroughly prepared with neat typed compositions, he had disappeared. He failed to show up for our regularly scheduled conference, and I received neither a note nor a phone call of explanation. A whole week went by. I wondered if Willie had finally been captured by the extremely current happenings in South Africa: passage of a new constitution that did not enfranchise the Black majority, and militant Black South African reaction to that affront. I wondered if he'd been hurt, somewhere. I wondered if the serious workload of weekly readings and writings had overwhelmed him and changed his mind about independent study. Where was Willie Jordan?

41　　One week after the first conference that Willie missed, he called: "Hello, Professor Jordan? This is Willie. I'm sorry I wasn't there last week. But something has come up and I'm pretty upset. I'm sorry but I really can't deal right now."

42　　I asked Willie to drop by my office and just let me see that he was okay. He agreed to do that. When I saw him I knew something hideous had happened. Something had hurt him and scared him to the marrow. He was all agitated and stammering and terse and incoherent. At last, his sadly jumbled account let me surmise, as follows: Brooklyn police had murdered his unarmed, twenty-five-year-old brother, Reggie Jordan. Neither Willie nor his elderly parents knew what to do about it. Nobody from the press was interested. His folks had no money. Police ran his family around and around, to no point. And Reggie was really dead. And Willie wanted to fight, but he felt helpless.

43   With Willie's permission I began to try to secure legal counsel for the Jordan family. Unfortunately, Black victims of police violence are truly numerous, while the resources available to prosecute their killers are truly scarce. A friend of mine at the Center for Constitutional Rights estimated that just the preparatory costs for bringing the cops into court normally approaches $180,000. Unless the execution of Reggie Jordan became a major community cause for organizing and protest, his murder would simply become a statistical item.

44   Again, with Willie's permission, I contacted every newspaper and media person I could think of. But the Bastone feature article in *The Village Voice* was the only result from that canvassing.

45   Again, with Willie's permission, I presented the case to my class in Black English. We had talked about the politics of language. We had talked about love and sex and child abuse and men and women. But the murder of Reggie Jordan broke like a hurricane across the room.

46   There are few "issues" as endemic to Black life as police violence. Most of the students knew and respected and liked Jordan. Many of them came from the very neighborhood where the murder had occurred. All of the students had known somebody close to them who had been killed by police, or had known frightening moments of gratuitous confrontation with the cops. They wanted to do everything at once to avenge death. Number One: They decided to compose a personal statement of condolence to Willie Jordan and his family, written in Black English. Number Two: They decided to compose individual messages to the police, in Black English. These should be prefaced by an explanatory paragraph composed by the entire group. Number Three: These individual messages, with their lead paragraph, should be sent to *Newsday*.

47   The morning after we agreed on these objectives, one of the

young women students appeared with an unidentified visitor, who sat through the class, smiling in a peculiar, comfortable way.

48 Now we had to make more tactical decisions. Because we wanted the messages published, and because we thought it imperative that our outrage be known by the police, the tactical question was this: Should the opening, group paragraph be written in Black English or Standard English?

49 I have seldom been privy to a discussion with so much heart at the dead beat of it. I will never forget the eloquence, the sudden haltings of speech, the fierce struggle against tears, the furious throw-away, and useless explosions that this question elicited.

50 That one question contained several others, each of them extraordinarily painful to even contemplate. How best to serve the memory of Reggie Jordan? Should we use the language of the killer—Standard English—in order to make our ideas acceptable to those controlling the killers? But wouldn't what we had to say be rejected, summarily, if we said it in our own language, the language of the victim, Reggie Jordan? But if we sought to express ourselves by abandoning our language wouldn't that mean our suicide on top of Reggie's murder? But if we expressed ourselves in our own language wouldn't that be suicidal to the wish to communicate with those who, evidently, did not give a damn about us/Reggie/police violence in the Black community?

51 At the end of one of the longest, most difficult hours of my own life, the students voted, unanimously, to preface their individual messages with a paragraph composed in the language of Reggie Jordan. *"At least we don't give up nothing else. At least we stick to the truth: Be who we been. And stay all the way with Reggie."*

52 It was heartbreaking to proceed, from that point. Everyone in the room realized that our decision in favor of Black English had doomed our writings, even as the distinctive reality of our Black lives always has doomed our efforts to "be who we been" in this country.

53 I went to the blackboard and took down this paragraph dictated by the class:

YOU COPS!
   WE THE BROTHER AND SISTER OF WILLIE JORDAN, A FELLOW STONY BROOK STUDENT WHO THE BROTHER OF THE DEAD REGGIE JORDAN. REGGIE, LIKE

MANY BROTHER AND SISTER, HE A VICTIM
OF BRUTAL RACIST POLICE, OCTOBER 25,
1984. US APPALL, FED UP, BECAUSE THAT
ANOTHER SENSELESS DEATH WHAT
OCCUR IN OUR COMMUNITY. THIS WHAT
WE FEEL, THIS, FROM OUR HEART, FOR WE
AIN'T STAYIN' SILENT NO MORE.

54   With the completion of this introduction, nobody said anything.
I asked for comments. At this invitation, the unidentified visitor, a
young Black man, ceaselessly smiling, raised his hand. He was, it so
happens, a rookie cop. He had just joined the force in September
and, he said, he thought he should clarify a few things. So he came
forward and sprawled easily into a posture of barroom, or fire-side
nostalgia:

55   "See," Officer Charles enlightened us, "Most times when you
out on the street and something come down you do one of two
things. Over-react or under-react. Now, if you under-react then you
can get yourself kilt. And if you over-react then maybe you kill
somebody. Fortunately it's about nine times out of ten and you will
over-react. So the brother got kilt. And I'm sorry about that, believe
me. But what you have to understand is what kilt him: Over-reaction.
That's all. Now you talk about Black people and White police but
see, now, I'm a cop myself. And (big smile) I'm Black. And just a
couple months ago I was on the other side. But it's the same for
me. You a cop, you the ultimate authority: the Ultimate Authority.
And you on the street, most of the time you can only do one of two
things: over-react or under-react. That's all it is with the brother.
Over-reaction. Didn't have nothing to do with race."

56   That morning Officer Charles had the good fortune to escape
without being boiled alive. But barely. And I remember the pride
of his smile when I read about the fate of Black policemen and other
collaborators, in South Africa. I remember him, and I remember the
shock and palpable feeling of shame that filled the room. It was as
though that foolish, and deadly, young man had just relieved himself
on his foolish, and deadly, explanation, face to face with the grief of
Reggie Jordan's father and Reggie Jordan's mother. Class ended
quietly. I copied the paragraph from the blackboard, collected the
individual messages and left to type them up.

57   *Newsday* rejected the piece.

58 *The Village Voice* could not find room in their "Letters" section to print the individual messages from the students to the police.

59 None of the TV news reporters picked up the story.

60 Nobody raised $180,000 to prosecute the murder of Reggie Jordan.

61 Reggie Jordan is really dead.

62 I asked Willie Jordan to write an essay pulling together everything important to him from that semester. He was still deeply beside himself with frustration and amazement and loss. This is what he wrote, unedited, and in its entirety:

> Throughout the course of this semester I have been researching the effects of oppression and exploitation along racial lines in South Africa and its neighboring countries. I have become aware of South African police brutalization of native Africans beyond the extent of the law, even though the laws themselves are catalyst affliction upon Black men, women and children. Many Africans die each year as a result of the deliberate use of police force to protect the white power structure.
>
> Social control agents in South Africa, such as policemen, are also used to force compliance among citizens through both overt and covert tactics. It is not uncommon to find bold-faced coercion and cold-blooded killings of Blacks by South African police for undetermined and/or inadequate reasons. Perhaps the truth is that the only reasons for this heinous treatment of Blacks rests in racial differences. We should also understand that what is conveyed through the media is not always accurate and may sometimes be construed as the tip of the iceberg at best.
>
> I recently received a painful reminder that racism, poverty, and the abuse of power are global problems which are by no means unique to South Africa. On October 25, 1984 at approximately 3:00 p.m. my brother, Mr. Reginald Jordan, was shot and killed by two New York City policemen from the 75th precinct in the East New York section of Brooklyn.

His life ended at the age of twenty-five. Even up
to this current point in time the Police Department
has failed to provide my family, which consists of
five brothers, eight sisters, and two parents, with a
plausible reason for Reggie's death. Out of the many
stories that were given to my family by the Police
Department, not one of them seems to hold water.
In fact, I honestly believe that the Police Department's assessment of my brother's murder is nothing short of ABSOLUTE BULLSHIT, and thus far
no evidence had been produced to alter perception
of the situation.

Furthermore, I believe that one of three cases
may have occurred in this incident. First, Reggie's
death may have been the desired outcome of the
police officer's action, in which case the killing was
premeditated. Or, it was a case of mistaken identity,
which clarifies the fact that the two officers who
killed my brother and their commanding parties are
all grossly incompetent. Or, both of the above cases
are correct, i.e., Reggie's murderers intended to kill
him and the Police Department behaved insubordi-
nately.

Part of the argument of the officers who shot
Reggie was that he had attacked one of them and
took his gun. This was their major claim. They also
said that only one of them had actually shot Reggie.
The facts, however, speak for themselves. According
to the Death Certificate and autopsy report, Reggie
was shot eight times from point-blank range. The
Doctor who performed the autopsy told me himself
that two bullets entered the side of my brother's
head, four bullets were sprayed into his back, and
two bullets struck him in the back of his legs. It is
obvious that unnecessary force was used by the
police and that it is extremely difficult to shoot
someone in his back when he is attacking or
approaching you.

After experiencing a situation like this and
researching South Africa I believe that to a large

degree, justice may only exist as rhetoric. I find it difficult to talk of true justice when the oppression of my people both at home and abroad attests to the fact that inequality and injustice are serious problems whereby Blacks and Third World people are perpetually short-changed by society. Something has to be done about the way in which this world is set up. Although it is a difficult task, we do have the power to make a change.

—Willie J. Jordan, Jr.
EGL 487, Section 58, November 14, 1984

It is my privilege to dedicate this book to the future life of Willie J. Jordan, Jr., August 8, 1985.

Silence

MAXINE HONG KINGSTON

Maxine Hong Kingston was born in 1940 of Chinese immigrant parents (laundry operators) in Stockton, California. She earned a B.A. at the University of California, Berkeley, in 1962. She taught English at high schools in Hawaii and California, taught creative writing at the University of Hawaii, and began publishing in *The New Yorker, The New York Times Magazine, Ms., The Iowa Review,* and other magazines and journals. She published her autobiography, *The Woman Warrior: Memoirs of a Childhood Among Ghosts* (1976), to high critical praise. She followed with *China Men* (1980). These two autobiographies use "talk-stories" of her parents and elders based on Chinese myths, legends, tales, and her own memories. She says, "Sometimes, our lives have plots like stories; sometimes we're affected by the stories or we try to live up to them or the stories give a color and an atmosphere to life." She wants her writing to distinguish reality from the legends and myth, especially the memories from childhood that profoundly affect the adult's sense of values.

"Silence," an excerpt from *The Woman Warrior,* describes a period during Kingston's childhood when, because she was unhappy at an American school, she went silent for three years, refusing to speak at the school, flunking kindergarten, and causing herself and her parents great consternation. However, she describes the joyful environment of the Chinese school that she attended during the evening. There, she did speak.

1.   Long ago in China, knot-makers tied string into buttons and frogs, and rope into bell pulls. There was one knot so complicated that it blinded the knot-maker. Finally an emperor outlawed this cruel knot, and the nobles could not order it anymore. If I had lived in China, I would have been an outlaw knot-maker.

2.   Maybe that's why my mother cut my tongue. She pushed my tongue up and sliced the frenum. Or maybe she snipped it with a pair of nail scissors. I don't remember her doing it, only her telling me about it, but all during childhood I felt sorry for the baby whose mother waited with scissors or knife in hand for it to cry—and then, when its mouth was wide open like a baby bird's, cut. The Chinese say "a ready tongue is an evil."

3.   I used to curl up my tongue in front of the mirror and tauten my frenum into a white line, itself as thin as a razor blade. I saw no scars in my mouth. I thought perhaps I had had two frena, and she had cut one. I made other children open their mouths so I could compare theirs to mine. I saw perfect pink membranes stretching into precise edges that looked easy enough to cut. Sometimes I felt very proud that my mother committed such a powerful act upon me. At other times I was terrified—the first thing my mother did when she saw me was to cut my tongue.

4.   "Why did you do that to me, Mother?"

5.   "I told you."

6.   "Tell me again."

7.   "I cut it so that you would not be tongue-tied. Your tongue would be able to move in any language. You'll be able to speak languages that are completely different from one another. You'll be able to pronounce anything. Your frenum looked too tight to do those things, so I cut it."

8.   "But isn't 'a ready tongue an evil'?"

9.   "Things are different in this ghost country."

10.   "Did it hurt me? Did I cry and bleed?"

11.   "I don't remember. Probably."

12.   She didn't cut the other children's. When I asked cousins and other Chinese children whether their mothers had cut their tongues loose, they said, "What?"

13.   "Why didn't you cut my brothers' and sisters' tongues?"

14.   "They didn't need it."

15.   "Why not? Were theirs longer than mine?"

16.   "Why don't you quit blabbering and get to work?"

17   If my mother was not lying she should have cut more, scraped away the rest of the frenum skin, because I have a terrible time talking. Or she should not have cut at all, tampering with my speech. When I went to kindergarten and had to speak English for the first time, I became silent. A dumbness—a shame—still cracks my voice in two, even when I want to say "hello" casually, or ask an easy question in front of the check-out counter, or ask directions of a bus driver. I stand frozen, or I hold up the line with the complete, grammatical sentence that comes squeaking out at impossible length. "What did you say?" says the cab driver, or "Speak up," so I have to perform again, only weaker the second time. A telephone call makes my throat bleed and takes up that day's courage. It spoils my day with self-disgust when I hear my broken voice come skittering out into the open. It makes people wince to hear it. I'm getting better, though. Recently I asked the postman for special-issue stamps; I've waited since childhood for postmen to give me some of their own accord. I am making progress, a little every day.

18   My silence was thickest—total—during the three years that I covered my school paintings with black paint. I painted layers of black over houses and flowers and suns, and when I drew on the blackboard, I put a layer of chalk on top. I was making a stage curtain, and it was the moment before the curtain parted or rose. The teachers called my parents to school, and I saw they had been saving my pictures, curling and cracking, all alike and black. The teachers pointed to the pictures and looked serious, talked seriously too, but my parents did not understand English. ("The parents and teachers of criminals were executed," said my father.) My parents took the pictures home. I spread them out (so black and full of possibilities) and pretended the curtains were swinging open, flying up, one after another, sunlight underneath, mighty operas.

19   During the first silent year I spoke to no one at school, did not ask before going to the lavatory, and flunked kindergarten. My sister also said nothing for three years, silent in the playground and silent at lunch. There were other quiet Chinese girls not of our family, but most of them got over it sooner than we did. I enjoyed the silence. At first it did not occur to me I was supposed to talk or to pass kindergarten. I talked at home and to one or two of the Chinese kids in the class. I made motions and even made some jokes. I drank out of a toy saucer when the water spilled out of the cup, and

everybody laughed, pointing at me, so I did it some more. I didn't know that Americans don't drink out of saucers.

20   I liked the Negro students (Black Ghosts) best because they laughed the loudest and talked to me as if I were a daring talker too. One of the Negro girls had her mother coil braids over her ears Shanghai-style like mine; we were Shanghai twins except that she was covered with black like my paintings. Two Negro kids enrolled in Chinese school, and the teachers gave them Chinese names. Some Negro kids walked me to school and home, protecting me from the Japanese kids, who hit me and chased me and stuck gum in my ears. The Japanese kids were noisy and tough. They appeared one day in kindergarten, released from concentration camp, which was a tic-tac-toe mark, like barbed wire, on the map.

21   It was when I found out I had to talk that school became a misery, that the silence became a misery. I did not speak and felt bad each time that I did not speak. I read aloud in first grade, though, and heard the barest whisper with little squeaks come out of my throat. "Louder," said the teacher, who scared the voice away again. The other Chinese girls did not talk either, so I knew the silence had to do with being a Chinese girl.

22   Reading out loud was easier than speaking because we did not have to make up what to say, but I stopped often, and the teacher would think I'd gone quiet again. I could not understand "I." The Chinese "I" has seven strokes, intricacies. How could the American "I," assuredly wearing a hat like the Chinese, have only three strokes, the middle so straight? Was it out of politeness that this writer left off strokes the way a Chinese has to write her own name small and crooked? No, it was not politeness; "I" is a capital and "you" is a lower-case. I stared at that middle line and waited so long for its black center to resolve into tight strokes and dots that I forgot to pronounce it. The other troublesome word was "here," no strong consonant to hang on to, and so flat, when "here" is two mountain-ous ideographs. The teacher, who had already told me every day how to read "I" and "here," put me in the low corner under the stairs again, where the noisy boys usually sat.

23   When my second grade class did a play, the whole class went to the auditorium except the Chinese girls. The teacher, lovely and Hawaiian, should have understood about us, but instead left us behind in the classroom. Our voices were too soft or nonexistent, and our parents never signed the permission slips anyway. They never

signed anything unnecessary. We opened the door a crack and peeked out, but closed it again quickly. One of us (not me) won every spelling bee, though.

24   I remember telling the Hawaiian teacher, "We Chinese can't sing 'land where our fathers died.' " She argued with me about politics, while I meant because of curses. But how can I have that memory when I couldn't talk? My mother says that we, like the ghosts, have no memories.

25   After American school, we picked up our cigar boxes, in which we had arranged books, brushes, and an inkbox neatly, and went to Chinese school, from 5:00 to 7:30 P.M. There we chanted together, voices rising and falling, loud and soft, some boys shouting, everybody reading together, reciting together and not alone with one voice. When we had a memorization test, the teacher let each of us come to his desk and say the lesson to him privately, while the rest of the class practiced copying or tracing. Most of the teachers were men. The boys who were so well behaved in the American school played tricks on them and talked back to them. The girls were not mute. They screamed and yelled during recess, when there were no rules; they had fistfights. Nobody was afraid of children hurting themselves or of children hurting school property. The glass doors to the red and green balconies with the gold joy symbols were left wide open so that we could run out and climb the fire escapes. We played capture-the-flag in the auditorium, where Sun Yat-sen and Chiang Kai-shek's pictures hung at the back of the stage, the Chinese flag on their left and the American flag on their right. We climbed the teak ceremonial chairs and made flying leaps off the stage. One flag headquarters was behind the glass door and the other on stage right. Our feet drummed on the hollow stage. During recess the teachers locked themselves up in their office with the shelves of books, copybooks, inks from China. They drank tea and warmed their hands at a stove. There was no play supervision. At recess we had the school to ourselves, and also we could roam as far as we could go—downtown, Chinatown stores, home—as long as we returned before the bell rang.

26   At exactly 7:30 the teacher again picked up the brass bell that sat on his desk and swung it over our heads, while we charged down the stairs, our cheering magnified in the stairwell. Nobody had to line up.

27   Not all of the children who were silent at American school found

voice at Chinese school. One new teacher said each of us had to get up and recite in front of the class, who was to listen. My sister and I had memorized the lesson perfectly. We said it to each other at home, one chanting, one listening. The teacher called on my sister to recite first. It was the first time a teacher had called on the second-born to go first. My sister was scared. She glanced at me and looked away; I looked down at my desk. I hoped that she could do it because if she could, then I would have to. She opened her mouth and a voice came out that wasn't a whisper, but it wasn't a proper voice either. I hoped that she would not cry, fear breaking up her voice like twigs underfoot. She sounded as if she were trying to sing through weeping and strangling. She did not pause or stop to end the embarrassment. She kept going until she said the last word, and then she sat down. When it was my turn, the same voice came out, a crippled animal running on broken legs. You could hear splinters in my voice, bones rubbing jagged against one another. I was loud, though. I was glad I didn't whisper. There was one little girl who whispered.

CLASSIC MULTICULTURAL ESSAYS ABOUT

Combating Prejudice

On Being Crazy

W. E. B. DUBOIS

W. E. B. DuBois (1868–1963) was born in 1868 in Great Barrington, Massachusetts. His years in Nashville, Tennessee (Fisk University, B.A., 1888), awakened him to racial prejudice and helped him launch his life's mission—to crusade for the abolishment of distinctions made on the basis of race. At Harvard University (M.A., 1891; Ph.D., 1896), he segregated himself from whites and set his mind to the task at hand—establishing a vanguard for the Civil Rights movement. His book *The Souls of Black Folk: Essays and Sketches* (1903) shocked both the white and black communities. In addition to portrayals of white cruelty and hypocrisy toward blacks, DuBois also attacked some black leaders, such as Booker T. Washington and his vocational training, which, to DuBois, merely perpetuated the caste system. DuBois helped found the National Negro Committee, which later became the National Association for the Advancement of Colored People (NAACP). He used his position as editor of *Crisis*, an NAACP journal, to speak boldly on all issues of the black movement. Becoming disillusioned with the United States, DuBois moved to Ghana in 1960. In 1961, he joined the Communist Party. In 1963, shortly before his death, he became a naturalized citizen of Ghana.

"On Being Crazy" first appeared in *An ABC of Color*. In it, he uses satire to demonstrate how illogical racial prejudice can become. Wherever the narrator turns, he finds whites resisting his presence because, while he wants a meal or a place to sleep, they do not want social equality. The situation achieves absurdity in the narrator's conversation with a white wayfarer on a muddy road.

1   It was one o'clock and I was hungry. I walked into a restaurant, seated myself, and reached for the bill of fare. My table companion rose.

2   "Sir," said he, "do you wish to force your company on those who do not want you?"

3   No, said I, I wish to eat.

4   "Are you aware, sir, that this is social equality?"

5   Nothing of the sort, sir, it is hunger—and I ate.

6   The day's work done, I sought the theatre. As I sank into my seat, the lady shrank and squirmed.

7   I beg pardon, I said.

8   "Do you enjoy being where you are not wanted?" she asked coldly.

9   Oh no, I said.

10   "Well you are not wanted here."

11   I was surprised. I fear you are mistaken, I said, I certainly want the music, and I like to think the music wants me to listen to it.

12   "Usher," said the lady, "this is social equality."

13   "No madame," said the usher, "it is the second movement of Beethoven's Fifth Symphony."

14   After the theatre, I sought the hotel where I had sent my baggage. The clerk scowled.

15   "What do you want?"

16   Rest, I said.

17   "This is a white hotel," he said.

18   I looked around. Such a color scheme requires a great deal of cleaning, I said, but I don't know that I object.

19   "We object," said he.

20   Then why, I began, but he interrupted.

21   "We don't keep niggers," he said, "we don't want social equality."

22   Neither do I, I replied gently, I want a bed.

23   I walked thoughtfully to the train. I'll take a sleeper through Texas. I'm a little bit dissatisfied with this town.

24   "Can't sell you one."

25   I only want to hire it, said I, for a couple of nights.

26   "Can't sell you a sleeper in Texas," he maintained. "They consider that social equality."

27   I consider it barbarism, I said, and I think I'll walk.

28   Walking, I met another wayfarer, who immediately walked to the other side of the road, where it was muddy. I asked his reason.

29   "Niggers is dirty," he said.

30   So is mud, said I. Moreover, I am not as dirty as you—yet.

31   "But you're a nigger, ain't you?" he asked.

32   My grandfather was so called.

33   "Well then!" he answered triumphantly.

34   Do you live in the South? I persisted, pleasantly.

35   "Sure," he growled, "and starve there."

36   I should think you and the Negroes should get together and vote out starvation.

37   "We don't let them vote."

38   We? Why not? I said in surprise.

39   "Niggers is too ignorant to vote."

40   But, I said, I am not so ignorant as you.

41   "But you're a nigger."

42   Yes, I'm certainly what you mean by that.

43   "Well then!" he returned, with that curiously inconsequential note of triumph. "Moreover," he said, "I don't want my sister to marry a nigger."

44   I had not seen his sister, so I merely murmured, let her say no.

45   "By God, you shan't marry her, even if she said yes."

46   But—but I don't want to marry her, I answered, a little perturbed at the personal turn.

47   "Why not," he yelled, angrier than ever.

48   Because I'm already married and I rather like my wife.

49   "Is she a nigger?" he asked suspiciously.

50   Well, I said again, her grandmother was called that.

51   "Well then!" he shouted in that oddly illogical way.

52   I gave up.

53   Go on, I said, either you are crazy or I am.

54   "We both are," he said as he trotted along in the mud.

from *A Long Way to Go*

ROSA PARKS

Rosa Parks was born in 1913 and lived in the quiet rural town of Pine Level, Alabama, yet she motivated a great social upheaval in 1955 when the Montgomery police arrested her for refusing to give up her bus seat to a white man. Dr. Martin Luther King, Jr., came to her defense, organized the blacks of the city in a boycott of the bus line, and eventually forced the city to desegregate the buses.

A Long Way to Go is Parks's celebration of the degree of freedom now found in the United States, but it also explains that "we still have a long way to go" as long as a person's race causes a trace of prejudice. The excerpt reprinted here uses the Statue of Liberty as a symbol of both freedom and bondage. When Parks was in school, the statue represented freedom, equality, and the pursuit of happiness, but, she says, "we had to face the fact that we were not as free as the books said." Years later, when visiting the statue during a trip to New York, she recognized again that *her* forefathers had never passed under the welcoming arm of Miss Liberty.

1   When I was coming up, I went to a one-room country school in Pine Level, Alabama, where all the pupils and the teachers were black. In the sixth grade, my mother sent me to Montgomery, where

I went to the Montgomery Industrial School, which was run by Miss Alice White. She was a very proper older woman who ran the school with a group of Northern white ladies who were sympathetic to the plight of Negroes. That's what they called us back then.

2   In school, we learned all of the civics lessons that children were supposed to learn. We had to memorize Abraham Lincoln's Gettysburg Address and portions of the Constitution. We recited the Pledge of Allegiance. We studied all of the Presidents—Washington, Jefferson, Lincoln—and we knew about all the wars.

3   I guess for most of us children, the Statue of Liberty was just something we read about in a civics book. We learned that poem about the statue, but it was just another lesson we had to recite, just like the Civil War poem about the Blue and the Gray, or the Gettysburg Address.

4   The Africans who came over on the slave ships never saw the statue. Of course, they didn't mention that in the history books. The studies we did in our books were based on freedom and equality and the pursuit of happiness and all. But in reality we had to face the fact that we were not as free as the books said. What they taught us in school didn't apply to us as a race. We were being told to be as submissive and as useful as possible to white people, to do their work and see to their comforts and be segregated from them when they saw fit for us not to be around.

5   Even Miss Alice White, who had all the best intentions in the world, was part of the system. In her lectures, she would tell us how horrible slavery was, but then she would say that at least it brought the Negro out of savagery in Africa. Of course, none of those slave traders ever asked the Africans whether they wanted to come to America. I imagine that if the Africans had come around after the statue was built, they would have had some terrible ideas about what it meant to them. I don't think they would have written any poems.

6   My family knew the brutality and disillusionment of not being treated like human beings. My grandfather was a slave. He was the son of the plantation owner, so he was very white in appearance. My grandfather used to say that the overseer took an instant dislike to him because he looked so white. He would always tell me how he had to dodge and hide to keep out of trouble with the overseer. Until the day he died, my grandfather had a fierce hatred of white people.

7   My mother had a mind of her own. She always held to the belief

that none of us should be mistreated because of our race. She was
pretty outspoken, and of course that didn't endear her to too many
whites. It didn't endear her to too many blacks, either, because in
those days the general attitude among our people was to go along
in silence. If you differed with that, you had to stand pretty much
alone.

8   I remember that one of the first books I read, back when I was
eight years old, was called *Is the Negro a Beast?* That was the kind
of attitude that white people had in Alabama in those days. It was
so different from what we were reading about in our American history
and civics lessons, with all the positive messages about life in this
country, and I could see that what we were being taught wasn't so,
at least as far as black people were concerned.

9   It didn't change much when I was working. I encountered all
kinds of discrimination. If you were black in the South, it was just
something you lived with all the time. I would just meet it in silence,
bite my lip, go on. I saw it a lot with the bus drivers. If they thought
you were about to make trouble, they would just shut the door on
you and drive on off. In fact, the same red-headed driver who arrested
me in 1955 [starting the Montgomery bus boycott led by Martin
Luther King] had evicted me from a bus in 1943. He didn't want
me to walk through the white section of the bus to get to the section
for blacks, and I told him I wasn't going to get off the bus while I
was already on. He took me by the sleeve of my winter coat and led
me off. When I got on his bus again twelve years later, I remembered
him very well, but I didn't expect him to disturb me a second time.

10   I didn't actually get to see the Statue of Liberty until about a year
after the boycott. By that time, my attitude was a little different. I
thought that saying—"Give me your tired, your poor . . ."—was
impressive, that we should help people who come to the United
States. This was a better place than where they had been.

11   I was invited to come to New York by Dr. Ralph Bunche and
met him at the United Nations. I stayed with a Quaker couple, Mr.
and Mrs. Stuart Meacham, who lived on Franklin D. Roosevelt Drive
in Manhattan, right on the East River. Mr. Meacham asked me what
was the first thing I wanted to do in New York. I told him, to see
the Statue of Liberty. I had always been fascinated by tall buildings
and monuments.

12   We went across the water by ferry about noon. It was just the

way I thought it would be, that big arm waving the torch high above everything. We walked up all those stairs to the very top, right in the crown. We looked out from the windows in the crown, and we could see for miles. When we went back down, Mr. Meacham took my picture at the foot of the statue.

13   I guess the statue should be a symbol of freedom. I would not want our young people to be so disillusioned that they couldn't feel a sense of awe about it. But I can't find myself getting overwhelmed. We are supposed to be loyal and dedicated and committed to what America stands for. But we are still being denied complete equality. We have to struggle to gain a little bit, and as soon as it seems we make some gains for all our sacrifices, there are new obstacles, and people trying to take away what little we have.

14   Certainly there is a degree of freedom in America that we can celebrate, but as long as a difference in your complexion or your background can be used against you, we still have a long way to go.

Letter from Birmingham Jail[1]

MARTIN LUTHER KING, JR.

Martin Luther King, Jr. (1929–1968) was born in Atlanta, the son of a minister and a teacher. He earned a B.A. at Morehouse College in 1948; a B.D. at Crozer Theological Seminary in 1951; a Ph.D. from Boston University in 1955; and a D.D. from Chicago Theological Seminary in 1957. He became an ordained minister and served as pastor at Dexter Avenue Baptist Church in Montgomery, Alabama. King founded the Southern Christian Leadership Conference in 1957. From that point on, his deeds and his honors escalated, including *Time* Man of the Year, 1953; Nobel Prize for Peace, 1964; and the Presidential Medal of Freedom, 1967.

His most famous writing is probably his "I Have a Dream" speech, but "Letter from Birmingham Jail" also holds a significant position in his writings. In 1963, King spearheaded a movement in Birmingham that brought his nonviolent methods to the forefront.

[1]This response to a published statement by eight fellow clergymen from Alabama (Bishop C. C. J. Carpenter, Bishop Joseph A. Durick, Rabbi Hilton L. Grafman, Bishop Paul Hardin, Bishop Holan B. Harmon, the Reverend George M. Murray, the Reverend Edward V. Ramage and the Reverend Earl Stallings) was composed under somewhat constricting circumstances. Begun on the margins of the newspaper in which the statement appeared while I was in jail, the letter was continued on scraps of writing paper supplied by a friendly Negro trusty, and concluded on a pad my attorneys were eventually permitted to leave me. Although the text remains in substance unaltered, I have indulged in the author's prerogative of polishing it for publication.

King used children and teenagers on the front lines of demonstrations. As they suffered from fire hoses and police dogs, media reports led to outrage at police tactics and support for King's cause. King, who spent time in jail during this campaign, wrote this letter in protest at injustice; he explained his philosophy of nonviolence, arguing that "injustice anywhere is a threat to justice everywhere. We are caught in an inescapable network of mutuality, tied in a single garment of destiny."

MY DEAR FELLOW CLERGYMEN:

1   While confined here in the Birmingham city jail, I came across your recent statement calling my present activities "unwise and untimely." Seldom do I pause to answer criticism of my work and ideas. If I sought to answer all the criticisms that cross my desk, my secretaries would have little time for anything other than such correspondence in the course of the day, and I would have no time for constructive work. But since I feel that you are men of genuine good will and that your criticisms are sincerely set forth, I want to try to answer your statement in what I hope will be patient and reasonable terms.

2   I think I should indicate why I am here in Birmingham, since you have been influenced by the view which argues against "outsiders coming in." I have the honor of serving as president of the Southern Christian Leadership Conference, an organization operating in every southern state, with headquarters in Atlanta, Georgia. We have some eighty-five affiliated organizations across the South, and one of them is the Alabama Christian Movement for Human Rights. Frequently we share staff, educational, and financial resources with our affiliates. Several months ago the affiliate here in Birmingham asked us to be on call to engage in a nonviolent direct-action program if such were deemed necessary. We readily consented, and when the hour came, we lived up to our promise. So I, along with several members of my staff, am here because I was invited here. I am here because I have organizational ties here.

3   But more basically, I am in Birmingham because injustice is here.

Just as the prophets of the eighth century B.C. left their villages and
carried their "thus saith the Lord" far beyond the boundaries of
their home towns, and just as the Apostle Paul left his village of
Tarsus and carried the gospel of Jesus Christ to the far corners of
the Greco-Roman world, so am I compelled to carry the gospel of
freedom beyond my own home town. Like Paul, I must constantly
respond to the Macedonian call for aid.

4   Moreover, I am cognizant of the interrelatedness of all communities and states. I cannot sit idly by in Atlanta and not be concerned
about what happens in Birmingham. Injustice anywhere is a threat
to justice everywhere. We are caught in an inescapable network of
mutuality, tied in a single garment of destiny. Whatever affects one
directly, affects all indirectly. Never again can we afford to live with
the narrow, provincial "outside agitator" idea. Anyone who lives
inside the United States can never be considered an outsider anywhere within its bounds.

5   You deplore the demonstrations taking place in Birmingham. But
your statement, I am sorry to say, fails to express a similar concern
for the conditions that brought about the demonstrations. I am sure
that none of you would want to rest content with the superficial
kind of social analysis that deals merely with effects and does not
grapple with underlying causes. It is unfortunate that demonstrations
are taking place in Birmingham, but it is even more unfortunate that
the city's white power structure left the Negro community with no
alternative.

6   In any nonviolent campaign there are four basic steps: collection
of the facts to determine whether injustices exist; negotiation; self-
purification; and direct action. We have gone through all these steps
in Birmingham. There can be no gainsaying the fact that racial injustice engulfs this community. Birmingham is probably the most thoroughly segregated city in the United States. Its ugly record of
brutality is widely known. Negroes have experienced grossly unjust
treatment in the courts. There have been more unsolved bombings
of Negro homes and churches in Birmingham than in any other city
in the nation. These are the hard, brutal facts of the case. On the
basis of these conditions, Negro leaders sought to negotiate with
the city fathers. But the latter consistently refused to engage in good-
faith negotiation.

7   Then, last September, came the opportunity to talk with leaders
of Birmingham's economic community. In the course of the negotia-

tions, certain promises were made by the merchants—for example, to remove the stores' humiliating racial signs. On the basis of these promises, the Reverend Fred Shuttlesworth and the leaders of the Alabama Christian Movement for Human Rights agreed to a moratorium on all demonstrations. As the weeks and months went by, we realized that we were the victims of a broken promise. A few signs, briefly removed, returned; the others remained.

8   As in so many past experiences, our hopes had been blasted, and the shadow of deep disappointment settled upon us. We had no alternative except to prepare for direct action, whereby we would present our very bodies as a means of laying our case before the conscience of the local and the national community. Mindful of the difficulties involved, we decided to undertake a process of self-purification. We began a series of workshops on nonviolence, and we repeatedly asked ourselves: "Are you able to accept blows without retaliating?" "Are you able to endure the ordeal of jail?" We decided to schedule our direct-action program for the Easter season, realizing that except for Christmas, this is the main shopping period of the year. Knowing that a strong economic-withdrawal program would be the by product of direct action, we felt that this would be the best time to bring pressure to bear on the merchants for the needed change.

9   Then it occurred to us that Birmingham's mayoral election was coming up in March, and we speedily decided to postpone action until after election day. When we discovered that the Commissioner of Public Safety, Eugene "Bull" Connor, had piled up enough votes to be in the run-off, we decided again to postpone action until the day after the run-off so that the demonstrations could not be used to cloud the issues. Like many others, we waited to see Mr. Connor defeated, and to this end we endured postponement after postponement. Having aided in this community need, we felt that our direct-action program could be delayed no longer.

10   You may well ask, "Why direct action? Why sit-ins, marches, and so forth? Isn't negotiation a better path?" You are quite right in calling for negotiation. Indeed, this is the very purpose of direct action. Nonviolent direct action seeks to create such a crisis and foster such a tension that a community which has constantly refused to negotiate is forced to confront the issue. It seeks so to dramatize the issue that it can no longer be ignored. My citing the creation of tension as part of the work of the nonviolent-resister may sound rather shocking. But I must confess that I am not afraid of the word

"tension." I have earnestly opposed violent tension, but there is a type of constructive, nonviolent tension which is necessary for growth. Just as Socrates felt that it was necessary to create a tension in the mind so that individuals could rise from the bondage of myths and half-truths to the unfettered realm of creative analysis and objective appraisal, so must we see the need for nonviolent gadflies to create the kind of tension in society that will help men rise from the dark depths of prejudice and racism to the majestic heights of understanding and brotherhood.

11   The purpose of our direct-action program is to create a situation so crisis-packed that it will inevitably open the door to negotiation. I therefore concur with you in your call for negotiation. Too long has our beloved Southland been bogged down in a tragic effort to live in monologue rather than dialogue.

12   One of the basic points in your statement is that the action that I and my associates have taken in Birmingham is untimely. Some have asked: "Why didn't you give the new city administration time to act?" The only answer that I can give to this query is that the new Birmingham administration must be prodded about as much as the outgoing one, before it will act. We are sadly mistaken if we feel that the election of Albert Boutwell as mayor will bring the millennium to Birmingham. While Mr. Boutwell is a much more gentle person than Mr. Connor, they are both segregationists, dedicated to maintenance of the status quo. I have hoped that Mr. Boutwell will be reasonable enough to see the futility of massive resistance to desegregation. But he will not see this without pressure from devotees of civil rights. My friends, I must say to you that we have not made a single gain in civil rights without determined legal and nonviolent pressure. Lamentably, it is an historical fact that privileged groups seldom give up their privileges voluntarily. Individuals may see the moral light and voluntarily give up their unjust posture; but, as Reinhold Niebuhr has reminded us, groups tend to be more immoral than individuals.

13   We know through painful experience that freedom is never voluntarily given by the oppressor; it must be demanded by the oppressed. Frankly, I have yet to engage in a direct-action campaign that was "well timed" in the view of those who have not suffered unduly from the disease of segregation. For years now I have heard the word "Wait!" It rings in the ear of every Negro with piercing familiarity. This "Wait" has almost always meant "Never." We must come to

see, with one of our distinguished jurists, that "justice too long delayed is justice denied."

14   We have waited for more than 340 years for our constitutional and God-given rights. The nations of Asia and Africa are moving with jetlike speed toward gaining political independence, but we still creep at horse-and-buggy pace toward gaining a cup of coffee at a lunch counter. Perhaps it is easy for those who have never felt the stinging darts of segregation to say, "Wait." But when you have seen vicious mobs lynch your mothers and fathers at will and drown your sisters and brothers at whim; when you have seen hate-filled policemen curse, kick, and even kill your black brothers and sisters; when you see the vast majority of your twenty million Negro brothers smothering in an airtight cage of poverty in the midst of an affluent society; when you suddenly find your tongue twisted and your speech stammering as you seek to explain to your six-year-old daughter why she can't go to the public amusement park that has just been advertised on television, and see tears welling up in her eyes when she is told that Funtown is closed to colored children, and see ominous clouds of inferiority beginning to form in her little mental sky, and see her beginning to distort her personality by developing an unconscious bitterness toward white people; when you have to concoct an answer for a five-year-old son who is asking, "Daddy, why do white people treat colored people so mean?"; when you take a cross-country drive and find it necessary to sleep night after night in the uncomfortable corners of your automobile because no motel will accept you; when you are humiliated day in and day out by nagging signs reading "white" and "colored"; when your first name becomes "nigger," your middle name becomes "boy" (however old you are) and your last name becomes "John," and your wife and mother are never given the respected title "Mrs."; when you are harried by day and haunted by night by the fact that you are a Negro, living constantly at tiptoe stance, never quite knowing what to expect next, and are plagued with inner fears and outer resentments; when you are forever fighting a degenerating sense of "nobodiness"—then you will understand why we find it difficult to wait. There comes a time when the cup of endurance runs over, and men are no longer willing to be plunged into the abyss of despair. I hope, sirs, you can understand our legitimate and unavoidable impatience.

15   You express a great deal of anxiety over our willingness to break laws. This is certainly a legitimate concern. Since we so diligently

urge people to obey the Supreme Court's decision of 1954 outlawing segregation in the public schools, at first glance it may seem rather paradoxical for us consciously to break laws. One may well ask: "How can you advocate breaking some laws and obeying others?" The answer lies in the fact that there are two types of laws: just and unjust. I would be the first to advocate obeying just laws. One has not only a legal but a moral responsibility to obey just laws. Conversely, one has a moral responsibility to disobey unjust laws. I would agree with St. Augustine that "an unjust law is no law at all."

16   Now, what is the difference between the two? How does one determine whether a law is just or unjust? A just law is a man-made code that squares with the moral law or the law of God. An unjust law is a code that is out of harmony with the moral law. To put it in the terms of St. Thomas Aquinas: An unjust law is a human law that is not rooted in eternal law and natural law. Any law that uplifts human personality is just. Any law that degrades human personality is unjust. All segregation statutes are unjust because segregation distorts the soul and damages the personality. It gives the segregator a false sense of superiority and the segregated a false sense of inferiority. Segregation, to use the terminology of the Jewish philosopher Martin Buber, substitutes an "I-it" relationship for an "I-thou" relationship and ends up relegating persons to the status of things. Hence segregation is not only politically, economically, and sociologically unsound, it is morally wrong and sinful. Paul Tillich has said that sin is separation. Is not segregation an existential expression of man's tragic separation, his awful estrangement, his terrible sinfulness? Thus it is that I can urge men to obey the 1954 decision of the Supreme Court, for it is morally right; and I can urge them to disobey segregation ordinances, for they are morally wrong.

17   Let us consider a more concrete example of just and unjust laws. An unjust law is a code that a numerical or power majority group compels a minority group to obey but does not make binding on itself. This is *difference* made legal. By the same token, a just law is a code that a majority compels a minority to follow and that it is willing to follow itself. This is *sameness* made legal.

18   Let me give another explanation. A law is unjust if it is inflicted on a minority that, as a result of being denied the right to vote, had no part in enacting or devising the law. Who can say that the legislature of Alabama which set up the state's segregation laws was democratically elected? Throughout Alabama all sorts of devious methods are used

to prevent Negroes from becoming registered voters, and there are some counties in which, even though Negroes constitute a majority of the population, not a single Negro is registered. Can any law enacted under such circumstances be considered democratically structured?

19   Sometimes a law is just on its face and unjust in its application. For instance, I have been arrested on a charge of parading without a permit. Now, there is nothing wrong in having an ordinance which requires a permit for a parade. But such an ordinance becomes unjust when it is used to maintain segregation and to deny citizens the First-Amendment privilege of peaceful assembly and protest.

20   I hope you are able to see the distinction I am trying to point out. In no sense do I advocate evading or defying the law, as would the rabid segregationist. That would lead to anarchy. One who breaks an unjust law must do so openly, lovingly, and with a willingness to accept the penalty. I submit that an individual who breaks a law that conscience tells him is unjust, and who willingly accepts the penalty of imprisonment in order to arouse the conscience of the community over its injustice, is in reality expressing the highest respect for law.

21   Of course, there is nothing new about this kind of civil disobedience. It was evidenced sublimely in the refusal of Shadrach, Meschach, and Abednego to obey the laws of Nebuchadnezzar, on the ground that a higher moral law was at stake. It was practiced superbly by the early Christians, who were willing to face hungry lions and the excruciating pain of chopping blocks rather than submit to certain unjust laws of the Roman Empire. To a degree, academic freedom is a reality today because Socrates practiced civil disobedience. In our own nation, the Boston Tea Party represented a massive act of civil disobedience.

22   We should never forget that everything Adolf Hitler did in Germany was "legal" and everything the Hungarian freedom fighters did in Hungary was "illegal." It was "illegal" to aid and comfort a Jew in Hitler's Germany. Even so, I am sure that, had I lived in Germany at the time, I would have aided and comforted my Jewish brothers. If today I lived in a Communist country where certain principles dear to the Christian faith are suppressed, I would openly advocate disobeying that country's antireligious laws.

23   I must make two honest confessions to you, my Christian and Jewish brothers. First, I must confess that over the past few years I have been gravely disappointed with the white moderate. I have

almost reached the regrettable conclusion that the Negro's great stumbling block in his stride toward freedom is not the White Citizen's Counciler or the Ku Klux Klanner, but the white moderate, who is more devoted to "order" than to justice; who prefers a negative peace which is the absence of tension to a positive peace which is the presence of justice; who constantly says, "I agree with you in the goal you seek, but I cannot agree with your methods of direct action"; who paternalistically believes he can set the timetable for another man's freedom; who lives by a mythical concept of time and who constantly advises the Negro to wait for a "more convenient season." Shallow understanding from people of good will is more frustrating than absolute misunderstanding from people of ill will. Lukewarm acceptance is much more bewildering than outright rejection.

24   I had hoped that the white moderate would understand that law and order exist for the purpose of establishing justice and that when they fail in this purpose they become the dangerously structured dams that block the flow of social progress. I had hoped that the white moderate would understand that the present tension in the South is a necessary phase of the transition from an obnoxious negative peace, in which the Negro passively accepted his unjust plight, to a substantive and positive peace, in which all men will respect the dignity and worth of human personality. Actually, we who engage in nonviolent direct action are not the creators of tension. We merely bring to the surface the hidden tension that is already alive. We bring it out in the open, where it can be seen and dealt with. Like a boil that can never be cured so long as it is covered up but must be opened with all its ugliness to the natural medicines of air and light, injustice must be exposed, with all the tension its exposure creates, to the light of human conscience and the air of national opinion, before it can be cured.

25   In your statement you assert that our actions, even though peaceful, must be condemned because they precipitate violence. But is this a logical assertion? Isn't this like condemning a robbed man because his possession of money precipitated the evil act of robbery? Isn't this like condemning Socrates because his unswerving commitment to truth and his philosophical inquiries precipitated the act by the misguided populace in which they made him drink hemlock? Isn't this like condemning Jesus because his unique God-consciousness and never-ceasing devotion to God's will precipitated the evil

act of crucifixion? We must come to see that, as the federal courts have consistently affirmed, it is wrong to urge an individual to cease his efforts to gain his basic constitutional rights because the quest may precipitate violence. Society must protect the robbed and punish the robber.

26   I had also hoped that the white moderate would reject the myth concerning time in relation to the struggle for freedom. I have just received a letter from a white brother in Texas. He writes: "All Christians know that the colored people will receive equal rights eventually, but it is possible that you are in too great a religious hurry. It has taken Christianity almost two thousand years to accomplish what it has. The teachings of Christ take time to come to earth." Such an attitude stems from a tragic misconception of time, from the strangely irrational notion that there is something in the very flow of time that will inevitably cure all ills. Actually, time itself is neutral; it can be used either destructively or constructively. More and more I feel that the people of ill will have used time much more effectively than have the people of good will. We will have to repent in this generation not merely for the hateful words and actions of the bad people, but for the appalling silence of the good people. Human progress never rolls in on wheels of inevitability; it comes through the tireless efforts of men willing to be co-workers with God, and without this hard work, time itself becomes an ally of the forces of social stagnation. We must use time creatively, in the knowledge that the time is always ripe to do right. Now is the time to make real the promise of democracy and transform our pending national elegy into a creative psalm of brotherhood. Now is the time to lift our national policy from the quicksand of racial injustice to the solid rock of human dignity.

27   You speak of our activity in Birmingham as extreme. At first I was rather disappointed that fellow clergymen would see my nonviolent efforts as those of an extremist. I began thinking about the fact that I stand in the middle of two opposing forces in the Negro community. One is a force of complacency, made up in part of Negroes who, as a result of long years of oppression, are so drained of self-respect and a sense of "somebodiness" that they have adjusted to segregation; and in part of a few middle-class Negroes who, because of a degree of academic and economic security and because in some ways they profit by segregation, have become insensitive to the problems of the masses. The other force is one of bitterness and hatred, and

it comes perilously close to advocating violence. It is expressed in the various black nationalist groups that are springing up across the nation, the largest and best-known being Elijah Muhammad's Muslim movement. Nourished by the Negro's frustration over the continued existence of racial discrimination, this movement is made up of people who have lost faith in America, who have absolutely repudiated Christianity, and who have concluded that the white man is an incorrigible "devil."

28   I have tried to stand between these two forces, saying that we need emulate neither the "do-nothingism" of the complacent nor the hatred and despair of the black nationalist. For there is the more excellent way of love and nonviolent protest. I am grateful to God that, through the influence of the Negro church, the way of nonviolence became an integral part of our struggle.

29   If this philosophy had not emerged, by now many streets of the South would, I am convinced, be flowing with blood. And I am further convinced that if our white brothers dismiss as "rabble-rousers" and "outside agitators" those of us who employ nonviolent direct action, and if they refuse to support our nonviolent efforts, millions of Negroes will, out of frustration and despair, seek solace and security in black-nationalist ideologies—a development that would inevitably lead to a frightening racial nightmare.

30   Oppressed people cannot remain oppressed forever. The yearning for freedom eventually manifests itself, and that is what has happened to the American Negro. Something within has reminded him of his birthright of freedom, and something without has reminded him that it can be gained. Consciously or unconsciously, he has been caught up by the *Zeitgeist*, and with his black brothers of Africa and his brown and yellow brothers of Asia, South America, and the Caribbean, the United States Negro is moving with a sense of great urgency toward the promised land of racial justice. If one recognizes this vital urge that has engulfed the Negro community, one should readily understand why public demonstrations are taking place. The Negro has many pent-up resentments and latent frustrations, and he must release them. So let him march; let him make prayer pilgrimages to the city hall; let him go on freedom rides—and try to understand why he must do so. If his repressed emotions are not released in nonviolent ways, they will seek expression through violence; this is not a threat but a fact of history. So I have not said to my people, "Get rid of your discontent." Rather, I have tried to say that this

normal and healthy discontent can be channeled into the creative outlet of nonviolent direct action. And now this approach is being termed extremist.

31   But though I was initially disappointed at being categorized as an extremist, as I continued to think about the matter I gradually gained a measure of satisfaction from the label. Was not Jesus an extremist for love: "Love your enemies, bless them that curse you, do good to them that hate you, and pray for them which despitefully use you, and persecute you." Was not Amos an extremist for justice: "Let justice roll down like waters and righteousness like an everflowing stream." Was not Paul an extremist for the Christian gospel: "I bear in my body the marks of the Lord Jesus." Was not Martin Luther an extremist: "Here I stand; I cannot do otherwise, so help me God." And John Bunyan: "I will stay in jail to the end of my days before I make a butchery of my conscience." And Abraham Lincoln: "This nation cannot survive half slave and half free." And Thomas Jefferson: "We hold these truths to be self-evident, that all men are created equal. . . ." So the question is not whether we will be extremists, but what kind of extremists we will be. Will we be extremists for hate or for love? Will we be extremists for the preservation of injustice or for the extension of justice? In that dramatic scene on Calvary's hill three men were crucified. We must never forget that all three were crucified for the same crime—the crime of extremism. Two were extremists for immorality, and thus fell below their environment. The other, Jesus Christ, was an extremist for love, truth, and goodness, and thereby rose above his environment. Perhaps the South, the nation, and the world are in dire need of creative extremists.

32   I had hoped that the white moderate would see this need. Perhaps I was too optimistic; perhaps I expected too much. I suppose I should have realized that few members of the oppressor race can understand the deep groans and passionate yearnings of the oppressed race, and still fewer have the vision to see that injustice must be rooted out by strong, persistent, and determined action. I am thankful, however, that some of our white brothers in the South have grasped the meaning of this social revolution and committed themselves to it. They are still all too few in quantity, but they are big in quality. Some—such as Ralph McGill, Lillian Smith, Harry Golden, James McBride Dabbs, Anne Braden, and Sarah Patton Boyle—have written about our struggle in eloquent and prophetic terms. Others have

marched with us down nameless streets of the South. They have languished in filthy, roach-infested jails, suffering the abuse and brutality of policemen who view them as "dirty nigger-lovers." Unlike so many of their moderate brothers and sisters, they have recognized the urgency of the moment and sensed the need for powerful "action" antidotes to combat the disease of segregation.

33   Let me take note of my other major disappointment. I have been so greatly disappointed with the white church and its leadership. Of course, there are some notable exceptions. I am not unmindful of the fact that each of you has taken some significant stands on this issue. I commend you, Reverend Stallings, for your Christian stand on this past Sunday, in welcoming Negroes to your worship service on a nonsegregated basis. I commend the Catholic leaders of this state for integrating Spring Hill College several years ago.

34   But despite these notable exceptions, I must honestly reiterate that I have been disappointed with the church. I do not say this as one of those negative critics who can always find something wrong with the church. I say this as a minister of the gospel, who loves the church; who was nurtured in its bosom; who has been sustained by its spiritual blessings and who will remain true to it as long as the cord of life shall lengthen.

35   When I was suddenly catapulted into the leadership of the bus protest in Montgomery, Alabama, a few years ago, I felt we would be supported by the white church. I felt that the white ministers, priests, and rabbis of the South would be among our strongest allies. Instead, some have been outright opponents, refusing to understand the freedom movement and misrepresenting its leaders; all too many others have been more cautious than courageous and have remained silent behind the anesthetizing security of stained glass windows.

36   In spite of my shattered dreams, I came to Birmingham with the hope that the white religious leadership of this community would see the justice of our cause and, with deep moral concern, would serve as the channel through which our just grievances could reach the power structure. I had hoped that each of you would understand. But again I have been disappointed.

37   I have heard numerous southern religious leaders admonish their worshipers to comply with a desegregation decision because it is the law, but I have longed to hear white ministers declare: "Follow this decree because integration is morally right and because the Negro is your brother." In the midst of blatant injustices inflicted upon the

Negro, I have watched white churchmen stand on the sideline and mouth pious irrelevancies and sanctimonious trivialities. In the midst of a mighty struggle to rid our nation of racial and economic injustice I have heard many ministers say: "Those are social issues, with which the gospel has no real concern." And I have watched many churches commit themselves to a completely otherworldly religion which makes a strange, un-Biblical distinction between body and soul, between the sacred and the secular.

38　　I have traveled the length and breadth of Alabama, Mississippi, and all the other southern states. On sweltering summer days and crisp autumn mornings I have looked at the South's beautiful churches with their lofty spires pointing heavenward. I have beheld the impressive outlines of her massive religious-education buildings. Over and over I have found myself asking: "What kind of people worship here? Who is their God? Where were their voices when the lips of Governor Barnett dripped with words of interposition and nullification? Where were they when Governor Wallace gave a clarion call for defiance and hatred? Where were their voices of support when bruised and weary Negro men and women decided to rise from the dark dungeons of complacency to the bright hills of creative protest?"

39　　Yes, these questions are still in my mind. In deep disappointment I have wept over the laxity of the church. But be assured that my tears have been tears of love. There can be no deep disappointment where there is not deep love. Yes, I love the church. How could I do otherwise? I am in the rather unique position of being the son, the grandson, and the great-grandson of preachers. Yes, I see the church as the body of Christ. But, oh! How we have blemished and scarred that body through social neglect and through fear of being nonconformists.

40　　There was a time when the church was very powerful—in the time when the early Christians rejoiced at being deemed worthy to suffer for what they believed. In those days the church was not merely a thermometer that recorded the ideas and principles of popular opinion; it was a thermostat that transformed the mores of society. Whenever the early Christians entered a town, the people in power became disturbed and immediately sought to convict the Christians for being "disturbers of the peace" and "outside agitators." But the Christians pressed on, in the conviction that they were "a colony of heaven," called to obey God rather than man. Small in number, they were big in commitment. They were too God-intoxicated to be "astro-

nomically intimidated." By their effort and example they brought
an end to such ancient evils as infanticide and gladiatorial contests.

41   Things are different now. So often the contemporary church is a
weak, ineffectual voice with an uncertain sound. So often it is an
archdefender of the status quo. Far from being disturbed by the
presence of the church, the power structure of the average community
is consoled by the church's silent—and often even vocal—sanction
of things as they are.

42   But the judgment of God is upon the church as never before. If
today's church does not recapture the sacrificial spirit of the early
church, it will lose its authenticity, forfeit the loyalty of millions, and
be dismissed as an irrelevant social club with no meaning for the
twentieth century. Every day I meet young people whose disappointment with the church has turned into outright disgust.

43   Perhaps I have once again been too optimistic. Is organized religion too inextricably bound to the status quo to save our nation and
the world? Perhaps I must turn my faith to the inner spiritual church,
the church within the church, as the true *ekklesia* and the hope of
the world. But again I am thankful to God that some noble souls
from the ranks of organized religion have broken loose from the
paralyzing chains of conformity and joined us as active partners in
the struggle for freedom. They have left their secure congregations
and walked the streets of Albany, Georgia, with us. They have gone
down the highways of the South on tortuous rides for freedom. Yes,
they have gone to jail with us. Some have been dismissed from their
churches, have lost the support of their bishops and fellow ministers.
But they have acted in the faith that right defeated is stronger than
evil triumphant. Their witness has been the spiritual salt that has
preserved the true meaning of the gospel in these troubled times.
They have carved a tunnel of hope through the dark mountain of
disappointment.

44   I hope the church as a whole will meet the challenge of this
decisive hour. But even if the church does not come to the aid of
justice, I have no despair about the future. I have no fear about the
outcome of our struggle in Birmingham, even if our motives are
at present misunderstood. We will reach the goal of freedom in
Birmingham and all over the nation, because the goal of America is
freedom. Abused and scorned though we may be, our destiny is tied
up with America's destiny. Before the pilgrims landed at Plymouth,
we were here. Before the pen of Jefferson etched the majestic words

of the Declaration of Independence across the pages of history, we were here. For more than two centuries our forebears labored in this country without wages; they made cotton king; they built the homes of their masters while suffering gross injustice and shameful humilia-tion—and yet out of a bottomless vitality they continued to thrive and develop. If the inexpressible cruelties of slavery could not stop us, the opposition we now face will surely fail. We will win our freedom because the sacred heritage of our nation and the eternal will of God are embodied in our echoing demands.

45   Before closing I feel impelled to mention one other point in your statement that has troubled me profoundly. You warmly commended the Birmingham police force for keeping "order" and "preventing violence." I doubt that you would have so warmly commended the police force if you had seen its dogs sinking their teeth into unarmed, nonviolent Negroes. I doubt that you would so quickly commend the policemen if you were to observe their ugly and inhumane treat-ment of Negroes here in the city jail; if you were to watch them push and curse old Negro women and young Negro girls; if you were to see them slap and kick old Negro men and young boys; if you were to observe them, as they did on two occasions, refuse to give us food because we wanted to sing our grace together. I cannot join you in your praise of the Birmingham police department.

46   It is true that the police have exercised a degree of discipline in handling the demonstrators. In this sense they have conducted themselves rather "nonviolently" in public. But for what purpose? To preserve the evil system of segregation. Over the past few years I have consistently preached that nonviolence demands that the means we use must be as pure as the ends we seek. I have tried to make clear that it is wrong to use immoral means to attain moral ends. But not I must affirm that it is just as wrong, or perhaps even more so, to use moral means to preserve immoral ends. Perhaps Mr. Connor and his policemen have been rather nonviolent in public, as was Chief Pritchett in Albany, Georgia, but they have used the moral means of nonviolence to maintain the immoral end of racial injustice. As T. S. Eliot has said, "The last temptation is the greatest treason: To do the right deed for the wrong reason."

47   I wish you had commended the Negro sit-inners and demonstra-tors of Birmingham for their sublime courage, their willingness to suffer, and their amazing discipline in the midst of great provocation. One day the South will recognize its real heroes. They will be the

James Merediths, with the noble sense of purpose that enables them to face jeering and hostile mobs, and with the agonizing loneliness that characterizes the life of the pioneer. They will be old, oppressed, battered Negro women, symbolized in a seventy-two-year-old woman in Montgomery, Alabama, who rose up with a sense of dignity and with her people decided not to ride segregated buses, and who responded with ungrammatical profundity to one who inquired about her weariness: "My feets is tired, but my soul is at rest." They will be the young high school and college students, the young ministers of the gospel and a host of their elders, courageously and nonviolently sitting in at lunch counters and willingly going to jail for conscience' sake. One day the South will know that when these disinherited children of God sat down at lunch counters, they were in reality standing up for what is best in the American dream and for the most sacred values in our Judaeo-Christian heritage, thereby bringing our nation back to those great wells of democracy which were dug deep by the founding fathers in their formulation of the Constitution and the Declaration of Independence.

48   Never before have I written so long a letter. I'm afraid it is much too long to take your precious time. I can assure you that it would have been much shorter if I had been writing from a comfortable desk, but what else can one do when he is alone in a narrow jail cell, other than write long letters, think long thoughts, and pray long prayers?

49   If I have said anything in this letter that overstates the truth and indicates an unreasonable impatience, I beg you to forgive me. If I have said anything that understates the truth and indicates my having a patience that allows me to settle for anything less than brotherhood, I beg God to forgive me.

50   I hope this letter finds you strong in the faith. I also hope that circumstances will soon make it possible for me to meet each of you, not as an integrationist or a civil-rights leader but as a fellow clergyman and a Christian brother. Let us all hope that the dark clouds of racial prejudice will soon pass away and the deep fog of misunderstanding will be lifted from our fear-drenched communities, and in some not too distant tomorrow the radiant stars of love and brotherhood will shine over our great nation with all their scintillating beauty.

Yours for the cause of Peace and Brotherhood,
MARTIN LUTHER KING, JR.

I'm Black, You're White, Who's Innocent?

SHELBY STEELE

Shelby Steele, who was born in 1946, exploded on the American conscience in 1990 with his book *The Content of Our Character: A New Vision of Race in America*. A professor at San Jose State University, he challenges both the black establishment and white supremacists. He argues that blacks have failed to achieve social equality because, in part, they prefer a second-class status so they can protest and complain about their condition. He condemns affirmative action because it keeps the recipients in a subservient role. Despite critics of his view, Steele won several awards for the book, including a National Book Critics Circle Award.

"I'm Black, You're White, Who's Innocent?" is an excerpt from *The Content of Our Character*. In it, he describes a moment at an integrated party when a black man raised a racial issue and the gathering rather quickly evaporated as both whites and blacks retreated from any discussion that might raise tempers or start an argument. He says, "I think those who provoke this sort of awkwardness are operating out of a black identity that obliges them to badger white people about race almost on principle." He refers to such provocations as "power moves" by which some blacks "try to freeze the enemy" in self-consciousness. He goes on to explain and explore his concept that "both races have a hidden investment in racism and

1   It is a warm, windless California evening, and the dying light that
covers the redbrick patio is tinted pale orange by the day's smog.
Eight of us, not close friends, sit in lawn chairs sipping chardonnay.
A black engineer and I (we had never met before) integrate the
group. A psychologist is also among us, and her presence encourages
a surprising openness. But not until well after the lovely twilight
dinner has been served, when the sky has turned to deep black and
the drinks have long since changed to scotch, does the subject of
race spring awkwardly upon us. Out of nowhere the engineer
announces, with a coloring of accusation in his voice, that it bothers
him to send his daughter to a school where she is one of only three
black children. "I didn't realize my ambition to get ahead would
pull me into a world where my daughter would lose touch with her
blackness," he says.

2   Over the course of the evening we have talked about money,
past and present addictions, child abuse, even politics. Intimacies
have been revealed, fears named. But this subject, race, sinks us
into one of those shaming silences where eye contact terrorizes.
Our host looks for something in the bottom of his glass. Two
women stare into the black sky as if to locate the Big Dipper
and point it out to us. Finally, the psychologist seems to gather
herself for a challenge, but it is too late. "Oh, I'm sure she'll be
just fine," says our hostess, rising from her chair. When she excuses
herself to get the coffee, the psychologist and two sky gazers offer
to help.

3   With four of us now gone, I am surprised to see the engineer still
silently holding his ground. There is a willfulness in his eyes, an
inner pride. He knows he has said something awkward, but he is
determined not to give a damn. His unwavering eyes intimidate even
me. At last the host's head snaps erect. He has an idea. "The hell
with coffee," he says. "How about some of the smoothest brandy
you've ever tasted?" An idea made exciting by the escape it offers.

Gratefully, we follow him back into the house, quickly drink his brandy, and say our good-byes.

4   An autopsy of this party might read: death induced by an abrupt and lethal injection of the American race issue. An accurate if superficial assessment. Since it has been my fate to live a rather integrated life, I have often witnessed sudden deaths like this. The threat of them, if not the reality, is a part of the texture of integration. In the late 1960s, when I was just out of college, I took a delinquent's delight in playing the engineer's role, and actually developed a small reputation for playing it well. Those were the days of flagellatory white guilt: it was such great fun to pinion some professor or housewife or, best of all, a large group of remorseful whites, with the knowledge of both their racism and their denial of it. The adolescent impulse to sneer at convention, to startle the middle-aged with doubt, could be indulged under the guise of racial indignation. And how could I lose? My victims—earnest liberals for the most part—could no more crawl out from under my accusations than Joseph K. in Kafka's *Trial* could escape the amorphous charges brought against him. At this odd moment in history the world was aligned to facilitate my immaturity.

5   About a year of this was enough: the guilt that follows most cheap thrills caught up to me, and I put myself in check. But the impulse to do it faded more slowly. It was one of those petty talents that is tied to vanity, and when there were ebbs in my self-esteem the impulse to use it would come alive again. In integrated situations I can still feel the faint itch. But then there are many youthful impulses that still itch and now, just inside the door of midlife, this one is least precious to me.

6   In the literature classes I teach I often see how the presence of whites all but seduces some black students into provocation. When we come to a novel by a black writer, say Toni Morrison, the white students can easily discuss the human motivations of the black characters. But, inevitably, a black student, as if by reflex, will begin to set in relief the various racial problems that are the background of these characters' lives. This student's tone will carry a reprimand: the class is afraid to confront the reality of racism. Classes cannot be allowed to die like dinner parties, however. My latest strategy is to thank that student for his or her moral vigilance and then appoint the young man or woman as the class's official racism monitor. But even if I get a laugh—I usually do, but sometimes the student is particularly

indignant, and it gets uncomfortable—the strategy never quite works. Our racial division is suddenly drawn in neon. Overcaution spreads like spilled paint. And, in fact, the black student who started it all does become a kind of monitor. The very presence of this student imposes a new accountability on the class.

7   I think those who provoke this sort of awkwardness are operating out of a black identity that obliges them to badger white people about race almost on principle. Content hardly matters. (For example, it made little sense for the engineer to expect white people to anguish terribly much over his decision to send his daughter to school with *white* children.) Race indeed remains a source of white shame; the goal of these provocations is to put whites, no matter how indirectly, in touch with this collective guilt. In other words, these provocations I speak of are *power* moves, little shows of power that try to freeze the "enemy" in self-consciousness. They gratify and inflate the provocateur. They are the underdog's bite. And whites, far more secure in their power, respond with self-contained and tolerant silence that is itself a show of power. What greater power than that of nonresponse, the power to let a small enemy sizzle in his own juices, to even feel a little sad at his frustration just as one is also complimented by it. Black anger always, in a way, flatters white power. In America, to know that one is not black is to feel an extra grace, a little boost of impunity.

8   I think the real trouble between the races in America is that the races are not just races but competing power groups—a fact that is easily minimized, perhaps because it is so obvious. What is not so obvious is that this is true quite apart from the issue of class. Even the well-situated middle-class (or wealthy) black is never completely immune to that peculiar contest of power that his skin color subjects him to. Race is a separate reality in American society, an entity that carries its own potential for power, a mark of fate that class can soften considerably but not eradicate.

9   The distinction of race has always been used in American life to sanction each race's pursuit of power in relation to the other. The allure of race as a human delineation is the very shallowness of the delineation it makes. Onto this shallowness—mere skin and hair—men can project a false depth, a system of dismal attributions, a series of malevolent or ignoble stereotypes that skin and hair lack the substance to contradict. These dark projections then rationalize the pursuit of power. Your difference from me makes you bad, and your

badness justifies, even demands, my pursuit of power over you—the oldest formula for aggression known to man. Whenever much importance is given to race, power is the primary motive.

10   But the human animal almost never pursues power without first convincing himself that he is *entitled* to it. And this feeling of entitlement has its own precondition: to be entitled one must first believe in one's innocence, at least in the area where one wishes to be entitled. By innocence I mean a feeling of essential goodness in relation to others and, therefore, superiority to others. Our innocence always inflates us and deflates those we seek power over. Once inflated we are entitled; we are in fact licensed to go after the power our innocence tells us we deserve. In this sense, *innocence is power*. Of course, innocence need not be genuine or real in any objective sense, as the Nazis demonstrated not long ago. Its only test is whether or not we can convince ourselves of it.

11   I think the racial struggle in America has always been primarily a struggle for innocence. White racism from the beginning has been a claim of white innocence and therefore of white entitlement to subjugate blacks. And in the sixties, as went innocence so went power. Blacks used the innocence that grew out of their long subjugation to seize more power, while whites lost some of their innocence and so lost a degree of power over blacks. Both races instinctively understand that to lose innocence is to lose power (in relation to each other). To be innocent someone else must be guilty, a natural law that leads the races to forge their innocence on each other's backs. The inferiority of the black always makes the white man superior; the evil might of whites makes blacks good. This pattern means that both races have a hidden investment in racism and racial disharmony despite their good intentions to the contrary. Power defines their relations, and power requires innocence, which, in turn, requires racism and racial division.

12   I believe it was his hidden investment that the engineer was protecting when he made his remark—the white "evil" he saw in a white school "depriving" his daughter of her black heritage confirmed his innocence. Only the logic of power explained his emphasis—he bent reality to show that he was once again a victim of the white world and, as a victim, innocent. His determined eyes insisted on this. And the whites, in their silence, no doubt protected their innocence by seeing him as an ungracious troublemaker, his bad behavior underscoring their goodness. What none of us saw was the underlying

game of power and innocence we were trapped in, or how much we needed a racial impasse to play that game.

13   When I was a boy of about twelve, a white friend of mine told me one day that his uncle, who would be arriving the next day for a visit, was a racist. Excited by the prospect of seeing such a man, I spent the following afternoon hanging around the alley behind my friend's house, watching from a distance as this uncle worked on the engine of his Buick. Yes, here was evil and I was compelled to look upon it. And I saw evil in the sharp angle of his elbow as he pumped his wrench to tighten nuts. I saw it in the blade-sharp crease of his chinos, in the pack of Lucky Strikes that threatened to slip from his shirt pocket as he bent, and in the way his concentration seemed to shut out the human world. He worked neatly and efficiently, wiping his hands constantly, and I decided that evil worked like this.

14   I felt a compulsion to have this man look upon me so that I could see evil—so that I could see the face of it. But when he noticed me standing beside his toolbox, he said only, "If you're looking for Bobby, I think he went up to the school to play baseball." He smiled nicely and went back to work. I was stunned for a moment, but then I realized that evil could be sly as well, could smile when it wanted to trick you.

15   Need, especially hidden need, puts a strong pressure on perception, and my need to have this man embody white evil was stronger than any contravening evidence. As a black person you always hear about racists but rarely meet any who will let you know them as such. And I needed to incarnate this odious category of humanity, those people who hated Martin Luther King, Jr., and thought blacks should "go slow" or not at all. So, in my mental dictionary, behind the term "white racist," I inserted this man's likeness. I would think of him and say to myself, "There is no reason for him to hate black people. Only evil explains unmotivated hatred." And this thought soothed me; I felt innocent. If I hated white people, which I did not, at least I had a reason. His evil commanded me to assert in the world the goodness he made me confident of in myself.

16   In looking at this man I was *seeing for innocence*—a form of seeing that has more to do with one's hidden need for innocence (and power) than with the person or group one is looking at. It is quite possible, for example, that the man I saw that day was not a racist. He did absolutely nothing in my presence to indicate that he was.

I invested an entire afternoon in seeing not the man but in seeing my innocence through the man. *Seeing for innocence* is, in this way, the essence of racism—the use of others as a means to our own goodness and superiority.

17 The loss of innocence has always to do with guilt, Kierkegaard tells us, and it has never been easy for whites to avoid guilt where blacks are concerned. For whites, *seeing for innocence* means seeing themselves and blacks in ways that minimize white guilt. Often this amounts to a kind of white revisionism, as when President Reagan declared himself "color-blind" in matters of race. The President, like many of us, may have aspired to racial color blindness, but few would grant that he ever reached this sublimely guiltless state. His statement clearly revised reality, moved it forward into some heretofore unknown America where all racial determinism would have vanished. I do not think that Ronald Reagan was a racist, as that term is commonly used, but neither do I think that he was capable of seeing color without making attributions, some of which may have been negative—nor am I, or anyone else I've ever met.

18 So why make such a statement? I think Reagan's claim of color blindness with regard to race was really a claim of racial innocence and guiltlessness—the preconditions for entitlement and power. This was the claim that grounded Reagan's campaign against special enti-tlement programs—affirmative action, racial quotas, and so on—that black power had won in the sixties. Color blindness was a strategic assumption of innocence that licensed Reagan's use of government power against black power. . . .

19 Black Americans have had to find a way to handle white society's presumption of racial innocence whenever they have sought to enter the American mainstream. Louis Armstrong's exaggerated smile hon-ored the presumed innocence of white society—*I will not bring you your racial guilt if you will let me play my music.* Ralph Ellison calls this "masking"; I call it bargaining. But whatever it's called, it points to the power of white society to enforce its innocence. I believe this power is greatly diminished today. Society has reformed and transformed—Miles Davis never smiles. Nevertheless, this power has not faded altogether and blacks must still contend with it.

20 Historically, blacks have handled white society's presumption of innocence in two ways: they have bargained with it, granting white society its innocence in exchange for entry into the mainstream, or they have challenged it, holding that innocence hostage until their

demand for entry (or other concessions) was met. A bargainer says, *I already believe you are innocent (good, fair-minded) and have faith that you will prove it.* A challenger says, *If you are innocent, then prove it.* Bargainers *give* in hope of receiving; challengers *withhold* until they receive. Of course, there is risk in both approaches, but in each case the black is negotiating his own self-interest against the presumed racial innocence of the larger society.

21   Clearly, the most visible black bargainer on the American scene today is Bill Cosby. His television show has been a perfect formula for black bargaining in the eighties. The remarkable Huxtable family—with its doctor/lawyer parent combination, its drug-free, college-bound children, and its wise yet youthful grandparents—is a blackface version of the American dream. Cosby is a subscriber to the American identity, and his subscription confirms his belief in its fair-mindedness. His vast audience knows this, knows that Cosby will never assault their innocence with racial guilt. Racial controversy is all but banished from the show. The Huxtable family never discusses affirmative action.

22   The bargain Cosby offers his white viewers—*I will confirm your racial innocence if you accept me*—is a good deal for all concerned. Not only does it allow whites to enjoy Cosby's humor with no loss of innocence, but it actually enhances their innocence by implying that race is not the serious problem for blacks that it once was. If anything, the success of this handsome, affluent black family points to the fair-mindedness of whites who, out of their essential goodness, changed society so that black families like the Huxtables could succeed. Whites can watch *The Cosby Show* and feel complimented on a job well done.

23   The power that black bargainers wield is the power of absolution. On Thursday nights, Cosby, like a priest, absolves his white viewers, forgives and forgets the sins of the past. And for this he is rewarded with an almost sacrosanct status. Cosby benefits from what might be called the gratitude factor. His continued number-one rating may have something to do with the (white) public's gratitude at being offered a commodity so rare in our time; he tells his white viewers each week that they are okay, and that this black man is not going to challenge them.

24   When a black bargains, he may invoke the gratitude factor and find himself cherished beyond the measure of his achievement; when he challenges, he may draw the dark projections of whites and become

a source of irritation to them. If he moves back and forth between these two options, as I think many blacks do today, he will likely baffle whites. It is difficult for whites either to accept or reject such blacks. It seems to me that Jesse Jackson is such a figure—many whites see Jackson as a challenger by instinct and a bargainer by political ambition. They are uneasy with him, more than a little suspicious. His powerful speech at the 1984 Democratic Convention was a masterpiece of bargaining. In it he offered a King-like vision of what America could be, a vision that presupposed Americans had the fair-mindedness to achieve full equality—an offer in hope of a return. A few days after this speech, looking for rest and privacy at a lodge in Big Sur, he and his wife were greeted with standing ovations three times a day when they entered the dining room for meals. So much about Jackson is deeply American—his underdog striving, his irrepressible faith in himself, the daring of his ambition, and even his stubborness. These qualities point to his underlying faith that Americans can respond to him despite race, and this faith is a compliment to Americans, an offer of innocence.

25   But Jackson does not always stick to the terms of his bargain as Cosby does on TV. When he hugs Arafat, smokes cigars with Castro, refuses to repudiate Farrakhan, threatens a boycott of major league baseball or, more recently, talks of "corporate barracudas," "pension-fund socialism," and "economic violence," he looks like a challenger in bargainer's clothing, and his positions on the issues look like familiar protests dressed in white-paper formality. At these times he appears to be revoking the innocence so much else about him seems to offer. The old activist seems to come out of hiding once again to take white innocence hostage until whites prove they deserve to have it. In his candidacy there is a suggestion of protest, a fierce insistence on his *right* to run, that sends whites a message that he may secretly see them as a good bit less than innocent. His dilemma is to appear the bargainer while his campaign itself seems to be a challenge.

26   There are, of course, other problems that hamper Jackson's bid for the Democratic presidential nomination. He has held no elective office, he is thought too flamboyant and opportunistic by many, there are rather loud whispers of "character" problems. As an individual, he may not be the best test of a black man's chances for winning so high an office. Still, I believe it is the aura of challenge surrounding him that hurts him most. Whether it is right or wrong, fair or unfair, I think no black candidate will have a serious chance at his party's

nomination, much less the presidency, until he can convince white Americans that he can be trusted to preserve their sense of racial innocence. Such a candidate will have to use his power of absolution; he will have to flatly forgive and forget. He will have to bargain with white innocence out of genuine belief that it really exists. There can be no faking it. He will have to offer a vision that is passionately raceless, a vision that strongly condemns any form of racial politics. This will require the most courageous kind of leadership, leadership that asks all the people to meet a new standard.

27   Now the other side of America's racial impasse: how do blacks lay claim to their racial innocence?

28   The most obvious and unarguable source of black innocence is the victimization that blacks endured for centuries at the hands of a race that insisted on black inferiority as a means to its own innocence and power. Like all victims, what blacks lost in power they gained in innocence—innocence that, in turn, entitled them to pursue power. This was the innocence that fueled the civil rights movement of the sixties and that gave blacks their first real power in American life—victimization metamorphosed into power via innocence. But this formula carries a drawback that I believe is virtually as devastating to blacks today as victimization once was. It is a formula that binds the victim to his victimization by linking his power to his status as a victim. And this, I'm convinced, is the tragedy of black power in America today. It is primarily a victim's power, grounded too deeply in the entitlement derived from past injustice and in the innocence that Western/Christian tradition has always associated with poverty.

29   Whatever gains this power brings in the short run through political action, it undermines in the long run. Social victims may be collectively entitled, but they are all too often individually demoralized. Since the social victim has been oppressed by society, he comes to feel that his individual life will be improved more by changes in society than by his own initiative. Without realizing it, he makes society rather than himself the agent of change. The power he finds in his victimization may lead him to collective action against society, but it also encourages passivity within the sphere of his personal life.

30   Not long ago, I saw a television documentary that examined life in Detroit's inner city on the twentieth anniversary of the riots there in which forty-three people were killed. A comparison of the inner city then and now showed a decline in the quality of life. Residents

feel less safe, drug trafficking is far worse, crimes by blacks against blacks are more frequent, housing remains substandard, and the teenage pregnancy rate has skyrocketed. Twenty years of decline and demoralization, even as opportunities for blacks to better themselves have increased. This paradox is not peculiar to Detroit. By many measures, the majority of blacks—those not yet in the middle class—are further behind whites today than before the victories of the civil rights movement. But there is a reluctance among blacks to examine this paradox, I think, because it suggests that racial victimization is not our real problem. If conditions have worsened for most of us as racism had receded, then much of the problem must be of our own making. To admit this fully would cause us to lose the innocence we derive from our victimization. And we would jeopardize the entitlement we've always had to challenge society. We are in the odd and self-defeating position in which taking responsibility for bettering ourselves feels like a surrender to white power.

31   So we have a hidden investment in victimization and poverty. These distressing conditions have been the source of our own real power, and there is an unconscious sort of gravitation toward them, a complaining celebration of them. One sees evidence of this in the near happiness with which certain black leaders recount the horror of Howard Beach, Bensonhurst, and other recent instances of racial tension. As one is saddened by these tragic events, one is also repelled at the way some black leaders—agitated to near hysteria by the scent of victim power inherent in them—leap forward to exploit them as evidence of black innocence and white guilt. It is as though they sense the decline of black victimization as a loss of standing and dive into the middle of these incidents as if they were reservoirs of pure black innocence swollen with potential power.

32   *Seeing for innocence* pressures blacks to focus on racism and to neglect the individual initiative that would deliver them from poverty—the only thing that finally delivers *anyone* from poverty. With our eyes on innocence we see racism everywhere and miss opportunity even as we stumble over it. About 70 percent of black students at my university drop out before graduation—a flight from opportunity that racism cannot explain. It is an injustice that whites can see for innocence with more impunity than blacks can. The price whites pay is a certain blindness to themselves. Moreover, for whites seeing for innocence continues to engender the bad faith of a long-disgruntled minority. But the price blacks pay is an ever-escalating poverty that

threatens to make the worst off a permanent underclass. Not fair, but real.

33   Challenging works best for the collective, while bargaining is more the individual's suit. From this point on, the race's advancement will come from the efforts of its individuals. True, some challenging will be necessary for a long time to come. But bargaining is now—today—a way for the black individual to *join* the larger society, to make a place for himself or herself.

34   "Innocence is ignorance," Kierkegaard says, and if this is so, the claim of innocence amounts to an insistence on ignorance, a refusal to know. In their assertions of innocence both races carve out very functional areas of ignorance for themselves—territories of blindness that license a misguided pursuit of power. Whites gain superiority by not knowing blacks; blacks gain entitlement by not seeing their own responsibility for bettering themselves. The power each race seeks in relation to the other is grounded in a double-edged ignorance of the self as well as of the other.

35   The original sin that brought us to an impasse at the dinner party I mentioned occurred centuries ago, when it was first decided to exploit racial difference as a means to power. It was a determinism that flowed karmically from this sin that dropped over us like a net that night. What bothered me most was our helplessness. Even the engineer did not know how to go forward. His challenge hadn't worked, and he'd lost the option to bargain. The marriage of race and power depersonalized us, changed us from eight people to six whites and two blacks. The easiest thing was to let silence blanket our situation, our impasse. . . .

36   What both black and white Americans fear are the sacrifices and risks that true racial harmony demands. This fear is the measure of our racial chasm. And though fear always seeks a thousand justifications, none is ever good enough, and the problems we run from only remain to haunt us. It would be right to suggest courage as an antidote to fear, but the glory of the word might only intimidate us into more fear. I prefer the word effort—relentless effort, moral effort. What I like most about this word are its connotations of everydayness, earnestness, and practical sacrifice. No matter how badly it might have gone for us that warm summer night, we should have talked. We should have made the effort.

Just Walk on By

BRENT STAPLES

Brent Staples was born in Chester, Pennsylvania, in 1951. He earned a B.A. from Widener University in 1973 and a Ph.D. in psychology from the University of Chicago in 1982. He began his career as a reporter for the *Chicago Sun-Times*. He then moved to New York to be an editor of the *New York Times Book Review*. He has served as a metropolitan editor of the *New York Times* since 1985.

"Just Walk on By" first appeared in 1986 in *Ms.* magazine under the title, "Just Walk on By: A Black Man Ponders His Power to Alter Public Space." In the essay, he discusses his power as a black man who, at night, could frighten women walking the streets. He says he could "alter public space in an ugly way." Realizing that he was "indistinguishable from the muggers who occasionally seeped into the area from the surrounding ghetto," he changed his behavior. Rather than exercising his "power to intimidate," he chose to make people comfortable about his presence by whistling melodies from Beethoven or Vivaldi.

1   My first victim was a woman—white, well dressed, probably in her early twenties. I came upon her late one evening on a deserted street in Hyde Park, a relatively affluent neighborhood in an otherwise mean, impoverished section of Chicago. As I swung onto the avenue behind her, there seemed to be a discreet, uninflammatory distance between us. Not so. She cast back a worried glance. To her, the

youngish black man—a broad six feet two inches with a beard and billowing hair, both hands shoved into the pockets of a bulky military jacket—seemed menacingly close. After a few more quick glimpses, she picked up her pace and was soon running in earnest. Within seconds she disappeared into a cross street.

2   That was more than a decade ago. I was twenty-two years old, a graduate student newly arrived at the University of Chicago. It was in the echo of that terrified woman's footfalls that I first began to know the unwieldy inheritance I'd come into—the ability to alter public space in ugly ways. It was clear that she thought herself the quarry of a mugger, a rapist, or worse. Suffering a bout of insomnia, however, I was stalking sleep, not defenseless wayfarers. As a softy who is scarcely about to take a knife to a raw chicken—let along hold it to a person's throat—I was surprised, embarrassed, and dismayed all at once. Her flight made me feel like an accomplice in tyranny. It also made it clear that I was indistinguishable from the muggers who occasionally seeped into the area from the surrounding ghetto. That first encounter, and those that followed, signified that a vast, unnerving gulf lay between nighttime pedestrians—particularly women—and me. And I soon gathered that being perceived as dangerous is a hazard in itself. I only needed to turn a corner into a dicey situation, or crowd some frightened, armed person in a foyer somewhere, or make an errant move after being pulled over by a policeman. Where fear and weapons meet—and they often do in urban America—there is always the possibility of death.

3   In that first year, my first away from my hometown, I was to become thoroughly familiar with the language of fear. At dark, shadowy intersections in Chicago, I could cross in front of a car stopped at a traffic light and elicit the *thunk, thunk, thunk, thunk* of the driver—black, white, male, or female—hammering down the door locks. On less traveled streets after dark, I grew accustomed to but never comfortable with people who crossed to the other side of the street rather than pass me. Then there were the standard unpleasantries with police, doormen, bouncers, cab drivers, and others whose business it is to screen out troublesome individuals *before* there is any nastiness.

4   I moved to New York nearly two years ago and I have remained an avid night walker. In central Manhattan, the near-constant crowd cover minimizes tense one-on-one street encounters. Elsewhere—vis-

iting friends in SoHo, where sidewalks are narrow and tightly spaced buildings shut out the sky—things can get very taut indeed.

5   Black men have a firm place in New York mugging literature. Norman Podhoretz in his famed (or infamous) 1963 essay, "My Negro Problem—and Ours," recalls growing up in terror of black males; they "were tougher than we were, more ruthless," he writes—and as an adult on the Upper West Side of Manhattan, he continues, he cannot constrain his nervousness when he meets black men on certain streets. Similarly, a decade later, the essayist and novelist Edward Hoagland extols a New York where once "Negro bitterness bore down mainly on other Negroes." Where some see mere panhandlers, Hoagland sees "a mugger who is clearly screwing up his nerve to do more than just *ask* for money." But Hoagland has "the New Yorker's quick-hunch posture for broken-field maneuvering," and the bad guy swerves away.

6   I often witness that "hunch posture," from women after dark on the warrenlike streets of Brooklyn where I live. They seem to set their faces on neutral and, with their purse straps strung across their chests bandolier style, they forge ahead as though bracing themselves against being tackled. I understand, of course, that the danger they perceive is not a hallucination. Women are particularly vulnerable to street violence, and young black males are drastically overrepresented among the perpetrators of that violence. Yet these truths are no solace against the kind of alienation that comes of being ever the suspect, against being set apart, a fearsome entity with whom pedestrians avoid making eye contact.

7   It is not altogether clear to me how I reached the ripe old age of twenty-two without being conscious of the lethality nighttime pedestrians attributed to me. Perhaps it was because in Chester, Pennsylvania, the small, angry industrial town where I came of age in the 1960s, I was scarcely noticeable against a backdrop of gang warfare, street knifings, and murders. I grew up one of the good boys, had perhaps a half-dozen fist fights. In retrospect, my shyness of combat has clear sources.

8   Many things go into the making of a young thug. One of those things is the consummation of the male romance with the power to intimidate. An infant discovers that random flailings send the baby bottle flying out of the crib and crashing to the floor. Delighted, the joyful babe repeats those motions again and again, seeking to duplicate the feat. Just so, I recall the points at which some of my

boyhood friends were finally seduced by the perception of themselves as tough guys. When a mark cowered and surrendered his money without resistance, myth and reality merged—and paid off. It is, after all, only manly to embrace the power to frighten and intimidate. We, as men, are not supposed to give an inch of our lane on the highway; we are to seize the fighter's edge in work and in play and even in love; we are to be valiant in the face of hostile forces.

9   Unfortunately, poor and powerless young men seem to take all this nonsense literally. As a boy, I saw countless tough guys locked away; I have since buried several, too. They were babies, really—a teenage cousin, a brother of twenty-two, a childhood friend in his mid-twenties—all gone down in episodes of bravado played out in the streets. I came to doubt the virtues of intimidation early on. I chose, perhaps even unconsciously, to remain a shadow—timid, but a survivor.

10   The fearsomeness mistakenly attributed to me in public places often has a perilous flavor. The most frightening of these confusions occurred in the late 1970s and early 1980s when I worked as a journalist in Chicago. One day, rushing into the office of a magazine I was writing for with a deadline story in hand, I was mistaken for a burglar. The office manager called security and, with an ad hoc posse, pursued me through the labyrinthine halls, nearly to my editor's door. I had no way of proving who I was. I could only move briskly toward the company of someone who knew me.

11   Another time I was on assignment for a local paper and killing time before an interview. I entered a jewelry store on the city's affluent Near North Side. The proprietor excused herself and returned with an enormous red Doberman pinscher straining at the end of a leash. She stood, the dog extended toward me, silent to my questions, her eyes bulging nearly out of her head. I took a cursory look around, nodded, and bade her good night. Relatively speaking, however, I never fared as badly as another black male journalist. He went to nearby Waukegan, Illinois, a couple of summers ago to work on a story about a murderer who was born there. Mistaking the reporter for the killer, police hauled him from his car at gunpoint and but for his press credentials would probably have tried to book him. Such episodes are not uncommon. Black men trade tales like this all the time.

12   In "My Negro Problem—And Ours," Podhoretz writes that the hatred he feels for blacks makes itself known to him through a variety

of avenues—one being his discomfort with that "special brand of paranoid touchiness" to which he says blacks are prone. No doubt he is speaking here of black men. In time, I learned to smother the rage I felt at so often being taken for a criminal. Not to do so would surely have led to madness—via that special "paranoid touchiness" that so annoyed Podhoretz at the time he wrote the essay.

13   I began to take precautions to make myself less threatening. I move about with care, particularly late in the evening. I give a wide berth to nervous people on subway platforms during the wee hours, particularly when I have exchanged business clothes for jeans. If I happen to be entering a building behind some people who appear skittish, I may walk by, letting them clear the lobby before I return, so as not to seem to be following them. I have been calm and extremely congenial on those rare occasions when I've been pulled over by the police.

14   And on late-evening constitutionals along streets less traveled by, I employ what has proved to be an excellent tension-reducing measure: I whistle melodies from Beethoven and Vivaldi and the more popular classical composers. Even steely New Yorkers hunching toward nighttime destinations seem to relax, and occasionally they even join in the tune. Virtually everybody seems to sense that a mugger wouldn't be warbling bright, sunny selections from Vivaldi's *Four Seasons.* It is my equivalent of the cowbell that hikers wear when they know they are in bear country.

Acknowledgments

Allen, Paula Gunn, "Where I Come from Is Like This," from THE
SACRED HOOP by Paula Gunn Allen. Copyright © 1986, 1992
by Paula Gunn Allen. Reprinted by permission of Beacon Press.

Baldwin, James, "If Black English Isn't a Language, Then Tell Me, What
Is?" From THE NEW YORK TIMES, July 29, 1979. Copyright ©
1979 by The New York Times Company. Reprinted by permission.

Bettelheim, Bruno. Reprinted with the permission of Simon & Schuster
from THE CHILDREN OF THE DREAM: Communal Child-Rear-
ing and American Education by Bruno Bettelheim. Copyright © 1969
by Macmillan Publishing Company.

Cary, Lorene. From BLACK ICE by Lorene Cary. Copyright © 1991
by Lorene Cary. Reprinted by permission of Alfred A. Knopf, Inc.

Deloria, Vine, Jr. Reprinted with the permission of Simon & Schuster
from CUSTER DIED FOR YOUR SINS: An Indian Manifesto by
Vine Deloria, Jr. Copyright © 1969 by Vine Deloria, Jr.

Du Bois, W. E. B., "On Being Crazy" from AN ABC OF COLOR.
Printed with permission of International Publishers, New York.

Ellison, Ralph. From SHADOW AND ACT by Ralph Ellison. Copyright
© 1953, 1964 by Ralph Ellison. Copyright © renewed 1981, 1992 by Ralph
Ellison. Reprinted by permission of Random House, Inc.

Galarza, Ernesto, "Growing into Manhood" from BARRIO BOY by
Ernesto Galarza. © 1971 by the University of Notre Dame Press. Reprinted
by permission of the publisher.

hooks, bell, "Straightening Our Hair" which appeared in Z MAGA-
ZINE, September, 1988. Reprinted by permission.

Hurston, Zora Neale, "Wandering," Chapter VI, pages 84–96 from
DUST TRACKS ON A ROAD by Zora Neale Hurston. Copyright
1942 by Zora Neale Hurston. Copyright renewed 1970 by John C.
Hurston. Reprinted by permission of HarperCollins Publishers, Inc.

Jordan, June, "Nobody Mean More to Me Than You and the Future
Life of Willie Jordan" as appeared in HARVARD EDUCATIONAL
REVIEW, August, 1988. Reprinted by permission of the author.

King, Martin Luther, Jr., "Letter from Birmingham Jail—April 16,
1963" from WHY WE CAN'T WAIT by Martin Luther King, Jr. Reprinted
by arrangement with The Heirs to the Estate of Martin Luther King,
Jr., c/o Joan Daves Agency as agent for the proprietor. Copyright
1963 by Martin Luther King, Jr., copyright renewed 1991 by Coretta
Scott King.

Kingston, Maxine Hong. From THE WOMAN WARRIOR by Maxine
Hong Kingston. Copyright © 1975, 1976 by Maxine Hong Kingston.
Reprinted by permission of Alfred A. Knopf, Inc.

Malcolm X. From THE AUTOBIOGRAPHY OF MALCOLM X by
Malcolm X with the assistance of Alex Haley. Copyright © 1964 by
Alex Haley and Malcolm X. Copyright © 1965 by Alex Haley and Betty
Shabazz. Reprinted by permission of Random House, Inc.

Mehta, Ved. Reprinted from THE LEDGE BETWEEN THE
STREAMS by Ved Mehta, by permission of W. W. Norton & Company, Inc. Copyright © 1982, 1983, 1984 by Ved Mehta.

Momaday, N. Scott, "The Way to Rainy Mountain," first published in
THE REPORTER, 26 January 1967. Reprinted from THE WAY
TO RAINY MOUNTAIN, © 1969, The University of New Mexico
Press. Used by permission.

Muniz, Maria L., "Back, but Not Home," from THE NEW YORK
TIMES, July 13, 1979. Copyright © 1979 by The New York Times
Company. Reprinted by permission.

Noda, Kesaya E., "Growing Up Asian in America." Reprinted by permission of the author, Kesaya E. Noda, from MAKING WAVES, by Asian Women United, © 1989 by Asian Women United.

Ortiz Cofer, Judith. From THE LINE OF THE SUN by Judith Ortiz Cofer. © 1989 by Judith Ortiz Cofer. Reprinted by permission of University of Georgia Press.

Puzo, Mario, "Choosing a Dream: Italians in Hell's Kitchen" by Mario Puzo, from THE IMMIGRANT EXPERIENCE by Thomas C. Wheeler. Copyright © 1971 by Doubleday, a division of Bantam Doubleday Dell Publishing Group, Inc. Used by permission of Doubleday, a division of Bantam Doubleday Dell Publishing Group, Inc.

Reed, Ishmael, "America: The Multinational Society." Excerpted from WRITIN' IS FIGHTIN': FORTY-THREE YEARS OF BOXING ON PAPER, © 1988 by Ishmael Reed. Reprinted by permission of Addison-Wesley Publishing Company, Inc. A new edition is scheduled for publication in Fall of 1996.

Rodriguez, Richard, "Aria," from HUNGER OF MEMORY by Richard Rodriguez. Reprinted by permission of David R. Godine, Publisher, Inc. Copyright © 1982 by Richard Rodriguez.

Soyinka, Wole. From AKE: THE YEARS OF CHILDHOOD by Wole Soyinka. Copyright © 1981 by Wole Soyinka. Reprinted by permission of Random House, Inc.

Staples, Brent, "Just Walk on By: A Black Man Ponders His Power to Alter Public Space," as appeared in MS., September, 1986. Reprinted by permission of author.

Steele, Shelby, "I'm Black, You're White, Who's Innocent?" from THE CONTENT OF OUR CHARACTER by Shelby Steele. Copyright © 1990 by Shelby Steele. Reprinted by permission of St. Martin's Press, Inc., New York, NY.

Wright, Richard. Chapter 13, pages 267–277 from BLACK BOY by Richard Wright. Copyright, 1937, 1942, 1944, 1945 by Richard

Index of Authors and Titles